# University Campus
# Barnsley

Telephone: 01226 216 885

Catalogue: **https://webopac.barnsley.ac.uk/**

Class No: ......822.33 PAL..........

**This book is to be returned on or before the last date stamped below. Thank you!**

| | | |
|---|---|---|
| | | |
| | | |
| | | |
| | | |
| | | |
| | | |
| | | |
| | | |
| | | |
| | | |
| | | |
| | | |

# DOING
# SHAKESPEARE

SIMON PALFREY

The Arden website is at
http://www.ardenshakespeare.com

*Doing Shakespeare*
first published 2005 by The Arden Shakespeare
Reprinted 2006

© 2005 Simon Palfrey

The Arden Shakespeare is an imprint of Thomson Learning

Thomson Learning
High Holborn House
50/51 Bedford Row
London WC1R 4LR

Typeset by LaserScript, Mitcham, Surrey

Printed in China

*British Library Cataloguing in Publication Data*
A catalogue record for this book is available from the British Library

*Library of Congress Cataloguing in Publication Data*
A catalogue record has been applied for

ISBN: 978-1-904271-54-3
NPN 9 8 7 6 5 4 3 2

For Georgia, Ella, Louis – and Jo

# THE AUTHOR

Simon Palfrey grew up in Australia and was a Rhodes Scholar at Oxford. He is the author of *Late Shakespeare: A New World of Words* (Oxford University Press, 1997; paperback 2000) and, with Tiffany Stern, *Shakespeare in Parts* (Oxford University Press, 2005). His essay, 'Macbeth and Kierkegaard' is published in *Shakespeare Survey 57* (2004). He is currently a lecturer in English at the University of Liverpool.

# CONTENTS

# PREFACE

This is a book about doing Shakespeare. First and foremost, the doing here is ours. And if we are doing Shakespeare, then we want to enjoy it and to understand it, not merely tick it off as an unpleasant rite of passage. We want to know why he has such a towering reputation, and to judge for ourselves whether the work deserves such acclaim rather than meekly taking it on trust. But how to do so? How do we make these famous, often fearful monuments work for us in fresh and intimate ways? How do we bring the plays to life, read or write about them in a fashion that is informed, engaging, and explorative rather than dutiful and second-hand? *Doing Shakespeare* offers answers to such questions. For the student new to his works it can be an invitation and introduction ('how do you do Shakespeare...'). For those who feel themselves all too familiar with the plays it can be a challenge and perhaps an invigoration. After all, if there are not always new ways of experiencing these so often done works, then there is little point in still doing them.

But the doing here is equally Shakespeare's. How does he do it? Why does he do it like he does? Why so excessive? Why so difficult? But more than that, to talk about doing Shakespeare is to emphasise that these plays are always in process. Shakespeare's art is before all a verbal one: something spoken (of course), but also something whose essence is in its verbs, its doing-things. *Doing Shakespeare* therefore describes both the forms of the plays and our experience of them: and it recommends the doing of each as similarly and symbiotically mobile.

## HOW TO USE THIS BOOK

The book does not need to be read lineally. It is structured so that each chapter is basically self-sufficient. Every chapter explores the significance of a particular formal technique or dramatic phenom-enon. These explorations are designed to answer questions that are frequently asked by readers or audiences, particularly those relatively new to the plays.

The first half of the book addresses questions about Shakespeare's language. Why does he use so many words? Why use two words when one will do? Why can't he say it more simply? Why so many metaphors? Why so bombastic? What is the difference between prose and verse, or rhymed and unrhymed dialogue? What is the point of all of those puns?

The second half of the book addresses questions about Shakespeare's characters. What language might we use to describe them? Where exactly do we locate them? Can we talk about them as though they are real? Is it illegitimate to wonder what they did before or after the play, or in scenes not shown? What are soliloquies for? If everything is spoken in character, then what can we believe? How do disguises and doubles contribute to characterisation? Is character criticism voyeuristic? Is it merely our projection? If it is, how does this bear upon a play's ethical challenges? What have all these complicated techniques got to do with the basic feelings that the characters evoke?

Each chapter is structured similarly. An opening section probes these questions, making brief allusions to particular plays; this is followed by selected longer set pieces, often increasing in detail and complexity, designed to illustrate possible responses to the question at issue. These set pieces are not meant to be exhaustive. They are meant to suggest methods of approach that can be developed or modified in thinking about any of Shakespeare's plays or characters. As a rule, the detailed examples are taken from plays most often studied and performed; the same techniques can be easily transferred to Shakespeare's less popular plays.

That said, a majority of the set pieces consider moments or characters in Shakespeare's tragedies. This is a result of the book's core preoccupations: the purpose of Shakespeare's difficulty or excessiveness; how Shakespeare's words and characters construct one another; the relationship between densely layered theatrical form and emotional and ethical responses. The questions are always there to be asked, but this is particularly the case for the plays written roughly between, say, *Julius Caesar* (around 1599) and *Antony and Cleopatra* (around 1607). Similarly, the book's exploration of character required repeated engagement with some of the most famous: above all Hamlet, Othello, Iago, and Macbeth. The discussions of individual characters do not come in one block, but are distributed throughout the book. Nevertheless, by using the character index it is easy enough to reconstruct an accumulative treatment of these (and other) important figures. The play index, giving details of scene and line, can be used similarly for the plays discussed at recurring points in the book.

Unless otherwise indicated, the Shakespeare text used for quotations and act, scene and line references is the Arden Shakespeare *Complete Works, Revised Edition* (2001), edited by Richard Proudfoot, Ann Thompson and David Scott Kaston.

# ACKNOWLEDGEMENTS

My father, Brian Palfrey, read large chunks of this book and helped to make it a lot better. In very different ways Deanne Williams, Tiffany Stern, John Gillies, and Philip Davis have offered galvanising advice or encouragement. Small sections were tried out at the 2000 and 2002 International Shakespeare Conferences at Stratford-upon-Avon, and I owe a particular debt to the thoughts of Jonathan Hope, Clara Calvo, Kent Cartwright, Penny Gay, and Paul Yachnin. Other pieces were rehearsed at the 1999, 2002 and 2003 Shakespeare Association of America meetings: among many, Mac Jackson, Suzanne Gossett, Martin Orkin, Peter M. Cummings, and Lynne Magnusson stand out for their stimulating responses. The people at Arden have been bright and encouraging throughout: initially Jessica Hodge and Andrew McAleer, latterly Margaret Bartley and Giulia Vincenzi. They have been unfailingly supportive of my wish to write the sort of book I have written. The chicken pox kids have been nothing but a hindrance, but they wouldn't have it any other way. And as for Jo, she thinks I've said quite enough already.

# INTRODUCTION

*This introduction has four brief sections. The first section looks at the instructions that Shakespeare's very first editors – fellow members of Shakespeare's theatre company – give as to how we might read him. They tell us that, for all of the plays' apparent ease and fluency, they can be difficult to understand. We have to expect a mixture of immediacy and withholding, and to read him carefully and repeatedly. The second part introduces the basic methods and premises of this book. That is, the best way of recovering the plays' urgency and immediacy is through sustained, sensitive attention to the movements described in the playtexts. There is no better way to retrieve the works as living things – whether in their originating time and place or in our own. The next two sections consider the viability of this approach in terms of the contexts of the plays' first production. First, we look briefly at the question of texts. Were the plays written to be read in book form? Can we even know what Shakespeare wrote? Second, we consider Shakespeare's audiences, both their differences from us and their differences from each other. They participated in a predominantly listening theatre, one in which the spoken word produced far more mental pictures than any visible spectacle. But they didn't listen like we do today: their attentive listening is closer to our close reading. There is nothing less anachronistic than a close attention to the spoken words. Whether our priority is to make the plays work freshly in our present, or to recover how they worked in their own historical moment, the best way is to re-imagine the possibilities inscribed in the playtext.*

## SHAKESPEARE'S VERY FIRST EDITORS

Shakespeare was very popular in his day, and he has remained very popular pretty much ever since. But Shakespeare is not easy. He has probably never been easy. Before we begin to unpack Shakespeare's difficulty, perhaps we can get some guidance from his very first editors, friends of Shakespeare and fellow shareholders in his theatre company. For certainly they recognised that many people might fail to get much at all from their prize playwright's works. They write this in their prologue to the first edition of Shakespeare's collected plays, the First Folio of 1623:

> But it is not our province, who only gather his works, and give them you, to praise him. It is yours that read him. And there we hope, to your diverse capacities, you will find enough, both to draw, and hold you: for his wit can no more lie hid, than it could be lost. Read him, therefore; and again, and again: And if then you do not like him, surely you are in some manifest danger, not to understand him.

This is one of the most suggestive things ever written about Shakespeare, not least because it brings us as close as we can get to the way Shakespeare's own company understood his work. And clearly they felt they had to both advertise and defend his way of writing. Shakespeare had been dead seven years. His posthumous fame was already in the making, but also somehow perilous. For the prologue implies that there are people about who 'do not like him'; that his work has been dismissed or insulted. They respond with a direction: look harder; do not expect what you usually expect; search for what lies hidden. And if it was necessary then, it is no less so now.

Here let us speculate a little. Shakespeare was the most successful playwright of his age. This success can be measured by performances of both old and new plays, in public and at court, and by the regular publication of cheap pirate editions of his work. However, playwriting was still only barely a properly literary pursuit; it still had the whiff of bear-baiting and prostitution, of being an occasion for coarse and easy communal arousal. There must have been many arbiters of taste who were unwilling to allow the plays the lasting prestige that only print might confer.

The publication of these plays in massive, expensive Folio form may have come as a provocation; it wasn't that long since Shakespeare's friend and rival Ben Jonson had been roundly ridiculed for doing the same with his plays. But anyone who had seen Shakespeare's plays must have noticed that there is much going on in them; that they tumble with conceits, images, and wordplay that go beyond the needs of an accessible popular yarn. Shakespeare's first fame was as a sexy young narrative poet. Perhaps it irritated educated traditionalists that some such poetic pretensions survived through two decades of writing for the popular stage. The impulse may have been to debunk his work as pretentious, exhibitionist, or emptily obscure.

Hence the editors' instructions. For what they stress is quite the opposite. They stress that Shakespeare's art works through a kind of silent, one-on-one mesmerism. It does so through drawing the reader into a web of concealment and revelation: 'we hope ... you will find enough, both to draw, and hold you'. The reader is to be held, suspended, in a stillness of concentration. Or it is a treasure hunt, with the treasure not so much open and displayed as there to be discovered and drawn out like needles from a golden haystack.

And if they recommend it in these terms, it is because they know what it's like. Again, they can give us guidance in our search for understanding. We should remember that these editors had lived with Shakespeare's plays for decades; some of the older ones for 30 years. They, like Shakespeare, were actors and investors in the company. They were present as one and then another play were suggested as possibilities, as they were sketched, composed, rehearsed, performed, toured with; as they were put away and then, perhaps years later, drawn out from the stack to be performed all over again. It is a relationship of immeasurable intimacy. We talk about theatre as a collaborative thing, and so we must imagine it here. Even if Shakespeare was the fabled solitary genius, he was writing always for others. He knew these others; he knew what they had said about the last play, their last part, how they spoke the words, responded to cues, what they enjoyed and what they did not. He knew his fellow King's Men as actors, businessmen, and, we can suppose, friends. We have to suppose a typical 'male' milieu, moving from playhouse to public house and back, rife with wit, puns, competitiveness, with personalities both inquisitive and exhibitionist. We have to suppose rivalries and ambition, a desire to get the good role or the biggest laughs.

It is an environment in which the actors are going to pick up on almost everything: not perhaps how the whole thing fits together – actors received only their own parts in a pasted together roll, not the whole play in book form – but certainly the details, any mischief or surprise, in their own speaking roles. Indeed they will expect hidden gems and secret hits. It is a process of composition and production that perfectly harnesses the dense and playful word use of Shakespeare. This interplay between play and company is all the more suggestive once we recall how Shakespeare's more popular plays (and there were many) remained in the repertoire. For the individual parts remain similarly alive. Whether it was the same actor playing an old part, or a new actor aware of his predecessor in the role, the professional instinct would be to keep things fresh, make the part new, find some unexploited 'wit' to play with. Shakespeare may or may not have been writing so as to keep readers busy for the next 500 years (we might suspect not). But certainly he was writing as he did for a company of players who would return, 'again, and again', to the reading, exploring, and performing of his parts.

So, these editors know exactly how much lies within these words, but they also know that to understand it takes effort. They might have lived with *Romeo and Juliet* and the hurly-burly obscurities of Mercutio for nearly three decades. This long-honed relationship to the plays might help explain the slightly ambiguous tone of this part of the prologue. It is a mingled tone, acknowledging both utter confidence and a certain nervousness: 'for his wit can no more lie hid, than it could be lost'. They are implying that his 'wit', precisely because it does in some crucial sense lie hidden, has in recent memory been endangered with loss. If you expect it to be the wit of farts and cartwheels, the kind of thing perhaps recalled from 'robustious' performances at the Globe, then it will indeed be 'lost'. Of course, as the editors know to their own benefit, much in Shakespeare's plays was spectacularly accessible. He retired by far the most successful dramatist of the age. But there are hints in the prologue that they too have been surprised by what they have discovered: that re-reading these 36 plays has made them realise just how much Shakespeare's splendid immediacy is laced through with barely noticed subtleties and complexities. This is the 'wit' they so wish us to share. Consequently, they effectively announce the movement of Shakespeare from a primary lodging on the stage to one on the page. Therefore 'read him': and again, and again. It is a remarkable and rather moving appeal not to allow all of this plenty to be wasted.

But it remains the fact that getting pleasure from such reading is a challenge. Shakespeare's meanings do not unfold effortlessly; he withholds things; he provokes questions that are not easily answered. But as Shakespeare's partners make clear, even though his words might be difficult, they are there to be understood. Here then is the premise with which this book (like the Folio) begins: that it is only by acknowledging Shakespeare's difficulty and unpredictability – dwelling within it, grappling with it – that we can begin to recover the particular energies of his plays. We cannot begin with expectant generalisations or would-be masterful agendas. We have to loosen the plays up from any such immobilising expectations. This means going back to the specific constituents of Shakespeare at work, recoverable in the various playtexts as we have received them. But at the same time it means recovering the processes that we are busy organising as we experience these works: again, Shakespeare's doing is inextricable from our own.

For as much as we might regret that we can never experience the primal heat of original composition and performance, we as readers should not feel that we are placed *now* in any inferior relation to the plays, or that we have somehow fatally missed the boat. It may well be that nothing beats a great performance. Equally, it is often the case that no stage performance can beat the ongoing performing of a play in the mind of someone who grows to love it. As Shakespeare's friends and partners end their prologue: 'And such Readers we wish him'.

## QUESTIONS AND APPROACHES

This book does not begin with the questions (concerning subjectivity, power relations, gender differences, family relations, national identities, etc.) that have been dominating university teaching and writing over the last decade or so. Those who are interested in these issues will find plenty here to challenge and stimulate them. But the book begins with the questions that *anyone* might ask, whether first-time reader or experienced actor, and pursues these questions via a method that tries to assume little more than a curious mind and a playtext.

Perhaps the most common demand made by those first coming to Shakespeare is that his work be 'relevant'. This need not mean that Shakespeare has to be dumbed down or dressed up. It simply means that the plays have to speak with immediacy and urgency. However, it is not always easy to feel either confident or enthusiastic about recovering any such thing. We might feel uneasiness or aversion to artefacts so distant and difficult. More than that, a suspicion develops that everything that could possibly be said or thought about the plays has already been thought and said, many times over and a long time ago. An assumption often hardens: if Shakespeare is going to be relevant to us, if he is to surprise us, then it can only be by making his plays work in some more immediately familiar framework. So, we work hard to see how his conflicts echo ours, or how his details tell us about life long ago, or how his stories can be adapted to more modern media and technologies.

All of this is appropriate when it comes to making the plays come alive in school or rehearsal. Many of us will need such 'hooks' to get engaged in the first place. But still there is a big problem. The assumption is that the plays as bare texts are somehow given and agreed. Any path so well trodden must be, in all essentials, thoroughly known. There is a considerable loss here. For there are limits to how much we can appeal to these extra-textual contexts – from the past or the present – before both they and the plays begin to seem static and self-reproducing. Perhaps we are doing both plays and history a disservice if we keep on mining one so as to supply fuel for an implicitly already known other. Perhaps we don't really know either of them very well: or at the very least it will do us no harm to pretend for a while that we don't.

This book, consequently, tries to go back to brass tacks: it tries to work out how the playtexts do whatever it is they do. There is nothing a-historical about such an engagement with form. Instead, we need to see how aesthetic form *is* history-in-action, just as it can embody a character's consciousness in process. We need to challenge any association of close attention to textual detail with political reaction or critical naivety. Sustained attention to text too often gets identified with a fabled 'new criticism' or 'structuralism' that disregards anything historical or political in favour of a transcendent text or mythic patterns. Where ambiguity or complexity are discovered, they are thought to serve and hallow only the sacred object – the poem or play – and not attest to conflicts or violence in any worlds to which the text owes its particular form. As a result, close attention to text has often only been acceptable if it can quickly be shown to lead to an overarching political or sociological master discourse.

This book assumes something slightly different: that the playtext is the most basic historical archive imaginable. But this doesn't mean an archive only of Elizabethan or early modern English history. It means a potential storehouse for anyone, now or to come, who recognises in the plays something of their own shape or possibilities. The plays have time and again seemed urgent and immediate, in all sorts of cultures and at all kinds of historical moments. This is because Shakespeare's plays both exceed their original informing contexts and elude final possession by anyone else's. There is always a detail to be mined, a joke to be rescued, a character to bring in from the margins. The plays always carry a quality of 'about to be': they swell with things latent or incipient, with things denied yet desired. And it is the dramatic forms that carry this energy. Every word, clause, figure and scene within a playtext is a 'site' of history, opening up or connecting to any number of other such sites. After all, there is nothing so intimate to the clash between opposing options or the coercions of historical circumstance, as the choice of a word that is to be spoken in a tense and super-policed public space. Shakespeare's words are themselves like dissentious bodies, housing movement and animating ongoing conflict. The same goes for his characters: they are (among other things) embodiments of the way theatrical form finds point and shape from its engagement with social excitement or agitation. Close attention to words and characters – both understood in their fullest capacity for internal movement and variation – need not imply interpretive naivety or political nostalgia. Once we recognise how one is always cut and chiselled by the other – words by their speakers, the speakers by their words – we come upon play-worlds marked by as much restlessness, novelty, and indeed difficulty as the play-forms in which they are represented.

So, if the plays embody material history or embattled citizens, they do so through their formal architecture. But to get at the fullness of one we must be careful not to pre-emptively curtail the other. It comes down to attentive, moment-by-moment listening. This doesn't mean studying only the words' referential content: it means being sensitive to how the words are working. This means recognising that every act of dramatic speech is a public one, and therein as much rhetorical as poetical, lyrical, descriptive, or conversational. There can be no over-simple assumption of a speech act that always performs a single declared action. In any play, words take effect in various rippling ways, invariably not limitable to the inferred intentions and definitions of a speaker in a specific moment. Above all, it means attending to the specific placement of any speaking: who is speaking, to whom, for what purpose, with whose language, with which listeners, and with what effect. How does a word or statement bear upon a particular dialogue, or a sequence of scenes, or a story? How do such things work to secrete, channel, or indeed explode meaning?

## Texts and contexts

It is sometimes thought that a close attention to words is anachronistic, because the people of Shakespeare's day did not have the plays there to read. Or alternatively, that it is anti-theatrical, because we are not dealing with a book but a play. But almost all of Shakespeare's most enduringly popular plays were published in book form during Shakespeare's lifetime: *Romeo and Juliet, Richard II, Richard III, A Midsummer Night's Dream, Much Ado About Nothing, Henry IV, Henry V, The Merchant of Venice, Hamlet, King Lear* (plus *Othello*, after Shakespeare's death but before the 1623 Folio). All of these plays were published in 'quarto' form. This refers to the four times that the sheet of paper is folded, so as to produce four leaves or eight pages; a few of these sheets would be sewn together to comprise the book. Quarto editions were therefore small and affordable, rather like a modern paperback. We do not know how many of the existing quartos were authorised by Shakespeare's company. Certainly not all of them: many were probably pirate editions, published to cash in on the popularity of a recently staged play. The prologue to the Folio distinguishes its 'perfect' authority from the 'diverse stolen, and surreptitious copies, maimed, and deformed by the frauds and stealths of injurious impostors'. The likelihood is that the company were hoarding the plays so as to make a killing on a collected edition (it was also not in their interests to have these popular scripts in easy circulation for others to perform). None-theless, in cases such as *Romeo and Juliet* and *Hamlet*, where two quarto editions were published in quick succession, it is probable that the second one, advertised as 'corrected' or 'augmented', was thus authorised. But what is abundantly clear is that there was indeed already an eager readership for Shakespeare's plays.

This is not to say that Shakespeare himself was writing for future readers. We simply don't know for sure where Shakespeare stood on the question of publication. He may have been a man of the stage who never gave a thought to his works' future readership. He may have been (as his first editors claim) always careful to keep his playtexts in safe keeping for their long-intended publication. Or perhaps he moved from one to the other as his career saw him inexorably becoming a 'classic' in his own lifetime. It is clear that the playtexts were habitually revised. Sometimes the differences between one version and another are small, sometimes profound.

But this does not in itself prove the argument either way. They may have been revised because the text was definitively a thing to be used. It was a script for performance, always susceptible to change or challenge, whether from the demands of time, an altered group of actors, a new stage space or audience, censorship, or whatever else. Alternatively, the revisions might precisely suggest an author taking considerable care over the details of a publishable text. So, Shakespeare might offer a shorter version for performance whilst keeping a fuller one in reserve for posterity (certainly his sonnets show a profound interest in the continuing life of a work of art after the death of its author).

The difference between Quarto and Folio texts present all sorts of interesting problems: concerning the relation of script to performance; the possibility or otherwise of defining 'the' play, whether as a general idea or in specifically problematic cases (like *King Lear*); the relative merits of one editorial practice over another. These are all important issues. However, to recognise that a play can exist in more than one version does nothing to reduce the validity of close textual reading: rather the opposite, if we want to recover evidence about the ways a play might have been cut, revised, or collaborated upon. Even if such matters are not our immediate subject, local differences between Quarto and Folio version are always worth tracing. They are no kind of scholarly luxury. Indeed, they frequently bear in important ways upon the very things this book is exploring (e.g. the situational potency of particular phrases or the limits of character).

## AUDIENCES

Shakespeare was writing in the first place for his public audiences. If we think that this fact excuses or precludes us from reading his playtexts as scrupulously as we can, then we are almost certainly falling for one or two widespread anachronisms. First, we might be superimposing modern notions of performance, with their stress upon production, props, and visualisation, upon the early modern period. Second, we might be assuming that early modern listening was akin to our own. In both cases we would be very wrong. We will be much closer to the mark if we liken the way Shakespeare's 'auditors' (probably a much more appropriate term than spectators) listened to his plays with the way we read them. For us the act most closely linked with education, and so with a directed willingness to think allusively and analytically, is reading. For people in Shakespeare's time it was just as likely to be listening. They didn't listen like we do, struggling to keep up with anything not immediately transparent, annoyed by long-windedness, embarrassed by fruitiness. They didn't require the spoken word to be one-paced and single-filed. They probably listened rather like we (if we really try) can sometimes read. Of course this doesn't deny the importance of all kinds of communicative immediacy: but we mustn't assume that our channels of immediacy were identical to theirs, or that what we see as over the top or abstruse was always so to them.

We have to remember the training in rhetoric that would have been shared by many in Shakespeare's audiences. Almost intuitively they would have an ear out for the numerous figures of repetition, antithesis, inversion and emphasis learnt in school. They would expect their listening to be abetted by simple rhetorical aids – modulations of stress, withheld rhymes, lines or speeches measured by deftly inscribed oppositions or symmetries. Similarly, they would be alive to different modes of address, to shifts between appeal and confession, epigram and proverb, and of course to scores of allusions, quotations, or misquotations. The other main subject of rhetorical training was tropes. That is, figures of speech that alter the meaning of a word or phrase through some form of substitution, comparison, or transposition: things like metaphors, similes, allegories, working both in large compass and in the tiniest details. Many in Shakespeare's audiences were thus trained to relish effects that we often view suspiciously, or as some sort of artificial excrescence upon straight talking and real meaning. There is nothing less foreign to Shakespeare's time or medium than intensive application to verbal effects.

Here we should recall the very high illiteracy of the age. Perhaps as few as 10 per cent of women could read and write, perhaps less than a third of men. But this needn't imply a lack of engagement with stories or ideas. It simply meant that they were read *to*. Most school learning was by rote, absorbed aurally: and so too was most knowledge of fables, stories, songs, ballads, news – and in a very real sense plays. Everyone was habituated to listening from infancy on. They didn't forget how to do it once reading came along; they weren't spellbound by spectacle. Listening was the main path to information and entertainment throughout most people's lives, and undoubtedly honed to an acuteness and sophistication that we can only guess at.

Merely to look at a facsimile of a sixteenth-century Shakespeare text will reinforce the fact that these audiences had a different relationship to the spoken and written word than we do. We will immediately notice how erratic spelling tends to be, and how inconsistent punctuation. Both things suggest a predominantly oral culture. The sound of words was more telling than their appearance. To recognise this should make us more rather than less sensitive to linguistic nuance, and to the volatile precision of Shakespeare's language. For instance, erratic spelling and aural awareness feed into an openness to puns. Similarly, if people are used to words looking irregular, they will be less resistant to irregular formations of words. This helps explain, for instance, Shakespeare's love of new-coined words, or of making nouns act as verbs or adjectives (and vice versa). The inconsistent punctuation of the period is similarly suggestive. It gives us all kinds of hints about stress and pronunciation. But more than that it suggests a medium suspended between speech and print. The question of priority between the two is much less important than the fact of their creative interplay. It is not just that words are composed to then be spoken, or that spoken speeches duly get written down. It is that the fluidity of speech – the fact that speech is constantly confusing or exceeding grammatical rules – has to find written form. To some degree this form will be like a cast, moulding the words into definitive shape. At the same time the fact that the words are written to be spoken, and come partly out of an oral culture whose forms are not set in stone, means that the shape they take on the page will retain much of this fluidity. The dramatic speech is thus as much a kind of motion picture as it is any kind of monument. This is as true of grammar as it is of the discrete words themselves. The changeable punctuation both records and contributes to this sense of word forms and speech forms in process. Above all, we have to get rid of any suspicion that language, vocabulary, and grammar are an oppressive inheritance, settled for all time. It may seem so at times to us, but Shakespeare and his colleagues in the popular theatre appear eagerly intent on showing that it would not be so for them.

Furthermore, we have to acknowledge just how various, and to a degree how unknown, Shakespeare's own audiences are. There is no space here for debates about the likely demographics of different playing arenas at different times. It is enough for us to remember that Shakespeare wrote for different stage spaces and different audiences. Most often the plays were written for the public stage, with the expectation that they might be asked for at court and that they could, in the event of plague closing the capital's theatres, be taken on tour to city inns or great houses in less contagious parts of the country. Occasionally his work may have been commissioned by the powerful (Queen Elizabeth reportedly wanted to see 'Falstaff in love', hence *Merry Wives of Windsor*), occasionally it may have been composed for specific occasions (*Midsummer Night's Dream* for a wedding). But the fact of an occasion cannot dictate responses to it. *A Midsummer Night's Dream* can hardly be understood as a sop to aristocratic self-celebration. There are many contexts in circulation at any time: none more decisive than those set in motion by the playtext.

Neither should any of Shakespeare's audiences be seen as homogeneous. The public stages ranged from the outdoor Rose and Globe (not built until nearly halfway through Shakespeare's career) to the indoor Blackfriars (available from 1608). It is likely that of these three the Rose franchise was the most populist, the Globe the most heterogeneous, and Blackfriars the most exclusive. But even so we have to posit all kinds of internal variations and demographic subsets. To be courtly or educated, for instance, as members of the wealthier Blackfriars' audience often were, in itself establishes very little about details of taste or politics. The same goes for 'the' court. There were in fact various courts, of king, queens, princes – at times singing from the same hymnbook, at others broodingly at odds. Depending upon who was doing the patronising – and of course who was in attendance – particular dramatic moments could bear subtly or starkly different significance. Again, such questions are fascinating, but not my particular subject. Suffice here to say that speculations about Shakespeare's audiences should never pre-empt openness to Shakespeare's meanings.

Something similar can be said for the different stage spaces. So, when Shakespeare's company got the lease for the indoor and more genteel Blackfriars, it may well be true that he was encouraged to write in new ways. The famously indefinable shape and genus of Caliban in *The Tempest*, for example, is explicable in terms of the new stage being candlelit. For the first time a staged body might be to the eye at once centre stage *and* in shadow. Visuals are beginning to catch up or correspond with the spoken word. Nevertheless, most of the work to make Caliban's body so pregnant with possibilities is still being performed by the language that would subdue or explain this body. More than anything, stage business here casts an even starker forensic spotlight upon linguistic details. Furthermore, it can be difficult to know which comes first: our guesses as to what technical or other possibilities the unique conditions of the new theatre (shape, sight lines, acoustics, lighting, clientele) might have suggested to Shakespeare; or our understanding of what 'already' characterises the post-Blackfriars plays. If we think that his late romances are unusually courtly or stately, we can ascribe this to the indoor theatre's higher class of person and plusher environment. If we think that these plays are sceptical and problematic, we can ascribe this similarly to a better educated clientele, or a space which because quieter and more comfortable was conducive to close attention to political questions. The fact that perhaps the most masque-like and processional play of all, *Pericles*, was a roaring success at the Globe, and the most argumentative and politicised, *Coriolanus*, coincides with the Blackfriars purchase, is perhaps sufficient to warn us off glib assumptions of cause and effect.

To get the fullest sense of Shakespeare we always need to move back and forth between playtexts and contexts. But the Shakespeare playtext is the most acute location for such contexts: both their representation and their analysis. It is above all a layered thing, poising one context within and against another. This is as powerful in its small details as in its larger structures. In this book, consequently, the concentration is upon the readable details of the playtexts, and the possibilities these inscribe. It remains the place where we can first and best get at whatever Shakespeare is doing.

# Part I
# WORDS

# 1

# WHY ALL OF THESE METAPHORS?

*This chapter considers the basic difficulty of Shakespeare's language. It asks why he writes in such a dense and complicated way. Why can't it be written more simply? If we understand enough to keep up with the story, then does it matter whether or not we get anything extra? What is the link between the difficulty of the language and its pleasures, or between meanings that are immediate and those that are withheld? Is Shakespeare's language not simply excessive? In order to answer these questions, this chapter looks carefully at the very basics of Shakespeare's use of metaphor. First, we distinguish Shakespeare's use of metaphor from more conventional ideas of how it works. We show that his metaphors are not used to dress up simple thoughts in fancy language. It is often the case that the metaphor itself is the thought – there is not a more basic meaning hiding inside the packaging. Instead, Shakespeare's meaning time and again gets body, substance, and character precisely from the implications of the metaphors. The chapter goes on to show that the best way of reading Shakespeare's language is simply to let it mean what it says, and to more or less take his metaphors literally. That is, we should trust that he uses words knowing what they mean. Almost nothing is wasted or haphazard; the referents are sown and plotted. The dramatic context is largely created by the words, and these contexts repeatedly show a full awareness of the referents of the words spoken, and a clear anticipation of how these referents will unfold, combine, or conflict. Shakespeare's words thereby often work like little stages, animating historical energies, housing conflict, and dramatising mental movement. Shakespeare's metaphors are truly originating: they embody*

*Shakespeare making up his worlds. To explore all of this, the chapter looks at a range of examples from some of Shakespeare's more linguistically challenging plays, including* Coriolanus, Othello, Macbeth, Hamlet, *and* The Tempest.

There was nothing to stop Shakespeare from adopting an elegant, even classical approach to dramatic language. His fellow playwright Ben Jonson did so with aplomb, advertising a decorum where every speech is appropriate to the speaker, the circumstance, and the consequent intention. Word and world are both securely in place. A word may have multiple meanings, but art is truest when it knows which one it wants, and makes the choosing clear. If we must use puns, for instance, then let clowns or conmen use them, but not princesses. Discretion, distinction, and discrimination equal decorum: to define is to choose rather than multiply.

But Shakespeare doesn't use words in this way. His words are at once overloaded and astonishingly rapid, giving the impression of a gushing torrent of words. Furthermore, these words are usually in verse, and stuffed full with figurative expressions. In his early plays the speeches are longest, and the extended similes and metaphors correspondingly drawn out. As his craft matures he is less likely to want to impress with the rotundity or grandeur of his conceits. But if this can seem like a small mercy, what gradually replaces it is perhaps even more forbidding. For in place of lengthy descriptions and declarative public rhetoric, we get dialogues unprecedented in popular drama for their metaphorical density, allusive networks, and forward and backward rhythms. He is long-winded and yet dense; elevated and yet punning; repetitious and yet elliptical. And one of the peculiar difficulties of Shakespeare is that he is very often all of these things at once. The most 'Shakespearean' language of all is at one and the same time long-winded, dense, grand, punning, repetitious, and elliptical: one in the other; each determined and framed by the other. Even if we get the gist we can simultaneously be aware of how much we are missing. This can be still more annoying because his words are not offered as exquisite linguistic miniatures to be pored over and dwelt upon. They are dramatic speeches, spoken in the course of unfolding action. An audience has no more power to stop or slow them down than we have of stopping or slowing down time itself. But of course they demand just such a pause for consideration – and almost certainly always have done.

What to do? For a start, we need to recognise that Shakespeare's language is often an interplay of immediacy and withholding. We need to distinguish between points where the appeal is immediate, is felt as something physical, as distinct from points where the effect reveals itself slowly, or resists being worked out unless it can be recollected (in memory) or revisited (in a second hearing or reading). Consider this from Iago: 'Arise, Arise/Awake the *snorting* citizens with the bell' (*Othello*, 1.1.88–9; my italics). The basic effect of the speech is simple enough. It is a rude wake-up call, specifically to Desdemona's father, Brabantio, implying that her marriage with Othello the Moor is an insult to all of Venice's respectable citizenry. But Iago's 'snorting' is doing more than describing a shared condition of sleep. It is a vivid word-picture, filling in for absent scenery, missing back-plot – and the speaker's concentrated menace. So, we should see a small vignette, a city's biography, as the previous evening's indulgence is slept ignorantly out. We should sense the professional soldier's contemptuous curl of lip, as Iago – the man who never sleeps – 'snorts' at the anaesthetised dopiness of these Venetians. Equally, these citizens can be imagined snorting *at* something. They sleep, yes, but they are dreaming hearty dreams, full of good horsy sport. The immediate context provides their dream. So, their snort is derision: they are laughing at Brabantio, the poor father, the only man in town who doesn't know that his innocent child is being had, right now, by a big black animal. But then there might be something more. In some dark place, the general and the child go to it. Consequently, the identification in the 'snorting' might simultaneously be with the 'Barbary horse' (1.1.110). For Othello too is 'snorting', the aged stud in the exhausting commission of fornication. In every dreamscape, therefore, Iago hears the same piggish purr, of decorum spread-eagled and secrecies breached. The 'snorting', in this sense, becomes the beast within. It speaks of wanting the very thing that will end all we treasure; it speaks of violation and voyeurism becoming the ethical norm. And above all – as perhaps we cannot immediately get, but will soon enough – it speaks of Iago, insinuating his own pathologies into his fatally sleepy compatriots.

Shakespeare's interfolding dialogues are often like this, at once strikingly immediate and full of latent layering; the 'through-line' is clear even though every connotation might not be. Equally often, however, the effects are less reassuring. No matter how trained in rhetoric, no first-time audience can ever have picked up all of the material that is stuffed into Shakespeare's denser constructions:

> Your enemies, with nodding of their plumes,
> Fan you into despair! Have the power still
> To banish your defenders, till at length
> Your ignorance – which finds not till it feels,
> Making but reservation of yourselves,
> Still your own foes – deliver you as most
> Abated captives to some nation
> That won you without blows!
>
> (*Coriolanus*, 3.3.126–33)

As is usually the case, many listeners will pick up the basic 'humour' or 'temperament' of Coriolanus's speech: here, bilious and splenetic. But none of it is easy. His talk of fanning 'plumes' and 'abated captives', for instance, lends a baroque sophistication to the soldier's almost infantile tantrum. The real difficulty, however, comes with the parenthesis of lines 129–31. The syntax is so contracted and elliptical, its message at once so violent and so abstract, that it is genuinely hard to channel the words into coherence. But even so we can seize upon small bits, severed from each other but still collecting into some kind of fractured whole: the alliterative contrast of 'finds not till it feels', the pithy summation of 'Still your own foes'. We can thus piece together the speech's prevailing confusion of motive and emotion. Even in semi-bewilderment we may understand that Coriolanus is here strung between dismay and disgust, instruction and insult, being dismissed and doing the dismissing. Invariably even Shakespeare's hardest language will work something like this. The words will offer a quick sense, concordant with the movement of plot and the broad delineation of mood, conflict and character, that can be taken up by even the least confident auditor. And simultaneously they will spark out other possibilities, ones that might confirm, counterpoint, or complicate this quick sense in any number of ways. Almost all of Shakespeare's more obscure dialogue is premised, as here, upon simultaneously different kinds of audience or readerly openness (or of course resistance).

But the recognition that there is often something extra in the language, something more than the attentive ear can quickly pick up, might also provoke a sceptical question. If the words are meant to serve a dramatic purpose, and are addressed to an audience, is there any point in hunting for more abundant meanings if we have identified how the speech fits in to the unfolding mood or action? Perhaps we should think of drama as most of us do music. We feel stuff when we hear it, and these feelings may include conscious recognitions and understandings. However, we rarely need to break anything down or distinguish this constituent from that to be able to believe that our experience of the music is worthwhile. Why can't Shakespeare be the same?

Of course we can answer here that Shakespeare is the same. If we see or read it for pleasure, as we usually hear music for pleasure, then it is quite enough to feel moved or excited, laugh or cry or simply enjoy the story. However complex the art or virtuoso the techniques, the point of the thing is its reception. Complicated means can produce very simple, albeit often very strong, responses. Furthermore, far more people study Shakespeare than study music. If more of us were presented with Beethoven or Eminem as a text to be analysed, and asked to explain why we think or feel what we do and how the text produces the effects it does, then the musical text would similarly be shown to be a network of all sorts of response-producing techniques, technologies, and rhetorical strategies. We can therefore offer the time-honoured justification of education: enjoyment is increased by understanding. There is pleasure to be gained from overcoming resistances, whether our own psychic blocks or the objective difficulties of a text. Curiosity nourishes itself, questions produce questions, and a whole world of possibilities begins to open up as soon as we care to look: and so on.

But still there are sceptical questions to be faced. We might grant that figurative speech can make the dramatic artefact more alluring, immediate, or striking. It can prevent the play from being too prosaic, too much like a news report; it can give us little puzzles and so the pleasure of solving them and moving on, both stirred and strengthened. It can give us something to grab hold of, to tussle with, to picture, and so help supply bare words with body and presence. But why go beyond such immediate comprehensibility? Is there a productive relationship between Shakespeare's difficulty and his pleasures? Does he not use too many words, too many metaphors, too many puns and pyrotechnics, many of which contribute nothing but an extravagant and self-pleasing sideshow to the main game? Could we not feel the pain of Othello or Macbeth without so much verbiage? To put it bluntly: couldn't they be simpler? Couldn't they be *shorter?*

Clearly, Shakespeare's torrent of language can provoke a torrent of questions. Let's see if we can offer any responses.

Ultimately, there is no separating Shakespeare's meaning from the many difficulties of his style. In many ways his language remains strange and difficult no matter how familiar we become with it. Or perhaps this can be rephrased: Shakespeare's language *should* continue to surprise and bewilder us; it should continue at times to feel estranged from our expectations or alien to our ease. If it doesn't feel like this, then it is almost certain that we are smoothing out the often 'tortive and errant' grain of Shakespeare to fit our own requirements of comfort (*Troilus*, 1.3.9). It can be precisely where the jokes are too many or the disguises too much that we should home in with our questions; precisely in this too many and too much that we find whatever answers are going. For it is simply not possible to bleach the murk and iron out the wrinkles and keep anything like the fabric's integrity. Shakespeare always resists such domestication. This isn't to say that every line is a perfect one. It is merely to say that we have to take the words as they are, in the order they are given and with the referents they evoke, and make of it what we can. We might simply hate Shakespeare's style, or like many readers before us think that there are good bits spoiled by his inveterately *Shakespearean* habits: not merely by the off-putting but (one supposes) unavoidable echo chamber of 'thous', thees' and 'prithees', but by things he did have a choice about, like all of those obscure metaphors, silly puns, and turgid rants. But one thing remains sure. Shakespeare's verbal manners are no kind of accident. He knew exactly what he was doing and – bad taste, overkill, impenetrable or not – there is not a word in Shakespeare that is not doing just what he wanted. Whatever other doubts or resistances we bring to the experience, we should have none whatsoever here.

## METAPHORS

Shakespeare's basic figure of speech is the metaphor. It will be useful here to compare Shakespeare's practice with customary notions of what 'metaphor' does and is. So, metaphor proposes a resemblance between two things, one being the thing said, the other being the thing meant. Consider 'the *blanket* of the dark' (*Macbeth*, 1.5.52). The thing said ('blanket') serves the things denoted (night-time, darkness, invisibility). This latter is what the speech is 'really' about. The figure of speech helps to give it force or colour, or gives a brief pleasure to the listener who identifies (usually instantaneously) the relation between the two parts. Rather confusingly, the word 'metaphor' can refer both to the whole phrase ('blanket of the dark') and to the figurative vehicle within it ('blanket'). This suggests how the figuring vehicle on its own carries an unusual charge of meaning, although one that is uniquely drawn from its connection to the particular context at hand.

This understanding of metaphor rests upon the assumption that the job of language is to transport something already thought. The mental picture exists independent of the words, and in a basic sense the words can be ditched once the message has been received. Metaphor exemplifies this idea of language because the colouring figure (often called the 'vehicle') is apparently so serviceable. It is like the fancy packaging for a gift: it may heighten expectation or add to the occasion; it may defer and so intensify the pleasures of reception. But once it is loosened from the gift that it burnishes, the packaging loses all shape, purpose, and indeed meaning.

But even in the most uncomplicated instances Shakespeare rarely works quite so straightforwardly. Let's consider 'the *blanket* of the dark' more closely. It is true enough to understand it as meaning that the night is 'like' a blanket: but hardly sufficient. So, the vehicle (blanket) is not here only, or even primarily, conveying the denoted object (dark). It is equally conveying a situational and psychological energy brought to bear specifically upon this object. It is Lady Macbeth's imaginary 'blanket', rather than the 'dark', that both generates and gathers in all of the situational specificity. In this sense, 'blanket' becomes almost a self-sufficient metaphor of its own, although its referents are still placed and enabled by 'the dark'. The image concentrates Lady Macbeth's anticipatory guilt. Each connotation of 'blanket' conjures up a narrative or psychological capsule, evoking the true past and safe future that she is about so fatally to scotch. We can see in the 'blanket' projections of childhood, the marriage bed, suffocation; with one glance she turns from 'heaven' into unrepentant brutality; with another, she turns to a childlike cocoon of safety, warmth, sleep – or of course amnesia. The word 'blanket' becomes a striking embodiment of the speaker's mind. Indeed, because its associations seem half-free of the Lady's conscious agency, the metaphor speaks all the more for the haunted world of *Macbeth*: one in which nothing is ever quite laid to rest, and in which a 'blanket' evokes at once the desire to hide from self-truth (in sleep or deception), and an unavoidable summons to the restless recapitulations of insomnia or sleepwalking.

Most speeches of any substance in Shakespeare include the basic type of metaphor, which is when one noun or noun-phrase stands in for another. For instance, in his final speech Othello speaks of himself as one 'unused to the melting mood', meaning tears (5.2.349). The image is overtly poetic, its alliterative prettification and gentle euphemism suggesting a man struggling to speak directly of grief and horror. Like much else in this speech, the euphemism hints at self-deflection, or of a struggle to recognise that it is really he who is denoted. A man, particularly a warrior like Othello, should be monumental; 'melting mood' is the sort of thing a woman suffers, with her capricious humours and bodily fluidity. This immediately suggests that the metaphor is more complicated than any 'this equals that' equation. For the phrase 'melting mood' does *not* in fact denote tears, at least not in any simple or finished way. Much more presently, it denotes exactly what it says: a 'mood' of 'melting' that Othello is struggling to acknowledge as his own. His substance truly is dripping away like wasted 'medicinable gum' (351), or like the throat-blood that he is all the time preparing to spill into. His state of mind is one of profound self-liquidation, but one that records and acts out his dissolution.

There is nothing very complicated about the metaphor. But we are barking up the wrong tree if we settle for any kind of 'substitution' hypothesis to explain how the language works. Of course there is the whole context of Othello's story to help fill out the words chosen and allow them their terrible pathos. But still the words of the metaphor have a palpable presence: a magnetism that draws the drama of the moment into these specific words.

There is another example a line or two earlier, when Othello describes how he 'threw a pearl away/Richer than all his tribe' (5.2.347–8). This couldn't perhaps be simpler: Desdemona is the 'pearl', and the metaphor proposes a simple substitution. But it is not really anything so neutral or nominal. For 'pearl' doesn't only evoke Desdemona's preciousness and nobility. Crucially, the pearl is white: in black contrast, he who plucked it from its shell is from a 'tribe'. (In medieval allegories the pearl could also evoke Christ's redeeming love: in the Folio text it is the base 'Judean' who threw it away, Othello thereby shading into Judas.) But even in admitting his guilt, Othello is busy repeating much of his error. For she remains to him exactly a 'pearl', a precious white gem to be worn glistening against his jet. The metaphor thus both concentrates and judges Othello's relation to the qualities he here recalls. He has not escaped from his tragedy; he has not ascended to some wise perch from which he can survey the wreck he has made and the reasons why he made it. He is still *in* it, still in the mind that made the whole game so easy to throw. In a sense, therefore, the shell that yielded this 'pearl' is nothing less than Othello's self-trapped mind. His is the sand that – now as before – chafes it into being. Furthermore, the 'pearl', as much as it is so very clearly Othello's word, is also a romantic cliché, an aspiration of all good hero-lovers to possess, in flesh or in verse (compare the cliché-sodden Troilus's evocation of Cressida, 'Her bed is India; there she lies, a pearl': *Troilus*, 1.1.99). It is one of numerous instances of Othello's slavishness before all things white and exemplary. Metaphor not only illustrates and reinforces Othello's entrapment, but contributes a killing and inescapable coda to it.

To think about metaphor in this way is to see in miniature a crucial part of the tragic narrative. It is also to see how this narrative in some fundamental sense could not be what it is without this instinct to think of, in almost a literal sense to construct, both one's self and others through metaphors. Here is the whole of Othello's self-epitaph:

> I have done the state some service, and they know't:
> No more of that. I pray you, in your letters,
> When you shall these unlucky deeds relate,
> Speak of me as I am. Nothing extenuate,
> Nor set down aught in malice. Then must you speak
> Of one that loved not wisely, but too well;
> Of one not easily jealous, but, being wrought,
> Perplexed in the extreme; of one whose hand,
> Like the base Indian, threw a pearl away
> Richer than all his tribe; of one whose subdued eyes,
> Albeit unused to the melting mood,
> Drops tears as fast as the Arabian trees
> Their medicinable gum. Set you down this,
> And say besides that in Aleppo once,
> Where a malignant and a turbanned Turk
> Beat a Venetian and traduced the state,
> I took by th' throat the circumcised dog
> And smote him – thus!        [*He stabs himself*]
>
> (5.2.339–56)

Othello gradually finds point and clarification only in extended metaphor. He begins with a fairly bald 'I', moves quickly into the anonymous third person ('one that loved not wisely ... one not easily jealous'), then to three successive non-occidental others, a 'base Indian' (or 'Judean' in Folio), an 'Arabian' tree, a malignant 'Turk', before circling in his penultimate move back into a state-serving 'Venetian' and then, terminally, into the 'circumcised dog' whom he slaughters. This rehearses Othello's definitive struggle for identity. Indeed it gives a potted life history, supplying what the play hitherto omits: as we suspected, every role and name he has worn has in some sense been borrowed. So, Othello's sequential displacing and discovery of self into others is also a self-constitution (and dissolution) through metaphor.

But we might also notice how the relationship between Othello and these self-allegories is akin to the relationship within a metaphor, between (to use I.A. Richards's terms) the tenor and the vehicle. So, the tenor here, the thing supposedly being spoken of, is Othello; the vehicles, in brief, are 'I', 'me', 'one', 'Indian', Arabian', 'Turk', 'Venetian', 'circumcised dog'. We might not usually think of 'I' or 'me' as at all metaphorical: they speak directly of the thing itself. But we should also see that the only substance that Othello can here deliver is when he is 'translated' into these externalised others – or into metaphor. When he tries to speak directly of 'I', his meaning is vague, vaporous, or deferred: 'I have done the state some service, and they know't:/No more of that'. Othello almost retreats into old habits of boastful modesty, but he stops himself. He is resolved to strip all such self-accounting down to the bone. But any such terminal self-accounting remains an act of self-figuring. He says 'Speak of me as I am', and duly proceeds to do so. For 'as I am' *is* a Turk, a Venetian, a dog, and so on, or that is as close to definition as he or we are ever going to get.

In much the same fashion, Shakespeare's meaning time and again derives body and substance from the metaphors that might at first glance appear merely to 'dress' it. Just as Othello's past and future is given to us through this sequence of aliens and alienation, so too a playworld's moving agitations are invariably given to us in the mini-narratives of the metaphors. Shakespeare repeatedly makes words per se three-dimensional, finding shape and motion in both time and space. His figures and clauses are often like little stages: enfolding or unfolding into stories, housing plots and movement, populated by divergent and often dissentious bodies. Of course Othello's reversion to self-allegories bears specifically upon his tragedy of an internal alien. Nevertheless, this 'metaphorised' identity, in which there is in some basic sense no essence other than these hypothesised resemblances, replicates the way that Shakespeare's metaphors work. They seem to serve or stand for some primary cohering reality: but the only access to and presence of this reality is the metaphors.

## WORDS AND EMBODIMENT

To grasp the import of Shakespeare's words we have to remember the limited means there were of sustaining illusion on the public stage. Usually performed in broad daylight, without many or any props, by actors that the audience had recently seen pretending to be someone else: costumes aside (which were often impressive) it was not a scene likely to zap one instantaneously into another world. It is the words that do most of the work of making such dramatic worlds visible to the mind. They are no kind of clear window onto an entire picture that exists without or before them. Modern productions or film versions of the plays invariably gain much of their impact from arresting sets and visuals. We can get the impression that the characters enter a world that is already there, independent of the dialogue that they speak. And of course we are asked to believe this: Lear is on a heath, Pericles at sea, Hermia and Helena in a forest. We are happy to allow these places a contingent reality, antecedent to the figures that inhabit them. But as much as this is a necessary fiction, it is also a fiction whose basic terms of permission are always there to be exploited.

Of course, a scene set in Verona or Fife might well draw upon the facts or fictions of that place as understood at the time. Every palace, forest, or city will be appealing to pre-existing associations, drawn from gossip, myth, generic tradition, contemporary reputation, or shared experience. Nevertheless, any such place is in some crucial sense unwritten and non-existent until we hear the words spoken by the characters 'in' it. This is the case even when the scene setting is at its most dramatically immediate. For instance, in *As You Like It* Duke Senior talks in his first line of 'brothers in exile', in his third line of 'these woods' (2.1.1–3). However, by instantaneously comparing the place to 'painted pomp' and the 'envious court' it becomes less a simple setting than a highly artificial tableau in which literary pastoral is set up for critique. In *The Winter's Tale* Antigonus's first lines clarify that 'our ship hath touch'd upon/The deserts of Bohemia' (3.3.1–2): but the geographical impossibility (Bohemia is landlocked) makes the place politically and even metaphysically estranging. Far from a pre-known historical place, it becomes pregnant with possibility because dissociated from habitual directions or understandings. Obviously not all of the play's places are so elusive (although plenty of them are). But the coast of Bohemia can stand for just how substantive, how embodying, Shakespeare's words have to be.

Often Shakespeare develops networks of words that accumulate into their own 'virtual' bodies, barely less real than any character. In *A Midsummer Night's Dream*, the Russian doll-like conceptual architecture finds an equivalence in the play's matrix of tropes evoking creation or transformation: the 'eyes' of poet or desire, 'love', 'dream', 'charm', 'spirits', 'imagination', 'madness', 'play'. Each stands for and contains the other; this 'right brain world' is at once embodied in the whole play and ever-present in each moment. No specific character ever quite epitomises it, but each scene is like a little detonation of the possibilities packed into these synonym-cum-metaphors. In *Troilus and Cressida* the remorseless images of a desired, diseased, or violated body begin to suggest that all of the play's fighting and lovemaking and posturing are forms of masturbation before this same humiliating piece of imaginary flesh. In *The Tempest*, historical action is repeatedly imagined as a movement between lulling imprisonment (in a tree, cloud, bottle, cave) and bursting bombast (from the same things). Geography develops a tangible political energy, identifiable equally with the island of the mind and the island that the characters struggle to possess.

There is always the option that this tentacle-like language can return to a central character. In *Antony and Cleopatra* an ideal heroic body is figured through repeated metaphors of marble, flower, fire, and liquid. This ideal body exists in a parallel mental space to the lovers, and variously shadows, mourns, and mocks the various Antonys that the play witnesses or recalls. No particular speaker directs this telepathic linking of metaphors: indeed its force derives from the fact that so many speakers share in its construction. That this ideal is so much more powerful, in a sense so much more palpable, than the diminishing soldier embodied on stage is the point. This is the externalising capability of Shakespeare's language – but also of course Antony's particular tragedy.

The spirit in *The Tempest*, Ariel, literally embodies this language use. So, Ariel has no material substance: or has none until s/he is put to use, when s/he can materialise into literally anything. Equally, although made of air (like words) once put on the stage s/he must *always* be embodied (even as the immaterial spirit waiting for instructions). Shakespeare's language treads the self-same boards:

> I boarded the King's ship: now on the beak,
> Now in the waist, the deck, in every cabin
> I flamed amazement.
>
> *(The Tempest, 1.2.196–8)*

What exactly is the airy spirit Ariel here describing? Is it the fire (in which case 'flamed amazement' might translate as an 'amazing flame')? Or is it rather the fear and wonder of the men on the ship, pictured particularly in the 'amazed' expressions on their faces, garishly lit by the surrounding flames? The effect of the phrase is that 'flamed' and 'amazement' both modify one another *and* emerge in leaping self-sufficiency. So, Ariel describes metamor-phosing into a flame: s/he wants to impress the master, and in this sense the 'amazement' works as awed commentary upon the ingenuity. At the same time the flame is only apparent; it doesn't scald and kill; it is designed for the mind of its recipients. In such a context, the real subject of the sentence is the 'infect'-ed reason of the men on the ship. In this speech (as in the whole play) matter is a screen for the mind, and mind is an effect of matter. The movements of Ariel in *The Tempest* often seem to shadow the movements of Shakespeare's words. The spirit's job is to be 'correspondent to command' (1.2.297): to translate words into all sorts of physical form. Ariel's paradoxical physicality – s/he is all air, but also (as the moulding force of fire implies) potentially all matter – is a symbol and exercise of Shakespeare's dramatic words.

## TAKING METAPHORS LITERALLY

For words to possess such substantive presence, or to animate such historical energies, often depends upon the way the words themselves are shown to have a history. Shakespeare will often use a word in such a way as gently to open up something like that word's hinterland. It is not that Shakespeare is full of etymological puns (like Spenser or Milton, who are constantly playing upon the differences between a word's Greek or Latin roots and its vernacular uses). But what he often does do is tap into the physical sources that underlie even the most abstract figure of speech. It is another aspect of his language's distinctive tangibility. Often he exploits this source whether or not it seems to be a working referent. So, it frequently happens that the physical reference is at odds with the more expected use of the word (the customary use that usually forgets the physical source). In turn it often happens that this physically precise meaning has a suggestive power far greater than the customary referent.

An example is Macbeth's: 'it hath *cow'd* my better part of man' (5.8.18). It is roughly clear what Macbeth means by 'cow'd' – something like overawed or subdued – but it is not at all clear exactly how it means this, or whether it implies anything more. This is because the derivation of 'cow'd' is itself unclear. Macbeth's is *OED*'s first record of the word being used as a verb; there is no traditional practice whatsoever of using 'cow'd' to mean 'subdued'. The dictionary appeals (rather hopefully) to the Old Norse 'kuga', meaning 'to oppress'. Perhaps some such transitive use was in circulation in one of Shakespeare's milieus, but it seems safer to look closer to home. If we do this, we quickly see three simple and appropriate possibilities. First, the past participle 'cowed' was in common enough circulation and meant simply 'cropped' or 'pruned' (as in a head or its hair). In this sense, for Macbeth's 'better part of man' to be 'cow'd' means, fairly starkly, that it has been cut off, or indeed emasculated. This leads into the second association, simpler still: to be 'cow'd' means to be made like a 'cow', that imperturbable, milky, *female* domestic bovine. Again, the humour cuts to Macbeth's bone. He is the man who is at the start of the play 'too full o'th milk of human kindness' (1.5.16), and who soon gets harried into self-loss by three witches and a wife. The cow thus floats bathetically into view – part deity, part daimon – as Macbeth's customary attendant spirit. Third, 'cow'd' is an abbreviation of 'coward' – picked up by Macduff in his immediate reply ('Then yield thee, coward') – and itself a tart joke about Macbeth's effeminising humiliation. A 'coward' invokes various animals in flight and more precisely 'turning tail', or having the tail drawn between the legs. Conveniently, this invokes respectively the emasculation and gender translation of the verb's two other likely sources. It is only by allowing the word's indecorous, rather bathetic associations full imaginative animation (as Macbeth himself mordantly does) that we bring the speech to proper dramatic life.

Or consider the conceit that begins Hamlet's first soliloquy: 'O that this too too sullied flesh would melt,/Thaw and resolve itself into *a dew*' (1.2.129–30). We might here ask a very basic question: is 'a dew' a metaphor? It might seem to represent a hankering for blank annihilation. Does it stand for something else, or is it in fact the thing itself, the element into which the prince wishes to dissolve? The answer, we might suggest, is somehow both, and in this it stands as a paradigm of Shakespeare's word use.

The placing of 'a dew' at the end of this statement of disgust might suggest that its function is simply to represent blank annihilation. But as much as the word completes the thought, it also stops one thought and inaugurates another; or perhaps secretes a certain wistfulness within the enveloping despair. For Hamlet concentrates himself – literally – into this image. Accordingly, the image itself becomes a concentration of the hero's dramatic possibilities.

So, 'a dew' can suggest dawn, youth, and freshness. It aestheticises both conception and birth, removing one from the taint of sperm, the other from the taint of woman. In devolving from flesh to dew, solid to liquid, Hamlet would become less massy, closer to air. The phrase's miniaturist transcendence perhaps suggests some kind of reincarnation or redemption; or perhaps hibernation, a burying away until circumstances are more auspicious. Some such thing is suggested by the solitude of '*a* dew', as though a particular private drop, as faceted as a crystal or a tear. In this limpid, pre-organic clarity the dew evokes, plaintively enough, a cleansing repair from the rank sweat and seed of the Elsinore jungle.

Once again, the single image shifts inside itself, houses movement: to press upon Shakespeare's conceits is to see something like a cell beneath a microscope, as putative singleness reveals a swarm of microbiological activity. But we should also see how all of this activity makes 'a dew' something more than a metaphor. It contains and concentrates the possibilities Hamlet so hankers for: and one such longing is for an end to metaphor, almost a fairy-tale longing for his wishes to take effect (as they might for a pampered child), and for him magically to become the thing he imagines for as long as he needs its release. In turn, these hints of a childish playing with options – as though he can always draw back from his depression, return to school, get on with his preparation for kingdom – feed into the word's slightly evasive multiplicity. (He hasn't yet met his father's ghost, which firms certain things up.) So, if we move from the image's connotations to the state of mind it expresses, we find an irresolute swarm of options. Hamlet has a paralysed sincerity; he is titanically sulky; he is rebellious, wishing to be self-making beyond false fathers, mothers, or gods; he is tempted by a showy, even fey exhaustion; his depression takes him to the edge of absolute bodily refusal.

Hamlet always seems neurotically aware of the way words turn into and away from one another, of the relations they establish, and of the options they leave hanging. In all of this, unsurprisingly, he resembles no one so much as Shakespeare. So, Hamlet is fully aware of literary cliché and generic models: but (like Shakespeare) he wants to shake the image out of any pastoral complacency and claim it as his own. Hence the three verbs (melt, thaw, resolve) that work to so concentrate the climactic noun. The effect is typical of Shakespeare. Time and again the simple surplus of meaning creates a sort of supra-context, an alternative world in which a play's or a character's most vital preoccupations find their air. So, the chosen word will evoke familiar things. But at the same time it will signal their passing into something fiercely private and unprecedented. This is what happens here with 'a dew'. The image possesses a layered – or indeed fractured – relation to space and time. In this it encapsulates its speaker's immediate placement: Hamlet's intense uneasiness in *any* given moment; his ambivalence toward literary or theatrical tradition; his evasion of the audience's easy possession. In this way, simple words like 'dew' can almost tremble with alternative projections as to what might be.

It is a common complaint that Shakespeare doesn't say what he means, or that he can never be taken 'literally' because he is so inveterately metaphoric. But examples such as these suggest a paradox: the best place to take Shakespeare literally is exactly when he is being most figurative. Inevitably this involves a paradox. 'Literally' is commonly used to suggest freedom from allusion, exaggeration, or figures of speech; it means giving priority to the 'relatively primary sense of a word, or to the sense expressed by the actual wording of a passage, as distinguished from any metaphorical or merely suggested reading' (*OED*, 'literal', 3b). This usually means that anything extreme or unusual tends to be phased out of view. Lateral or tangential vision is, 'by definition', not the issue. What matters is what is 'really' being said: invariably a predictable sentiment, endorsed by common sense and everyday assumptions. But it needn't mean anything so dispiriting. There are many worse ways of coming to grips with Shakespeare than, very simply, giving priority to 'the actual wording of a passage'. It means placing in abeyance our faith in, or indeed our need for, the 'normal', 'customary', or 'primary' meaning. We have to let Shakespeare's words mean what they say. This seems obvious, but the history of much teaching of and writing about Shakespeare has been all about something almost opposite: partly through humility and good manners, partly through a resistance to extravagance, partly because Shakespeare must be our mirror and therefore the great reflector of everything *we already know*, Shakespeare has been treated as though he wasn't responsible for his own meanings. It is assumed that his metaphors run away from him and are best let go, or that they are invoked for momentary effect and then left behind in the galloping impatience of his brilliance. Let us try something different: let's assume he chooses his words with care; that he knows what he is doing in choosing them; and that he can see the implications of so doing.

## ORIGINAL AND ORIGINATING METAPHOR

For all of its reference points in literary history, the chronicles, and contemporary preoccupations, there is a crucial edge in Shakespeare's language use that is new. For instance, he invents large abstract nouns that take a mild verb and lay claim to it ('oppugnancy', *Troilus and Cressida*, 1.3.111). These big new nouns can be almost intimidating, seeming to force through to the particular space in the world waiting just for them ('assassination', *Macbeth*, 1.7.2). But he is just as likely to take a common noun and through an unleashing violence 'verb' it into entirely fresh and often troubling possibilities ('un*seam'd* him from the nave to th' chops', *Macbeth*, 1.2.22). Once-settled things are electrified into sudden and unknown movement ('un*sex* me here', *Macbeth*, 1.5.40). Above all, this sort of language use shows Shakespeare – literally – making up his world. The words are rushed through with a strange restlessness of becoming, a felt consciousness of audacity, and an awareness that they themselves, both the images and what they imagine, might indeed not even be: what seems to be given is in fact astonishingly provisional.

Consider Iago's 'if ever mortal eyes do see them *bolster*' (*Othello*, 3.3.402). A 'bolster' is an under-pillow; Iago uses the noun as a verb, basically meaning having sex (because in bed together); this in turn connects with 'bolster' as a prop or support. So, the bodies of Cassio and Desdemona are in the bed ('bolster' 1), they are taking each other's bodily pressure ('bolster' 2), they are aiding and abetting each other's secret crime ('bolster' 3). The fact that the vision is one of imaginative voyeurism ('if ever eye did see') clinches its horrifying mix of physical and ethical pornography. We are not there, it is not happening: but we crane our necks to try to see it, and so end up secretly in the bedroom (as though holding our breath under the 'bolster'). The point to notice is the connection between linguistic, speculative, and ethical violence. Iago wrenches the word from its normal use: this mirrors and channels the wrenching insult of the imagined act. Throughout this great temptation scene (3.3) Iago's keywords perform the same – characteristically Shakespearean – operation: invoking customary meanings or expectations, splitting them in two, and watching unprecedented possibilities sprout and spawn from the fissure.

To summarise this introduction to Shakespeare's figurative language: a drama committed to *original* metaphor as a primary means of making its worlds means one thing above all. It means that language is not primarily there to describe what is already known and observed. Instead, it is itself finding out what might be present; it is its own barometer of possibility. It is at once tangible and speculative, rooted in the body's immediacy but committed to an almost magical apprehension of what might be. Above all, it gives us minds and societies in process. Dramatic character, plot, and scene – indeed all of the things we engage with – can be understood as experiments in language's capability of embodiment. There is nothing safe or static about this sort of language. Everything is up for grabs, and as perilous as precious. We might be used to characterising Shakespeare's protagonists in some such way. But it is equally true of his language. It gives us a clue why his work can be so exciting and so daunting.

# 2

# WHY USE TWO WORDS WHEN ONE MIGHT DO?

*This chapter continues to examine some of Shakespeare's more complex linguistic habits. Shakespeare's relentless metaphors can be difficult, but understanding them is made still more challenging by the grammatical framework in which they are usually placed. Shakespeare's lines and sentences are not structured in the same reliable fashion as modern English. Their syntax is often dense and elliptical. The relation between one word and another is often ambiguous. It can be impossible to say which word qualifies which, or to identify what is the subject of a clause. But at the same time as his language is marked by gaps and inversions, it can also seem oddly repetitive. One common example of this is when Shakespeare uses two very similar words, separated by the conjunction 'and', to characterise a single thing. This is the figure of speech called* hendiadys. *This chapter explores why he uses this figure of speech. If the repetition is not pointless and excessive, then it must be that the twinned words are doing more than simply complementing each other. Perhaps the single words mean things on their own as well as in relation to their neighbours; perhaps it is the words' differences as much as their similarities that Shakespeare is exploiting; perhaps the relation between the two words is more of a wrestle, more of a drama, than any notion that they simply reinforce each other could allow. In other words, this chapter explores hendiadys as a typical example of how Shakespeare's clauses generate meaning in different directions at once. This figure of speech exemplifies Shakespeare's construction of concentrated units of speech that can simultaneously embody different states of mind, different perspectives, and different situations in space*

*and time. And because the supposedly colouring or qualifying word is*
*given its own freestanding status, it is another example of how*
*Shakespeare invests his words with dramatic body, presence, and energy.*

If Shakespeare's word use is often marked by metaphorical density, elliptical sentence structure, and ambiguous syntax, then a copybook example of this word use is the figure of speech called *hendiadys*. This is where two substantive words, usually nouns but quite often adjectives, are joined by the conjunctive *and*: for example, Macbeth's 'the *bank* and *shoal* of time' (1.7.6) or Horatio's 'the dead *waste* and *middle* of the night' (*Hamlet*, 1.2.198). Normally we would find either a noun phrase (adjective/ noun as in 'incestuous sheets', *Hamlet*, 1.2.157) or a noun and a dependent noun ('the winds of heaven', *Hamlet*, 1.2.141). The word 'hendiadys' literally means 'one through two'. This suggests why the trope is so suggestive and characteristic an example of Shakespeare's use of language. For we may well ask why we need two words to supply one referent. At least a pun, which gives us the opposite – two through one – has the benefit of cleverness and concentration, perhaps of a certain surprise, or furtiveness, or explosiveness. But what can this 'one through two' trope suggest but a slack indulgence in words for their own sake, or a fundamentally pointless piling up of pseudo-adjectives in disguise? Or was it simply Shakespeare's way of filling out the pentameter? Stuck with an eight-foot rather than ten-foot thought, he started habitually adding 'and *blah*' to keep his meter ticking.

What is the 'one' that the 'two' serves? If the two words are roughly synonymous, the answer to this may be simple enough. So, the 'and' joins the two words together into a single unit, like two brotherly adjectives modifying a noun. Each word basically reinforces the other. The parallel structure of hendiadys therefore helps furnish a coordinate meaning. In such cases the repetition might be more about atmosphere than anything more semantically exact: for example, Macbeth's 'Thou *sure and firm-set* earth/ Hear not my steps' (2.1.56–7). It is often the case that the second term helps to define the first. So, rather than invoking referential multiplicity, the repetition might help to concentrate meaning, or to unfold a character's very particular preoccupations. An example of this is Claudius's words about Hamlet:

> There's something in his soul
> O'er which his melancholy sits on brood,
> And I do doubt the *hatch and the disclose*
> Will be some danger...

(3.1.165–8; my italics)

The speech balances simultaneous semantic fields, one a mother hen cherishing her egg, the other Hamlet's brooding depression. The hendiadys completes the effect by drawing the two fields together in a single picture: so, the hatched egg is also a 'hatch' opening, as in a secret trapdoor (on a stage, for instance); Hamlet the mother gives birth to Hamlet the conspirator; the thing disclosed is both this 'hatch' and the ghostly secrets that Hamlet *and* Claudius have been sitting upon. In this sense, 'disclose' works back upon 'hatch' to make it primarily about speech. Claudius is frightened less of the 'danger' of a plot than of public disclosure – the very thing that from the start Hamlet has been forbidden.

If we look at how Shakespeare uses the device, we will find that it is rarely so simple as to give two synonyms or near-synonyms. The two words often sound like synonyms, or can be construed as synonyms, but there is also a contrary pull away from sameness. So, though occasionally the repetition channels a more focused image, more often than not – this being Shakespeare – it also animates profound oppositions or uncertainties. Here is the Chorus in *Henry V*:

> And leave your England as dead midnight still,
> Guarded with grandsires, babies and old women,
> Either past or not arrived to *pith and puissance.*

(3.0.19–21; my italics)

The phrase 'pith and puissance' sounds rather like undistinguishing hyperbole, an impression reinforced by the alliteration. In this sense, the words can be taken as one to mean 'patriotic strength'. But the relationship between the two nouns is in fact more interesting. So, the Old English 'pith' denotes the physical strength and backbone that might allow any Latinate 'puissance', meaning a more generalised or poeticised authority. Without the little people's resilience there is no national greatness; the fact that the home country has been left to babies and the aged to defend reinforces the fact that the war itself is being fought by the 'pith' of common men. As much as 'pith' and 'puissance' conflate into one image of power, they also separate in rather proud independence: 'pith' is home-grown and individuated, a thing of brain and sinew; 'puissance' is idealised and mythic, a creature of politics and reputation. The second might require and direct the first, but it is the first that allows and protects the second. This simple hendiadys thus concentrates *Henry V*'s most basic questions concerning the origins and the costs of power.

As the example from *Henry V* suggests, the difficulties that the figure raises are also opportunities. The 'and' does not necessarily mean 'equals', but can imply a range of possible relationships between the two halves of the proposition. We need to see it as a prototypically dramatic sort of space, its content as up for grabs and open to influence as any other theatrical moment. It is a kind of pause, but one full of echoes and anticipations; it proposes relations but does not determine them; it allows equally for union and distinctness. Typical of Shakespeare, the figure's difficulties are often to do with the hierarchy or ordering of sense: to which do I give priority? However, this problem is different from how it would be with a pun, or even with an oxymoron. To recognise a pun is to recognise some sort of subversion or splitting of sense; to recognise an oxymoron is to enjoy the fact of apparently paradoxical cohabitation. There can be pleasure, self-awareness, or release in these recognitions. Hendiadys, however, is different. There is no laughter in hendiadys, no kind of shared or even sharable response. If we suspect some shifting out of dependency between the two nouns, then it is difficult to know what to do with this difference except – if we don't simply suppress it – follow it in its paths.

## PART AND SUM

The fact that the partnership between the two words in hendiadys has already been assumed – by their juxtaposition, and by their serving of identical grammatical functions – means that we cannot simply undo this identity by recognising that it is inexact, or complicated by some co-existing alternative. Almost because the doubling invites the assumption of similarity, it can also invite the most basic questions of interpretation. How exactly do the two thus fit together? In what ways and to what ends? Depending upon what assumptions? Revealing what prejudices, violence, forgetfulness, or special pleading? To assert identity may be to question it. The consequence for making sense of the thing is simple, and applicable far beyond hendiadys. We have to allow equal referential and dramatic potential to *both* the sum of the parts and the parts of the sum.

Some of Shakespeare's most famous phrases are examples of this 'one through two' figure: 'slings and arrows', 'sound and fury', 'lean and hungry'. Anyone familiar with these phrases knows what they 'mean', but generally without thinking carefully about the twinned words' lexical connotations. This is the way with clichés, as their popularity gradually robs them of much force or precision. But of course these phrases weren't always clichés, and even if we tend to hear them as a gestural unit, we should assume that Shakespeare first wrote them with at least some investment in the respective connotations of each substantive word. Let's consider 'Yond Cassius has a lean and hungry look:/He thinks too much: such men are dangerous' (*Julius Caesar*, 1.2.193–4). How do the two adjectives here link? They might be simple synonyms. Alternatively, the second might be a conclusion drawn from the first: so, Cassius is 'lean'; he hasn't eaten much; he must be 'hungry'. But the dietary signification is hardly primary. Caesar's point is less the observed physical fact than the inferred mental attribute. That is, Cassius's sensuous asceticism suggests an interest in appetites less easily satisfied. In the world of Rome this means matters of civic health and political digestion. Again, the first 'twin' presents the picture, while the second interprets and clinches it. The hendiadys is not so much repeating a physical observation as presenting a sort of unpacked metaphor: 'lean' and 'hungry' depart from their roots in the body and evoke an itchy and unsatisfied mind. It is often the case with hendiadys (as here) that the second of the pair seems to be the defining one, the one with a greater force of *is*). Nevertheless, the figure's symmetrical construction always potentially allows referential equality or competition between the two parts. So, Cassius might be 'lean' because he is (always) 'hungry'. The sense then is that Cassius feeds off himself, aggravating his restless knowledge of self-lack next to Caesar. In this case, the second of the two turns upon the first, like a dog biting its own tail. The two words are close to being simply dependent: that they are not, that it is ambiguous which depends upon the other, encapsulates one of the key dramatic questions of the play's early scenes. That is, whether the state of things is determined by the visible and accountable public body, or by more private and insidious mental gnawings.

Still better known is Hamlet's '*slings and arrows* of outrageous fortune' (3.1.58). It offers a basic picture of battle. The most immediate sense is of being fortune's victim, and wounded by 'arrows' makes clear enough sense. But what should we make of 'slings'? Slings do not fire arrows, after all. We might think that the alternative 'bows and arrows of outrageous fortune' sounds comically unlikely, but this is probably because the phrase chosen has become so famous: 'bows and arrows' at least has the (supposed) virtue of consistency. But if Hamlet had said 'bows and arrows' the power of the phrase would largely be lost: exactly because the two substantives would indeed collapse into a single noun phrase.

The collocation of 'slings' with 'arrows' has a subtly dislocating effect. We don't picture so much a material function (as we would if 'bow' were used) as a sort of aerial scene, one that is not concentrated solely in the body of the subject (whether archer or target) but is instead diffused into a whole hemisphere of vaulting attrition and pelting danger. If the arrows are indeed flung from a sling we get something rather less ordered than we might expect from serried ranks of archers. It evokes unexpectedness and unpredictability, a world of crossed purposes and oblique diagonals. It suggests something arbitrary, something careless and imprecise. Above all, perhaps, it suggests the combined childishness and monstrosity of 'fortune'. For we should take each part of the twin as a distinct image, offering its own distinct narrative projection. The 'slings' of fortune evokes being slung or flung this way and that, as though helplessly tossed upon a 'sea of troubles'. The 'arrows' of fortune evokes a martyr's prolonged pain, experienced as an intensely quizzical concentration upon its multiple and haphazard causes (Hamlet here as a faithless St Sebastian, staring ruefully at the arrows in his – or others' – flesh). Taken as a picture of a single mental state, Hamlet's construction makes of both injury and survival a pained bewilderment. He is both watching it and enduring it. In other words Hamlet, speaking at once from personal experience and for anybody, uses 'slings and arrows' to place himself both inside and outside the canvas. The hendiadys suspends him between activity and passivity, just as any agency in the image is both within and oddly detached from the battle. In both things, the figure epitomises Hamlet's ambiguous place in his own story.

## GRAMMATICAL OPENNESS

Hendiadys is a good example of the difficulties of interpretation caused by Shakespeare's very free and unpredictable grammatical structures. Hendiadys always contributes to what is called a noun phrase (or nominal group). This refers to the group of words that can act as the subject of a sentence: in other words, the thing about which something is stated or predicated. The only necessary element in a noun phrase is the head; there may however be other words in the noun phrase that modify, qualify, or determine the meaning of this head. In modern English the function of all the words in a noun phrase is usually clear. This is not the case in Shakespeare: he simply played by different grammatical rules (or at times, it can seem, none at all). Shakespeare's freedom with noun phrases goes hand in glove with some of his most notorious habits: most particularly, the unpredictable word order and extreme compression of much of his verse. Often we can be unsure how one word or clause relates to the next. Does the word work by modifying or being modified by a preceding or a succeeding word? What is it dependent on? Or does it work 'on its own'? Shakespeare frequently excludes linking words that are common in modern English and that oil and measure the semantic flow. Instead a bunch of words, all of them potentially substantive, are stacked one against another without direction as to which takes priority.

It is perhaps tempting to understand these habits as simple laziness, even perversity. But they are instead finely tuned techniques for giving his speech-acts – *and* many of the individual words or clauses within them – their dramatic combination of body and movement. We see this repeatedly in hendiadys. So, in most of the instances we have looked at there is no absolute priority between the two substantives. The descriptive word is not being used merely as a modifier, as it is in the case of an adjective serving its noun. Rather, a substantive in hendiadys can be at once a modifier to the subject of the clause, or to its twin, and an alternative head in its own right. Each of the pairs can possess its own 'mini-world'; rather like any figure in a painting, however marginal, has the potential to hold the gaze and thereby suggest its own story within the story. In other words, Shakespearean hendiadys invariably offers four different noun phrases: those belonging discretely to each of the twins, to the pair as a unit, and to the subject that they are supposedly serving. Any number of relationships might be in motion; the different 'heads' may be equal to one another, or wrestling with one another, or arranged with a clear sense as to which is subordinate to which. That the figure of hendiadys is most regularly used either in Shakespeare's more metaphysical tragedies (*Hamlet, Macbeth, Othello*) or his problem plays (*Measure for Measure, Troilus and Cressida, All's Well That Ends Well*) suggests the thematic ambition that the figure is helping to express. He wants concentrated units of language to crystallise both coordinated and divergent perspectives upon any particular phenomenon. As Hamlet's 'slings and arrows' perfectly suggest, this can include different cognitive or emotional states, and different situations in space and time.

Linked to this is the way hendiadys lends a feeling of eloquent forethought to even the most trivial sentiments. This is partly a consequence of using substantive words to do the describing or colouring work that adjectives normally do. It can give this describing energy a grounded, even statuesque form of self-certainty. This is reinforced by the use of 'and' to separate the two substantives. The descriptive words are not offered one on top of another in some undistinguishing list. Instead, the pause furnishes each word with an aura of being chosen, and therefore its own specific gravity. Even when the twinned words are adjectives (e.g. 'lean and hungry') they operate just as nouns do. So, nouns can uniquely claim a sort of spatial right of being: an existential presence and foothold that is rarely the property of an adjective. When adjectives are used in hendiadys, they are partly detached from the noun they are supposedly colouring. This allows each adjective both to serve the larger unit of the phrase or sentence and for that larger unit to serve it. In collecting these surrounding energies, the adjective achieves a rare self-sufficiency; it too houses its own little world of movement and possibility. It is a typical example of how Shakespeare invests individual words with a palpability, a force of presence, that is rarely found in more everyday discourse.

An example is Hamlet's 'things *rank* and *gross* in nature' (1.2.136). Compare this with the possible alternative, 'rank, gross nature': 'nature' here becomes the beginning and endpoint of the description; the noun possesses the qualities indicated by the adjectives. By way of contrast, 'things rank and gross in nature' gives ontological priority to the adjectives. They become almost microbiologically dynamic. These 'things' (the plural is significant and appropriate) are not only defining nature: they are exceeding its proper bounds. The adjectives thereby perform their own meaning: both 'rank' and 'gross' connote over-fertility and luxuriant growth. By giving the adjectives a function that is not limited to modifying the grammatical head ('nature'), Shakespeare makes the adjectives similarly overgrow their normal boundaries. They 'become' whatever nature is here represented, and in this sense serve as proxy-nouns; equally, it is they that *do* this becoming, and in that sense become proxy-verbs as well. Importantly, this effect is not here achieved by semantic doubling. Hamlet (unusually) is not punning. The phrase still teems with

Shakespeare's trademark multiplicity: but the multiplication is of grammatical functions, as adjective, noun and verb coalesce in a striking example of theatrical embodiment. It is an entirely characteristic example of Shakespeare's word use: at once incarnate and animating, and innovative in both.

Examples such as these show how the sense in Shakespeare is often working independently of conventional syntax. His meanings are often not generated lineally. They can find focus or agency in multiple points and directions at once. Of course this can be forwards, so that the earlier word determines the later; equally it can be backwards, with a later word qualifying or altering an earlier. As we have seen, it can be grounded in single words that secrete or spark off their own narratives. An excellent example of this is Prospero in *The Tempest*:

> What seest thou else
> In the dark backward and abysm of time?
>
> (1.2.49–50)

We can get Prospero's basic meaning fairly easily: he is asking his daughter what else she can remember from long ago. But the particular relation of one word to another in the second line is very hard to pin down. Grammatically the head of the noun phrase seems to be 'time'. If this is the case, then 'dark backward and abysm' has to be working as a single modifying phrase. However, the fact that it is a phrase means that we can take it as a unit on its own: we might then try to identify a subordinate head within it (the subject being served). But which is this head? It could be any and all of 'dark', 'backward', 'abysm', or 'dark backward'. So, 'dark backward' and 'abysm of time' might be twinned and virtually synonymous phrases, each self-sufficient but mutually reinforcing; or 'dark backward' and 'absym' might both work as modifiers of 'time'. The problem comes from Shakespeare's use of nouns when we might expect adjectives. All of these words are more forceful and vivid than 'time'; more than that, they possess a spatial tangibility all their own.

Consider 'abysm'. In some ways it works neatly as a metonym, signifying 'unknown' or 'deep'. And indeed, if 'abysm' only denoted a deep profound space it might well suit Prospero's evocation of something at once dizzying to the mind and immeasurable in itself. But in 1611 it was nothing like so 'safely' metaphoric. 'Abysm' could mean two distinct great deeps. Both were imaginatively fearsome and, in the way of pre-modern mental geography, cosmologically exact: it meant either a subterraneous reservoir of waters or the bottomless pit of hell. 'Abysm', consequently, is far too specific and indeed terrifying a thing to be able quietly to modify the head 'time'.

Furthermore, 'abysm' has a peculiar suitability for this play. *The Tempest* begins at sea, or rather at a sea distempered by magic. In this it suggests 'abysm' as a subterranean reservoir. It then moves to an island infamously unlocatable, neither out of nor quite of the mapped world. Here the various exiles have to relive their crimes, to which end they get immersed in varieties of salty, stormy, muddy mockeries of punishment: that is, evoking 'abysm' as hell (or as Ferdinand, the king's son, Miranda's future suitor, and first man overboard, cries, 'Hell is empty,/And all the devils are here', 1.2.214–15). The island is called many different things by many different figures, but we might well add 'abysm' to the list. This is still more appropriate when we recall how the island is perhaps pre-eminently a *mental* space, one of perilous remembrance, projection and self-rehearsal. Again, it is an 'abysm': Shakespeare gives to the supposed grammatical modifier a fearful kind of virtual force. The effect is that the single noun phrase posits genuinely rivalrous, parallel, co-existent worlds.

Furthermore, Prospero is here the 'micro' to this 'macro'. For it is *his* 'dark backward' about which he seems so agitated. It is indeed 'dark' for him, a place both of sibling villainy ('i'th' dead of darkness', 1.2.130) and inscrutable metaphysical secrets. Prospero's play will in due course attempt to remedy both of these things. So, the play's action is partly about repeating what has been done in the past (various forms of conquest, temptation, crime, education). Prospero's ambition is nothing less than to re-engineer time itself, and the agencies at work within it. In the big things, inevitably, he fails: he cannot rule hearts, but only dictate actions. He can never forestall the march of time precisely into the darkness of death, whether understood as a backward return or a forward falling.

The play thus ends with a triple return to the 'dark backward': Prospero's 'dark' brother is 'abysmally' unrepentant; Prospero is going home; his every 'third thought' shall be his 'grave' (5.1.313). Much of this is foretold in Prospero's 'dark backward and abysm of time'. Evoking time, memory, and ethical accounting (reinforced by the straight association of 'abysm' with hell), this 'abysm' *is* his working element. But it is not only Prospero's. The shifty possession of agency in the noun-phrase corresponds to the shifty political agencies in the play. The 'dark backward' is at once a spatio-temporal realm beyond Prospero's knowledge or intervention *and* a private seat of memory and volition for every single individual – including, not least, the daughter whose thoughts he cannot finally govern.

In being such a home for these things, hendiadys is an archetypal Shakespearean construction. More than that, its very structure epitomises an art-form that is always recasting conventional expectations as to hierarchy, precedence, and progression.

## SATIRE AND CHARACTERISATION

Shakespeare was well aware of the potential in hendiadys – as in all linguistic conceits – for pomposity, pretension, or pointless verbiage. So, as with many of Shakespeare's stylistic extravagancies, a particular instance of the device's use is parodic, or on a cusp between respect and ridicule. At the far end of satirical hendiadys we have Pistol's absurdities in *2 Henry IV*, characterised by bathetic diminution, as the second substantive trivialises or vulgarises the first's attempt at nobility: 'in base durance and contagious prison,/Hal'd thither/By most mechanical and dirty hand' (5.5.34–6). This satiric excessiveness is partly about publishing this play's differences from rival tub thumpers (Pistol jovially misappropriates some famous lines from Marlowe's *Tamburlaine* at 2.4.162). But it also contributes to a performance that is all about mock-tragic grandeur, tautological repetition, and the inflating of degradation. Pistol's imitation-heroics thereby shadow and counterpoint the similarly spurious nobility and hawked idealism of the principals on both sides in the civil war.

By the middle years of Shakespeare's career hendiadys becomes one of the primary signatures of self-regarding military-political bombast. The opening speech of Agamemnon in *Troilus and Cressida* is an extreme example:

> Checks and disasters
> Grow in the veins of actions highest reared,
> As knots, by the conflux of meeting sap,
> Infects the sound pine and diverts his grain
> *Tortive and errant* from his course of growth.
> Nor, princes, is it matter new to us
> That we come short of our suppose so far
> That after seven years' siege yet Troy walls stand,
> Sith every action that hath gone before,
> Whereof we have record, trial did draw
> *Bias and thwart*, not answering the aim
> And that unbodied figure of the thought
> That gav't surmised shape. . . .
> The fineness of which metal is not found
> In Fortune's love; for then the *bold and coward*,
> The *wise and fool*, the *artist and unread*,
> The *hard and soft*, seem all *affined and kin*.
> But in the *wind and tempest* of her frown,
> Distinction, with a *broad and powerful* fan,
> Puffing at all, winnows the light away,
> And what hath *mass or matter* by itself
> Lies rich in *virtue and unmingled*.

> (1.3.5–30; my italics)

The speech is an exercise in tortuous obfuscation. There is nothing here that couldn't be said in a couple of lines, as Agamemnon recycles various ways of saying 'cheer up, great actions are never easy, nobility appears most when it is tested most'. In a sense the whole scene is a parody of political rhetoric. (This speech is met by the equally verbose Nestor's dry putdown, 'Great Agamemnon, Nestor shall apply/Thy latest words' – the 'latest', we surmise, in a long and tedious line.) The satiric note in the speech is partly suggested by the banal list of abstract contraries ('the bold and coward, the wise and fool. . .'). But it is more particularly focused in the way Agamemnon's attempts at novelty are above all self-describing. It is *this* speech that is 'tortive' (strangled and labyrinthine) and 'errant' (wayfaring), which shows 'bias' (swerving away from its aim) and 'thwart' (going crossways or side to side rather than straight). Hence the peculiar ambiguity of the closing lines. The image is supposedly of how bad fortune sorts the wheat ('what hath mass or matter') from the chaff ('the light'). But it is Agamemnon who is described by the image of 'Distinction' (he is the highest of the Greeks), 'Puffing at all' (with his windy rhetoric), and winnowing 'the light away' (any clarity or enlightenment). It is Agamemnon's roundabout oratory (*periphrasis*) that ensures nothing at all 'Lies rich in virtue and unmingled'. The hendiadys is used exactly to foreground the perils of its use (pretentiousness, hollowness, orotundity, obscurity). The style is itself the subject matter, and therein the medium of Shakespeare's satirical purposes.

This line between stylistic seriousness and pastiche can be a difficult one to judge. The best example is probably Othello, particularly in his early scenes. Before we meet him we witness Iago's contemptuous mockery of Othello's self-regarding speech: 'a bombast circumstance/Horribly stuffed with epithets of war' (1.1.12–13). We might then be unusually prepared to hear just the kinds of over-stuffed padding – epitomised in hendiadyses – that Othello's first speeches duly provide: 'I fetch my *life and being*/ From men of royal siege' (1.2.21–2), 'I would not my unhoused free condition/Put into *circumscription and confine*/For the sea's worth' (1.2.26–7), 'I have married her./The very *head and front* of my offending/Hath this extent, no more'(1.3.80–2). What is immediately noticeable, and very different from most uses of the device, is that the second noun is pretty much redundant. It either repeats the first or deflates it – a vaguely humiliating detumescence where inflation is the aim.

Shakespeare is again using the rhetorical habit as itself a sign of character. So, Othello tends to use it when speaking of himself, as part of a speech in which he is also talking about rhetorical manners: 'when I know that boasting is an honour' (1.2.20), 'Rude am I in my speech/And little blest with the soft phrase of peace'

(1.3.82–3). The climax of Othello's self-justification before the senators is, predictably, also a climax of excessive hendiadyses:

> And heaven defend your good souls that you think
> I will your *serious and great* business scant
> When she is with me. No, when light-winged toys
> Of feathered Cupid seel with wanton dullness
> My *speculative and officed* instrument,
> That my disports *corrupt and taint* my business,
> Let housewives make a skillet of my helm
> And all *indign and base* adversities
> Make head against my estimation.
>
> (1.3.268–76; my italics)

In a sense everything here performs the closing line, making ironic 'head' against Othello's 'estimation'. It is difficult not to hear the lines as pastiche, a snip and paste job gleamed from some unholy mix of official documents and ancient romance. Accordingly, it is easy enough to identify this borrowed sublimity with Othello's well-rehearsed insecurities (black man in a white world, infidel in a Christian society, African in Europe, all of which make him the overcompensating epitome of the smug occident and its discourses of authority). In Othello's case the elements of irony should not overwhelm the portrait of genuine dignity and power. But still more importantly, Othello's bloated and half-borrowed discourse is a crucial marker of his incipient tragedy. Stylistic pastiche can serve the gravest and most pathos-ridden ends.

The main point is simple enough: rhetorical practice per se can both express and comment upon a particular character or world-view. In this hendiadys is no different from any number of tropes or figures, particularly when used excessively. In the case of hendiadys, we might recognise its over-abundant use and see it as a sign of a mind too fond of its own exempla, or too certain that both the world and the word will go on supplying endless congenial analogies. Perhaps the best example of this is Laertes in *Hamlet*. He uses the trope too relentlessly for it to be an accident; in this he is his father's son, and hendiadys an apposite technique for the family devotion to self-affirming tendentiousness. Because in Laertes' case the figure is so intimately linked both to characterisation and theme, it is an appropriate example with which to finish. Here is some of Laertes' advice to his sister Ophelia:

> For Hamlet, and the trifling of his favour,
> Hold it a *fashion* and a *toy* in blood,
> A violent in the youth of primy nature,
> Forward, not permanent, sweet, not lasting,
> The *perfume* and *suppliance* of a minute,
> No more.

OPHELIA     No more but so?
LAERTES                    Think it no more.
                           (1.3.5–10; my italics)

Laertes either speaks in antitheses ('sweet, not lasting') or reinforcements. Hamlet's favour is a 'fashion' (a passing, vain, whimsical plaything) and a 'toy' (the thing thus played and parted with). It is a 'perfume' (as a noun a seductive burning vapour, as a verb the impregnating of such a scent) and a 'suppliance' (a beseeching petition which as a 'perfume' will 'supply' no more than air). The twinned nouns basically reinforce one another, not quite repeating each other, but lending to the partner a distinctive flavour and limit. His subject seems, very simply, to be Hamlet's desire. Laertes' repetitions are meant to reiterate that this desire cannot last. Accordingly, 'blood' evokes lust and probably lineage. The fact that Hamlet is a prince dictates both the difficulty of resistance and the likelihood of post coital dismissal; these blue bloods buy and discard women of the court like they do their coats ('fashion'). Accordingly, the 'minute' is the tiny duration of Hamlet's flame. Here we can see how Laertes, out of prurience, or delicacy, or rivalrous malice, is including in this 'minute' the act of sex itself.

Laertes is therefore saying more than that she shouldn't trust him, or that Hamlet's desire is a whim that won't last. He is saying, much more menacingly, that Hamlet will use her and dismiss her; that she will be a sexual plaything, left unwanted and abandoned once he has had his way with her. This is the added portent of Laertes' twinned nouns. As well as describing Hamlet's 'favour', they dramatise this sexuality in action: they evoke the movement from Hamlet's desire to its prey. Consequently, as much as the nouns picture Hamlet as subject, they also picture Ophelia as that subject's object. *She* will be 'a toy' and 'suppliance': the thing to be played with, and the thing that gets supplied. In other words, the 'minute' is a shared one: Ophelia possesses it just as much as Hamlet. (This suggests a wry sexual humour to the shared line: 'The perfume and suppliance of *a minute*, No more' *Oph.* 'No more but so?' *Lae.* 'Think it no more'.) The same goes for a 'toy in blood'. In Laertes' projection, his virgin sister might get as overheated in lust as her 'primy' suitor ('your chaste treasure open/To his unmaster'd importunity', 1.3.31–2).

Here we can see the dramatic and psychological adaptability of hendiadys. Because the nouns are not directly tied to a nominal head, they are free to turn and to animate the half-puns that dwell in their use. In this way, the hendiadys opens up the referential context, making fruitfully ambiguous who or what the twinned nouns are actually describing. So, Laertes' lesson goes on and on, as do his hendiadyses:

> For nature crescent does not grow alone
> In *thews* and *bulk*, but as this temple waxes,
> The inward service of the mind and soul
> Grows wide withal...
> He may not, as unvalu'd persons do,
> Carve for himself, for on his choice depends
> The *sanity* and *health* of this whole state;
> And therefore must his choice be circumscrib'd
> Unto the *voice* and *yielding* of that body
> Whereof he is the head. Then if he says he loves you,
> It fits your wisdom so far to believe it
> As he in his particular *act* and *place*
> May give his saying deed...
> And keep you in the rear of your affection
> Out of the *shot* and *danger* of desire....
> And in the *morn* and *liquid dew* of youth
> Contagious blastments are most imminent.
>
> (1.3.11–42; my italics)

For the most part Laertes seems to be talking about something other than his sister's body. However, we keep on witnessing a repeat of the dramatic snapshots concentrated in his earlier hendiadyses ('fashion/toy', 'perfume/suppliance'). He is imagining the sex act between his sister and Hamlet, and projecting its unwished for physical consequences. So, 'thews and bulk' describes the outward show of 'nature crescent': basically, a growing body. It is an odd image to stick on when describing fully grown adults. Unless we understand him as meaning that people often get heavier as they get older, then we have to attribute the peculiarly magnifying intensity of 'thews and bulk' to a sexualised vision of 'nature crescent'. The word 'crescent' usually invokes the moon; in this case, the 'crescent' is waxing, or growing toward a full moon. Again the twinned nouns telescope a certain narrative drama: in this case, the movement from Hamlet's phallic erection (the horned crescent shape) to Ophelia's pregnancy (the full moon). This movement is predicted in the similar movement between the two nouns: 'thews' represents a specifically muscular, *male* physical power (and also, appropriately enough, it meant an apparatus for punishing and humiliating 'disorderly' women); 'bulk', by contrast, evokes a container, whether a ship or belly, and so a specifically *female* volume. The other twinned nouns concentrate a similar division of agency or possession: the hendiadys both gestures toward a shared condition (shared by the state or by the 'lovers') and splits according to the respective roles of the two lovers in the union. In each case the first noun is Hamlet, the second Ophelia: 'sanity' (imperilled mind) and 'health' (imperilled body); 'voice' (aural command) and 'yielding' (physical submission); 'act' (positive doing) and 'place' (space of doing); 'shot' (ejaculative violence) and 'danger' (target); 'morn' (rising son/sun) and 'liquid dew' (female juices).

Laertes' use of hendiadys is much more than smug or vapid repetition. It concentrates a very specific narrative – one given surreptitious force by the fact that the 'making' energy between the twinned words is only implied. Laertes' mix of furtiveness and reiteration thereby feeds into some of the play's more elusive mysteries: the virginity or otherwise of Ophelia; the subliminally incestuous motives of her brother. By connection, the compacted repetitions lay the ground for Laertes' rivalry with Hamlet: a queasy sense in which he inhabits this 'act and place' with as much imaginative passion as Hamlet ever might or could have. There is a barely displaced voyeurism about his returning snapshots of sister sex, anticipating the equally unedifying battle for possession between brother and lover in Ophelia's grave (5.1).

Laertes' obsessive tutorial is a consummate example of Shakespeare's ability to make single rhetorical figures contain their own 'mini-dramas'. They work as encapsulated narratives, both embodying the present moment and predicting future unfoldings. Similarly, these speeches ride a cusp between a speaker's conscious intention and more subversive insinuations: of vicarious desires or unconscious implications; or tacit commentaries upon such intentions or implications. Either Laertes is not absolutely in control of his meanings, or he is anxious that his addressee should not be. Either way, once we get these meanings, we get access to motives or compulsions that the character would wish to keep a lid upon.

Hendiadys is an example and concentration of many of Shakespeare's favourite verbal and grammatical effects. It illustrates Shakespeare's use of irregular syntactic order, backward and forward rhythms, overdetermined pauses and silence, philological multiplicity, and latent puns. All of these techniques have meaning both as substantial things in themselves, and in the relational networks to which they contribute. Character, sexuality, politics and the rest: all are embodied in the most basic structural, prosodic, and figurative devices.

# 3

# WHY THE REPETITION?

*This chapter looks at some of the basic uses of phrasal repetition. It begins by acknowledging how fundamental repetition is to organising Shakespeare's rhythms and meanings. It looks briefly at the way predictably symmetrical and antithetical phrases are used to pace speaking and listening, to ensure clarity, and to point any surprises or disjunctions. The chapter goes on to look at Shakespeare's technique of repeating the same word in quick succession. He does this often in his sonnets, and it is also a device familiar from punning clowns. In this chapter, however, we look at its dramatic use in tragedy. The brisk repetition can be done to mark simple emotional emphasis. More often than not, it is also done so that a probing light is shone upon the claims of the repeating word. The repetition does not work simply to reiterate one particular meaning. Rather, it tends to split the word in two. The more the word is spoken, the less it remains single and reliable. In this way, Shakespeare's repetitions have the effect of dramatising the word. The use of the word re-enacts the struggles informing that word; it reveals how the word bears witness to ongoing battles over identity, history, or knowledge. Examples are taken from* Othello, King Lear, *and* Hamlet. *The chapter closes with an extended analysis of a single repeating word in* Macbeth. *In this case, the repetition draws out latent possibilities in the word, which in turn dramatise the possibilities of this peculiarly intense dramatic moment.*

For all of Shakespeare's frequent complexity, some of his most characteristic verbal techniques are extremely simple. A favourite device is to repeat the same word or phrase within a short space of time, a technique drawn directly from the training in rhetoric common to Shakespeare, his fellow players, and many in his audiences. Perhaps the majority of common rhetorical figures involve some type of repetition, whether for purposes of emphasis, clarity, contrast, paradox, inversion, rhythm, symmetry, wit, or humour. The verse of Shakespeare's earlier plays is saturated with such effects: varieties of repetition are an indispensable means of measuring the speech, of orchestrating its humours and directing its listening. Here is Richard II:

> Ay, no; no, ay; for I must nothing be.
> Therefore no 'no', for I resign to thee....
> With mine own tears wash away my balm,
> With mine own hands I give away my crown,
> With mine own tongue deny my sacred state,
> With mine own breath release all duteous oaths...
>
> *(Richard II*, 4.1.201–10)

Here Shylock:

> I am a Jew. Hath not a Jew eyes? hath not a Jew hands, organs, dimensions, senses, affections, passions? fed with the same food, hurt with the same weapons, subject to the same diseases, healed by the same means, warmed and cooled by the same winter and summer as a Christian is? – if you prick us do we not bleed? if you tickle us do we not laugh? if you poison us do we not die? and if you wrong us shall we not revenge?
>
> *(The Merchant of Venice*, 3.1.54–62)

Here Hermia and Helena:

HERMIA   I frown upon him; yet he loves me still.
HELENA   O that your frowns would teach my smiles such skill!
HERMIA   I give him curses; yet he gives me love.
HELENA   O that my prayers could such affection move!
HERMIA   The more I hate, the more he follows me.
HELENA   The more I love, the more he hateth me.
HERMIA   His folly, Helena, is no fault of mine.
HELENA   None but your beauty; would that fault were mine!
> *(A Midsummer Night's Dream*, 1.1.194–201)

Whatever the emotion – indeed whatever the expected attitude to the emotion – repetition of word, phrase, and rhythm was able to underscore it. The ubiquity of these figures of speech is suggested not least by their openness to irony or burlesque. Everyone would recognise the rhetorical custom informing the (misdirected) mourning of Juliet's Nurse; equally, they would recognise its extravagant indecorum:

> O woe! O woeful, woeful, woeful day.
> Most lamentable day. Most woeful day
> That ever, ever I did yet behold.
> O day, O day, O day, O hateful day.
> Never was seen so black a day as this.
> O woeful day, O woeful day.
>> (*Romeo and Juliet*, 4.5.49–54)

There is nothing at all difficult about any of these repetitions here: and that is basically the point. The repetitions make clear to actor and auditor the key themes and passions of any moment. In a predominantly listening auditorium such as Shakespeare's, there could be no more useful device.

Throughout his writing Shakespeare relies heavily upon figures of repetition. However, as his career progresses he becomes less likely to organise his blank verse around the kinds of symmetries seen above, with their predictable rhythms of reiteration, correspondence, and inversion. We get less patterned, more jagged constructions, closer to the surprises and abruptness of thought. But still we can recognise familiar rhythms. Here is the tortured Angelo:

> O fie, fie, fie!
> What dost thou, or what art thou, Angelo?
> Dost thou desire her foully for those things
> That make her good? O, let her brother live!
>> (*Measure for Measure*, 2.2.172–5)

Here Macbeth:

> From this moment,
> The very firstlings of my heart shall be
> The firstlings of my hand. And even now,
> To crown my thoughts with acts, be it thought and done:
> The castle of Macduff I will surprise...
>> (*Macbeth*, 4.1.146–50)

The thoughts in each speech are framed by familiar rhythms of repetition and antithesis. But this familiarity is also here a kind of permission for strangeness or novelty, for conceptual as much as merely structural inversion. It allows Shakespeare to say difficult and audacious things and still for the words to feel accessible: with Angelo, the paradox of desiring beauty so as to foul it, and of questioning both one's actions and one's very identity; with Macbeth, the way in which an image of newborn innocence, 'firstlings', gets instantaneously defined by its annihilation, facilitating an alarming connection in the repetition between the act of thinking and infanticide. In both cases, the symmetrical structure sets up an almost comforting expectation – of conformity to patterns, of mental familiarity – which then opens the door to its utter confuting. We get the dissolving of self in act, or of thought in deed. In both cases, the repetition both frames an enormous inhumanity and allows this inhumanity to remain somehow close to us. The thought processes are intimately threatening or tempting, precisely because their structural form is so intuitively possessed by us.

## REPEATING SINGLE WORDS

Alongside this intellectually structuring use of repetition, Shakespeare develops a mode of blunt, stark, phrasal repetition that – almost because of its bluntness – can split open each play's most pressing questions. It is a technique familiar from his sonnets, which display literally hundreds of examples. But many of Shakespeare's most famous dramatic moments involve just such repetition. We might think of Hamlet's 'To be or not to be'; Iago's 'I am not what I am'; Othello's 'Put out the light, and then put out the light'; Lear's 'Never, never, never, never, never'; Lady Macbeth's 'To bed, to bed, to bed'. Often the repeated word is simple but resonant, of the kind meant to help organise social and ethical relations: honour, nature, king, father, duty, honesty, virtue, fair, foul; alternatively, the repeated word will evoke a very basic function of experience: sense, see, done, be, am. In other words, these are 'axial' words, ones to spin a society or a story around.

This sort of repetition can alert us to the very basic Shakespearean machinery: everyday words, but full of the movement that characterises their everyday use; simple surfaces, subterranean agitations. Accordingly, most often the effect is to dramatise the repeated word. Moving with claim and counterclaim, the word itself embodies the larger playworld's exploration of competing origins or uncertain authority. For these echoing words invariably embody a play's most profound struggles over history, identity, or knowledge. With his customary uncanny feeling for the playwright's craft, Iago employs the repeating technique to murderous effect:

IAGO    Did Michael Cassio, when you wooed my lady,
    *Know* of your love?
OTHELLO                    He did, from first to last.
    Why dost thou ask?
IAGO    But for a satisfaction of *my thought*,
    No further harm.
OTHELLO                Why of *thy thought*, Iago?
IAGO    I did not *think* he had been acquainted with her.
OTHELLO    O yes, and went between us very oft.
IAGO    *Indeed*?
OTHELLO    *Indeed? Ay, indeed. Discern'st* thou aught in that?
    Is he not *honest*?
IAGO    *Honest*, my lord?
OTHELLO    *Honest*? Ay, *honest*.
IAGO    My lord, for aught I *know*.
OTHELLO    What dost thou *think*?
IAGO    *Think*, my lord?
OTHELLO    *Think*, my lord! By heaven, thou echo'st me
    As if there were some monster in thy *thought*
    Too hideous to be *shown*. . . . If thou dost *love* me
    *Show* me thy *thought*.
IAGO                        My lord, you *know* I *love* you.
OTHELLO    I *think* thou dost.
    And for I *know* thou'rt full of *love* and *honesty*
    And weigh'st thy words before thou giv'st them
        breath,
    Therefore these stops of thine fright me the more. . . .
IAGO                    For Michael Cassio,
    I dare *be* sworn, I *think*, that he is *honest*.
OTHELLO    I *think* so too.

IAGO                    Men should *be* what they *seem*,
    Or those that *be* not, would they might *seem* none.
OTHELLO   Certain, men should *be* what they *seem*.
IAGO   Why then I *think* Cassio's an *honest* man.

                              (*Othello*, 3.3.94–132; my italics)

The keywords here, 'know', 'thought', 'think', 'indeed', 'honest', 'discern'st', 'shown', 'seem', 'be', all press upon the same space: one where subject and object try (and fail) to settle into clarity and distinctiveness. Each of the words equivocates between thought and fact, or conception and birth. Iago forces us to ponder exactly what claims are made by each word: so, to 'think' is and is not to know; to 'see' is and is not to witness; to 'seem' is and is not to 'be'; 'indeed' is and is not to execute. Othello tries desperately to adjudicate what might be from what is, but he is trapped in Iago's web of paradox (e.g. 'Show me thy thought'). In thematic terms, the subject of the repetitions is the quicksand of any 'knowledge' dependent upon nothing but inference: and what 'knowledge', in the end, is not? The repetition thus harps upon the play's central tragic chord: the impossibility of knowing what is or has been, or of knowing another, or, finally, of knowing one's self.

The repeating words are fatally disembodied. Floating free of any grounding, non-abstract noun, they mutate in Othello's mind into a tribe of self-fracturing, self-hatching monstrosities. Iago's repetitions do not describe things that already are. Nor do they conform to the kind of world upon which Othello's substance depends: one that is as it appears; one that sustains itself through the fundamental identity of like and like, premise and conclusion. Instead, Iago's repetitions hatch a world where language embodies nothing but possibility, or imagination, or things 'coming-to-be'. It is a consummate Shakespearean space and energy – albeit one that kills all of his heroes.

This technique of repeating a single foundational word so as to create a kind of dramatic black hole – at once inceptive and annihilating – is seen again in the terrible line of Lear's spoken over his child's dead body: 'Never, never, never, never, never' (5.3.307). The line suggests a paradox, being so apparently empty of nuance or poetry and yet so moving. But such aesthetic denial is partly the point: a whole pentameter is given over to a single word; we know what a line *can* hold, and in the refusal to allow any such variation or inventiveness the repeated word collects into itself an other-obliterating authenticity. At the same time, it is so plaintively 'like life' to thus hopelessly moan or curse or roar. This helps make the moment very powerful in performance: there is a sheerness and starkness in the recognition that something so blank can be set free of its habitual banality.

But there is a further paradox. The apparent desolation of the line is in fact permitted by all kinds of words and moments from earlier in the play. That is, stuff that can neither be seen nor heard as Lear cries, and yet here operates in a busily associative silence. Beginning with Cordelia's astonishing denial ('Nothing, my lord') of her father's request for evermore exorbitant flattery, *King Lear* makes the idea of 'nothing' echo with possibilities. And above all, in almost fairy-tale fashion, it echoes with the possibility or hope that love might return to 'save the day'. In turn 'nothing' becomes perhaps the chief conceit of the play, as a trope not only of abandoned love but also of linguistic impasse, cosmic apocalypse, property loss, and social chaos. It finds further application in a sequence of characters forced to renounce all and begin from scratch ('Edgar I *nothing* am', and so on). The question in *Lear* is always whether anything can come from 'nothing' (silence, poverty, nakedness, namelessness), whether it secretes any rare love or resilient truth, or whether there is any virtue or opportunity in a return to ground zero. If the question repeatedly poises a defiant wistfulness against nihilism, then Lear's 'Never, never, never, never, never' is its apogee. The long stretch of its reiterations at once evokes unquenchable stubbornness and terminal exhaustion. The line takes the play's ubiquitous trope of 'nothing' and at once concentrates and multiplies it as the clinching tragic equation.

A variation upon this emotionally heightened repetition (called *epizeuxis* in the rhetoric books) is the seemingly pointless repetition of apparent synonyms. We can return here to one of Hamlet's famous conceits: 'O that this too too sullied flesh would melt/Thaw and resolve itself into a dew' (1.2.129–30). He repeats *almost* the same verb three times (melt, thaw, and resolve). In a sense he means nothing more than 'Oh that my flesh would melt, and melt, and melt into a dew'. But of course there is more. He imagines not an instantaneous metamorphosis, but an immense, deliberative, languishing process of *de*-creation. Equally, it suggests that he has thought this very thought time and time again. The repetition gives to Hamlet's words the illusion of intense precognition, a strained and violent wistfulness through which Hamlet's mind has indeed become almost porous with longing for dissolution. The apparent verbal superfluousness, consequently, *is* the mental exactitude. We witness the paralysis of depression and the circularity of obsession. In turn this allows the 'dew' to teem with its own long-brewed narratives of self-possibility.

But the words are similar, not identical. Each verb will imply its own distinct activity; the surplus within one word can then be set up in dialogue with that of the other. So, 'melt' suggests a movement into absence, formlessness, or indistinction. The words 'melt' and 'thaw' are close but not quite identical: one might 'melt' from being overheated, and the word has a bias toward warmth and flow; 'thaw', however, is a more negative condition, beyond appetite, and remains beholden to the ice it modifies. So, whereas 'melt' retains a sensual allegiance, 'thaw' is further along the passage beyond humanness (no one 'thaws' with desire). In turn, 'resolve' implies a decision, a resolution; the constituent parts have been identified, separated, and finally distilled. In completing the verbal trio, 'resolve' figures an end, a 'solution'. In this, it gathers a meta-dramatic allure (for Hamlet) as an alternative end to the tragedy he already sees coming.

The subtle gradations between Hamlet's verbs therefore suggest a single identifiable process: a cumulative, compounded 'verb-act' of self-dissolution and self-resolution. In this way, the verbs become a noun-phrase all their own. They are at once before the 'dew' (as preparation for it) and the very substance of this 'dew'. In other words, the thing Hamlet recommends is precisely this process of melting. The 'dew' is not so much the end result as the enacting of the verbs. Hamlet does indeed desire some slow osmosis, but the pervasive sense is that he doesn't quite know into what. It is not a simple dream of escape, or transformation, or extinction: there is in a sense no place of refuge, nothing except this lust never *quite* to be absorbed. The almost static, barely flowing repetitions thus offer a suggestive variation upon Hamlet's notorious 'delay'. However much the speech teases with death-wish, the last thing he wants is completion.

Much later in the play Hamlet offers a different sort of knowing repetition:

> Was't Hamlet wrong'd Laertes? Never Hamlet.
> If Hamlet from himself be ta'en away,
> And when he's not himself does wrong Laertes,
> Then Hamlet does it not, Hamlet denies it.
> Who does it then? His madness. If't be so,
> Hamlet is of the faction that is wrong'd,
> His madness is poor Hamlet's enemy.
>
> (5.2.232–8)

Hamlet's hair-splitting reasoning is satirising the self-pleasing casuistry of court or legalese (exemplified by Laertes' father, Polonius). More to the point, however, is how Hamlet's worrying at a self-subverting, divisible 'Hamlet' shows him taking on the play's chief concern and perspective as his own. He adopts the role of his own concerned onlooker, at once mocking those who affect to find motive in his outward shows and offering pseudo-lessons in interpretive clemency. Partly he advertises some essential Hamlet, lying safely 'behind' any passing eccentricities; partly he mocks any such faith as sentimental mystification. The transparent bogusness of his rationalisation dares us to judge him solely by his (often cruel or petty) actions. At the same time, the very brazenness of his lie, and our knowledge that elsewhere he flatly dismisses talk of his 'madness', returns us via a kind of double-bluff to some still deeper but inexpressible inwardness. Hamlet acts here as though he is meta-dramatically ascendant, anticipating and orchestrating likely audience responses. But – crucially – he yet remains the victim of all he diagnoses.

To see how this works we need to remember the wider context of the word's use in the play. In all of Shakespeare no other name is spoken so often as 'Hamlet': more than 80 times, as opposed to about 30 for Othello and 40 for Macbeth. But the first two times this name is mentioned it refers not to 'Hamlet' – not to *the* Hamlet – but to his dead father. Why does Shakespeare have the name spoken twice about someone else? It cannot have been accidental: and indeed we find that merely to ask the question is to open up, or go grasping after, something like the play's 'questionable' heart. So, who exactly is Hamlet? Which is Hamlet? Is Hamlet indeed Hamlet? Has he come into 'himself', inherited himself, assumed the mantle? What exactly is the relationship between the ghostly father and the haunted son? How absolute is this haunting? How much is Hamlet's identity his own? We should see that these questions are exactly the questions that we ask of the play and, equally, that Hamlet asks of himself. When 'the' Hamlet is finally referred to by name – 175 lines into the play, or a good 10 minutes – he is '*young* Hamlet'. The differentiation is necessary, not only because it distinguishes between this Hamlet and the previously invoked one, but also because it reinforces that he is yet 'young', he has work to do, and that this tragedy will at least partly be about fully possessing, after initial prevarications, the fullness of a revenge tragedian's name.

Consequently, the way Hamlet teases with his name to Laertes can be taken as a self-parodying metaphor of Hamlet's burdensome inheritance: here it is in pseudo-playful miniature. This is why Hamlet's play with his name recapitulates his broader tragedy. We see this in the double appropriateness of 'Hamlet is of the faction that is wrong'd', where 'Hamlet' refers both to the name and to the 'inner being'. A 'factious' party is one prone to dissension and turbulence: Hamlet's mischievous irony cannot mask his self-mutiny. As he said in the previous scene with Horatio, 'in my heart there was a kind of fighting' (5.2.4). Hamlet ridicules what he knows to be his basic truth. He has indeed been taken away from himself: taken hostage by melancholy, by a foul imagination, by news from some other world that should not enter our own. His disgraceful performance before Laertes is in the fullest sense 'his own' even as it is an instance in which Hamlet 'forgot himself'. The repetition therefore reprises Hamlet's fear of self-diminution. At each repetition of his name, a little bit more of the majesty, mystery, and redeemable promise is lopped away. It speaks of Hamlet's anxiety that he has become nothing more than a subtraction from his own fullness. Again, the repetition embodies an irreparable and fully self-policed division of identity.

## REPETITION AS LATENT DOUBLE MEANING

Perhaps the most characteristic use to which Shakespeare puts his flat word-repetitions is when the word 'repeats' upon itself, and thereby unfolds otherwise subdued double meaning. A good example is Macbeth's words as he enters thinking about whether or not to kill the king. Once again we might at first glance conclude that the repetitions are semantically unnecessary, or given only to achieve a simple theatrical immediacy:

> If it were done, when 'tis done, then 'twere well
> It were done quickly...
>
> (1.7.1–2)

The nominal head of the sentence is, we might suppose, 'it'. The 'it' he alludes to is ostensibly the murder of Duncan, his choice of 'it' representing an evasive and euphemistic referent for the sacrilegious act that cannot be named. But the 'it' is also swallowed up by the syntax: Macbeth's recourse to ''tis' and ''twere' means that 'it' cannot really be heard. Instead, 'it' is slid over, the briefest preparation for the effective grammatical head: that is, the verbal mesh of 'dones', past participle of the most basic 'doing word' of all. In typical Shakespeare fashion, the verb becomes a type of noun-in-the-making. Equally typically, it is repeated so as to suggest subjective and situational multiplicity: more than one time frame, more than one state of mind, as possibilities are sketched in simultaneous instantaneity.

The expression involves a curious mixture of bluntness and evasion. This is partly to do with the repeated verb, 'done', which advertises finality but specifies absolutely nothing. But still more it is because Macbeth says the word three times. If he had said, 'if it were done, then 'twere well it were done quickly', there would be no problem: 'Do it, and do it now', would then be the meaning. As the words are given, some such resolve hangs in the air: but we have to skip over the actual words if we want to settle upon any such comfortable sense. It is the middle 'repeat' ('when 'tis done') that hangs loose. It creates a logical caesura, a backtracking parenthesis, in Macbeth's attempt at decisiveness. Repeating 'done' three times thus has the paradoxical effect of both reinforcement and weakening. More importantly, it makes the words 'hang' in the air, as though the very space of Macbeth's present mind. So, it invites psychological inference. We might think that if Macbeth were certain of his course he wouldn't need to remind himself so often; the repetition is (yet another) act of self-persuasion. We might identify obsessive familiarity: we witness him in mid-thought; he doesn't need to spell it out. Alternatively, we might hear a nervous stutter, an evasive circumlocution, a thumping palpitation, or merely an emphatic reiteration: or perhaps all of these at once.

The repetition, therefore, is at once self-explanatory *and* a puzzle. Similarly, although the words almost physically enact Macbeth's mental state, the fact that this state is one of evasion and repression requires that we peel away masks and burrow more deeply for its substance. But, paradoxically, there is neither mask nor depth except the repeating 'dones'. Whatever Macbeth here means – whatever he here is – has to be discovered in the relational context of these repetitions.

So, 'If it were done' and 'when 'tis done' can be a logically building sentence meaning something like 'If I am going to do it, then when I do it/have done it...'. Or it can be two abbreviated attempts to get at the thought of getting it over with, in which case 'if it were done' and 'when 'tis done' mean exactly the same thing. 'If it were done' combines a future, past, and present tense in one. 'If' looks forward to something 'not yet'. The phrase 'were done' suggests that the act is performed and thereby 'done with'. This thereby passes into a sort of projected present tense, whereby the speaker imagines himself in the position of someone who has 'done it', and is therefore free of 'it'. Equally, however, 'were done' implies the ellipsis to be: that is, 'if it were to be done'. This again evokes the speaker considering how he might go about 'doing' the deed. We are back before any beginning.

The second verb phrase ('when 'tis done') inscribes a similarly forward-and-backward sense of time. 'When' modified by 'is' again anticipates the subject looking back upon something 'done'. Importantly, however, it can also refer to the experience of the act of doing it. In this sense, 'done' means 'being done', or 'when it is being done'. Macbeth is envisaging the physical performing of murder, or the mind engaged in the doing. He sees right through all fancies and abstractions to the mechanisms of achievement. How exactly should I kill him? With what instruments, what movements, in what particular place on the king's body? The phrase might therefore evoke a kind of quick grace, that of the practised killer, seeing the enormity of what he is contemplating, too keenly aware of the meekness and virtue of his mark, and so determined to do it right, in a sporting, brisk and painless fashion. This rehearsal of a saving chivalry then passes into thoughts of redemption: if it is 'done' this way, 'then' all will be 'well'. He will overcome the primal stain or the predetermined doom if only he gets this thing done. The murder becomes a sort of sacrament, a sacrificial propitiation.

Clearly, however, such thoughts are at best sketched: indeed everything here is almost decisively unarticulated, or present only as the most awesomely shadowing implication. The semantic evasiveness is in a way almost wistful: to name might be to kill the thing he is as well as the thing he should serve and revere (his king, name, duty, hospitality). In this sense, euphemism carries a frightful weight of responsibility; to peep behind the blanket of euphemism is to see true terror. But above all, perhaps, Macbeth's words seem to want doubt 'done' with: to render language as flat and depthless as action, in some final sense to be bereft of lurking power (of the kind so menacingly possessed by the witches). It is as though the repetition here is a brief (and quickly abandoned) experiment in a language *without* metaphor: reaching out to nothing elsewhere, transporting into nothing. In struggling to arrest the cell-like fissions of figurative language, Macbeth can be seen making one final effort to at once shut down and facilitate his 'ambition'. Macbeth frequently fears or hopes that speech has some power to cast a spell, or weave a self-protective halo. Here is another such superstitious gesture.

But the irony is that the language's very lack of content means that its significance is discovered less in the act it purports to describe (murder a king) than in the very evasions, doubts, and angst that compel Macbeth's choice of word. Ironically, then, the words become almost radically metaphoric. In the neutrality and featurelessness of 'it' and 'done', in the vast unspeakable gaps they traverse, a world of possibilities is at once born, deferred, and somehow aborted. So, the one moment might be every moment, the one act every act, not merely because he would barter all of future time for that one moment to be achieved, but because for all activity to be parcelled into a thrice-repeated 'done' is to render all action, before commission, in the past. There are no verbs left to 'do'.

Accordingly, far from some liberation into decision and finesse, Macbeth's repetitions frustrate any decisive martial or humanist action. They are more like a lulled hibernation, a wishful curling up into a deep objectless sleep. Each 'done' drums home the previous 'done', as though digging an arid well. In this way the null enormity of 'done' begins simply to mean death: whether of life or of thought, the theme is (self-) abdication via (self-) usurpation. The words 'it' and 'done' then stand in for a manner of universal abhorrence: a vacuum from which all matter is sucked, a black hole whose force field traps the lot (in both aspects rather like Macbeth himself).

Finally, the repetitions encapsulate the play's suspended, co-parallel take upon time. Macbeth enters the stage as though drawn by the witches. From this moment on events are at once shockingly abrupt, and experienced as a kind of memory of something that has already been anticipated, and in some predetermined sense has already been 'done'. By the same token, the phrase prepares for ghosts and shadows: it won't be done even when it is done; these things return to haunt. What is 'done' can never be 'done' with, and to say the word is almost to mean its opposite. It is typical that Macbeth's grimly drumming lines should set up such an enveloping and terrible metaphysical joke (the phrase continues to haunt in Lady Macbeth's sleepwalking, 5.1.69). When Shakespeare repeats these simple, weighty words, whole worlds can be found repeating in them.

# 4

# WHY THE HIGH STYLE?

*In this chapter we look at Shakespeare's use of very grand or florid language. We start with examples of long-winded public rhetoric. Often this can all sound the same, and we might find ourselves wondering why it couldn't all be said much more quickly and simply. So, this section looks at ways of breaking down a few speeches so that we might see more of their colour, humour, and particularity. The first examples are taken from the history plays* Henry VI *and* Henry V. *The second section looks at the often very rich language of* Romeo and Juliet. *Here, it is less a case of grand-sounding oratory and more one of seemingly excessive floweriness. We show how any style needs to be put in its context, and particularly the context of its particular speaker. In this play, each character has his or her distinctive style of speech, and each style can be contrasted with or mocked by someone else's style. We will see that very ornate language – just like military or political 'bombast' – can be as ironic a way of speaking as any joke. The chapter closes with an extended analysis of a single lyrical speech of Horatio's in* Hamlet. *Horatio's language is not usually particularly 'poetical', and the point of this analysis is to show why Shakespeare might have given him such ornate language on this particular occasion. What does the high style reveal about character and theme? Once again, it is a question of recovering the context of the particular speech-act – and of how the specific details of the speech contribute to forming that context.*

One of the most common complaints about Shakespeare is that his language is inflated and over-grand. The term used at the time was 'bombast', referring to high-sounding language used to pad out trivial or commonplace sentiments. This application derives from the meaning most commonly used at the time: that is, cotton wool, and particularly the sort of wool used to stuff clothes or pad doublets. *OED* dates the first specifically linguistic application in 1589, from the satiric pen of Thomas Nashe: 'To outbrave better pens with the swelling bombast of a bragging blank verse'. Nashe here links bombastic padding with a particular style of macho pretentiousness. More specifically, he is railing against the new rage of the public theatres – the thundering, often militaristic rhetoric that saturates plays like Marlowe's *Tamburlaine* and Shakespeare's *Henry VI*. Although such plays were for a time irresistibly popular, the fashion for what 20 or so years later Ben Jonson termed the 'furious vociferation' of the 'late Age' did not really survive much beyond the early 1590s. Shakespeare himself can be seen clearly enough parodying this style with the 'swaggerer' Pistol in *Henry IV* and *Henry V*. But even if he doesn't long keep on writing in the grand style of the early histories, Shakespeare continues to write in what has often been thought inflated or over-fussy language. This is true even of his most praised works: in writing of the 'horror' of *Macbeth* in the 1670s, the poet and critic John Dryden is referring not to its searing portrait of despair and evil but (with quite equal aversion) to the play's awful 'bombast speeches . . . which are not to be understood'. The inflation turns inward, perhaps, rather than being shouted upon the parapets. But all we get is would-be meditative speech cankered by swelling tumours: for everyone's sake they are best cut out.

There seems little doubt on which side of the argument the young Shakespeare stood. He was, with Marlowe, the most reckless purveyor of what Ben Jonson (perhaps scornfully) called the 'mighty line'. Shakespeare's early plays – *Titus Andronicus, 1, 2, 3 Henry VI, Richard III* – are stocked to the brim with loud and long declamations. And so it was that a famous insult found its mark, from another rival playwright, Robert Greene:

> There is an upstart crow, beautified with our feathers, that with his *Tiger's heart wrapped in a player's hide*, supposes he is as well able to bombast out a blank verse as the best of you.
>
> (Chambers 1930: II.188)

Greene may have collaborated with Shakespeare in writing the first in the *Henry VI* trilogy, and here he parodies a line from the third (the accusation of plagiarism suggesting a less than amicable separation). Greene makes one telling alteration to Shakespeare's line, replacing 'woman's hide' with 'player's hide'. Greene perhaps writes as a scorned and hurt partner to the cruel 'tiger' Shakespeare; perhaps as a university educated dramatist indignant that a mere *player* should presume to write anything so ennobling as verse (as though to say 'you've got a *hide*'); perhaps as a debauched and dying man (for so he was) raging against the decay of poetic standards. Whatever his motives, there is no doubt that he tries to skewer the upstart as all cotton puff and no muscle. And perhaps he is half-right. Here is the offending speech. It will serve as well as scores of others to illustrate the early Shakespeare at his most apparently 'bombastic'; and, perhaps unfortunately, it seems appropriate to quote the whole thing:

> She-wolf of France, but worse than the wolves of France,
> Whose tongue more poisons than the adder's tooth!
> How ill-beseeming is it in thy sex
> To triumph like an Amazonian trull
> Upon their woes whom Fortune captivates!
> But that thy face is vizard-like, unchanging,
> Made impudent with use of evil deeds,
> I would assay, proud queen, to make thee blush.
> To tell thee whence thou cam'st, of whom deriv'd,
> Were shame enough to shame thee, wert not shameless.
> Thy father bears the type of King of Naples,
> Of both the Sicils, and Jerusalem,
> Yet not so wealthy as an English yeoman.
> Hath that poor monarch taught thee to insult?
> It needs not, nor it boots thee not, proud queen;
> Unless the adage must be verified,
> That beggars mounted run their horse to death.
> 'Tis beauty that doth oft make women proud;
> But God he knows thy share thereof is small.
> 'Tis virtue that doth make them most admir'd;
> The contrary doth make thee wonder'd at.
> 'Tis government that makes them seem divine;
> The want thereof makes thee abominable.
> Thou art as opposite to every good

As the Antipodes are unto us,
Or as the south to the Septentrion.
O tiger's heart wrapp'd in a woman's hide!
How could'st thou drain the life-blood of the child,
To bid the father wipe his eyes withal,
And yet be seen to bear a woman's face?
Women are soft, mild, pitiful, and flexible;
Thou stern, indurate, flinty, rough, remorseless.
Bid'st thou me rage? Why, now thou hast thy wish.
Would'st have me weep? Why now then hast thy will.
For raging wind blows up incessant showers,
And when the rage allays, the rain begins.
These tears are my sweet Rutland's obsequies,
And every drop cries vengeance for his death
'Gainst thee, fell Clifford, and thee, false Frenchwoman.
                                              (*3 Henry VI*, 1.4.111–49)

The speaker is the Duke of York, about to be executed by his addressees here, Queen Margaret and Clifford. This then is the first half (he rises to a similar pitch in a moment's time) of York's departing tirade against his enemies in the civil wars. The whole speech can in a sense be understood as a single speech-act. So, each aspect of the rhetoric serves a departing howl of protest and defiance. But there remain things about the speech that resist being dismissed as the one-note jottings of immature bluster.

We might notice, for instance, how the speech is laced with subtly ingratiating humour. He begins and ends the speech by linking Margaret to France, bracketing all he says as a nationalistic trumpet call. In turn the speech is structured by repeated more or less xenophobic allusions: she is Amazonian, of Naples, Sicily, Jerusalem, of the Antipodes. Perhaps she is vulnerable, in the great royal tradition, to slurs concerning foreign lineage; perhaps this asserts the Yorkist's more home-sown claims to sovereignty. York then sustains his insults by linking the Queen's corruption with sexual immodesty: 'But that thy face is vizard-like, unchanging,/ Made impudent with use of evil deeds,/I would assay, proud queen, to make thee blush./To tell thee whence thou cam'st, of whom deriv'd,/Were shame enough to shame thee, wert not shameless'. Here 'impudent' connotes unblushing shamelessness and, by association, the gross openness of that of which she should be ashamed, her 'pudend' or privy parts. The appeal is at once populist, nationalistic, anti-popish, and slyly obscene: all in all unlikely to play badly in a popular theatre around 1590–92 (two or so years after the defeat of the Spanish Armada).

The use made of conventional rhetorical figures is similarly alert and flexible. York's patterns are ones of repetition and antithesis, but Shakespeare is careful to avoid any tediously predictable jog-trot rhythm. So, York shifts from question to assertion to proverb; he has successive lines free of pauses, each enjambing the next in a cascade of denunciation (113–15), and then follows it with a set of five lines (116–20) which make liberal use of pauses and caesura, slowing the pace down, gathering his (and our) breath so as to keep fresh the sense and relish of his theme. But more than this, Shakespeare also gives to York an overheated, exasperated quality, measured by an occasionally frayed observance of rhetorical symmetry. So, we hear an over-abundance of repetitions ('Were shame enough to shame thee, wert not shameless'); or this:

> Women are soft, mild, pitiful, and flexible;
> Thou stern, indurate, flinty, rough, remorseless.
>
> (141–2)

York's theme here is that Margaret betrays the natural order: she is a woman opposite to womankind, and thereby a kind of barely human Gorgon. The 'natural' qualities of women decree an elegantly decorous rhythm: the four soft verbs of line 141 scan neatly and to measure. By contrast, the 'rough' qualities of Margaret decree a correspondingly rough rhythm. This is marked by the second line's metrical exceeding of the first. Its fifth and final adjective, 'remorseless', is one more than the four that York could muster in praise of 'women'. There is here a small self-referential joke – 'remorseless' is exactly what York's dispraise is becoming. But the further point of this violation of rhetorical expectation is that it brings into doubt York's control of his *own* symmetries. As his next line seems to recognise – 'Bid'st thou me rage? Why, now thou hast thy wish' – the extra adjective or hanging foot suggests a man at the end of his tether, overcome by a more 'remorseless' enemy, and at the point of losing control over the one remaining thing – persuasive discourse – that can assert civic respect and ethical (if not military) power.

We also have to place the 'bombast' in its visible staged context. A cursory reading of the scene might suggest that York's 'tiger's hide' speech is yet one more piece of invective in a scene – a play, a trilogy, a history cycle – jam-packed with slowly ricocheting tirades. But we should see instead that it is minutely orchestrated, and in fact bubbles out of York's almost heroically extended muteness. For York hasn't appeared to want to speak, preferring in his defeat the dignity of silence. He is taunted into speech by Margaret, who stages his capture so as to maximise his humiliation: she sits him on a molehill, goads him with memories of his murdered 'darling' son Rutland, bids York wipe his tears with a napkin stained with Rutland's blood, insults him as a clownish carnival king by decking his head with a paper crown. All of these insults have a particular and very theatrical effect, drawn from the rituals of festival. The molehill is a parody version of the 'mountain' he would have conquered: accordingly, it is York's mock-throne, his mock-seat, and his mock-stage. He is to be laughed at as a ridiculous impostor, and in doing so his line's absurd claims to the real crown should similarly be mocked into destruction: 'Stamp, rave, and fret, that I may sing and dance./ Thou would'st be fee'd, I see, to make me sport' (1.4.91–2). Margaret is baiting York, exactly like a dog might a chained bear in one of the other entertainments so beloved of Elizabethan visitors to the Bankside. In other words, she is partly setting him up *for* the audience: for our admiration, pity, or thirst. We await and need his response; being so ritualistically set up, York's response gathers into itself a culminating and hypnotic force.

The point to notice is how one generic mode – Margaret's satiric pantomime – prepares for another – York's promise-carrying pathos. In one sense, of course, he is about to die. But in another sense his 'bombast' survives her cruel comedy – is in a basic way released by it – and bears the power of narrative and historical prediction. So, Margaret is triumphant in this moment, but will in due course be defeated; York is defeated in this moment, but in due course the Yorkist line will triumph. Margaret's sarcastic introduction to York's long speech works similarly: 'Nay, stay; let's hear the orisons he makes'. She knows that he is going to curse her, and so she calls the curse a prayer ('orisons') to show how little she cares and, with demonic relish, how little anything he says can take effect. We hear the mockery, and listen to the 'orison' with this mockery in the air. However, we do not as we hear the speech share in the mockery: we are pushed toward a kind of redeeming of the notion of 'orisons'. It is not that York's bombast delivers the humility and charity that has been missing: not at all. But the speech *is* moving toward some such thing even as it reiterates present devastation. This is what makes his 'tiger' speech so effective. It is a perfect symptom of its moment, indeed of the war itself, swaying this way and that and 'tugging' an audience accordingly (2.5.1–13). Hence the response of his supposed enemy Northumberland: 'Beshrew me, but his passion moves me so/ As hardly I can check my eyes from tears' (1.4.150–1). We, the audience, are invited to move in between Margaret's sadistic irony and Northumberland's surprised empathy. York duly dies upon two prayers, one for vengeance upon his killers, and one for God's mercy. This final prayer ('Open thy gate of mercy, gracious God!') is immediately and savagely mocked: 'Off with his head, and set it on York gates;/So York may overlook the town of York', 1.4.179–80). But then the very next scene shows that York's first prayer – for vengeance – will indeed be heard: York's sons hear of his death and effectively determine to make his final prayer come true. In other words, the speech is speaking *to* various different things at once, all of which listening positions an audience can inhabit: to York's immediate addressees; to the witness of hidden justice; to future history; and to the rest of the play.

To summarise: we should see that there is nothing at all indiscriminate about this 'bombast' or its placement. We need to listen to the words carefully, and hear how thunderous rhetoric, that might seem at first glance to be a one-note exercise in monotony, is in fact very carefully scored with variations. Equally, we need to place the speech in its specific scene, invariably one of diverse poses and competing perspectives. What is the speech responding to? Who is being addressed? What visual scene? Which generic framework? Does it reflect back upon what has been? Does it look forward to what is to come? Even the most apparently monumentalising speech is always flushed with movement.

## WIT IN BOMBAST: *HENRY V*

It is easy to miss how layered and indeed witty Shakespeare's long-winded public rhetoric can be. This is particularly so when the speaker – say a more or less anonymous duke or bishop – appears to be doing little more than providing details of the story. We pick up the basic fact that so and so is a rebel, so and so a loyal subject, but basically these long speeches appear to be defined (to risk sounding rather circular) by no more than they appear to *do*. That is, they can be reduced to an action-efficient, serviceable summary: this one is off to war, that one is mourning his sons, that other one has been banished. It can be as though we don't expect or even wish for anything individuated in any kind of political or military blank verse. Such dismissive suspicions can be a convenient refuge from what has become to many an unfashionable and inhospitable mode of delivery. But the suspicion is mistaken, and we miss much that is funny and subversive in Shakespeare if we are not alive to the fact that high-sounding blank verse can be absolutely as ironic a mode of discourse as the most brazen joke.

The early scenes of *Henry V* offer some typical examples. Here is the Archbishop of Canterbury speaking of the king:

CANTERBURY   The King is full of grace and fair regard.
ELY   And a true lover of the holy Church.
CANTERBURY   The courses of his youth promised it not.
  The breath no sooner left his father's body
  But that his wildness, mortified in him,
  Seemed to die too; yea, at that very moment,
  Consideration like an angel came
  And whipped th'offending Adam out of him,
  Leaving his body as a paradise
  T'envelop and contain celestial spirits.
  Never was such a sudden scholar made,

> Never came reformation in a flood
> With such a heady currence scouring faults,
> Nor never Hydra-headed wilfulness
> So soon did lose his seat, and all at once,
> As in this king.
>
> (1.1.22–37)

The speech serves the purpose of quickly reminding an audience that the king of this play is the same man as the prince Hal last witnessed ascending to the throne at the end of Shakespeare *2 Henry IV*, performed perhaps a year or two earlier. We are reminded of how Hal slummed it for a long time in alehouses and the like, how he was a rebellious and disappointing son, and how absolute was his eventual 'reformation'. This former libertine, we are told, is now a kind of saint. The archbishop then tells us what we need to know: the king of *this* play, unlike those of the earlier productions by this company of *Henry VI, Richard II, Richard III*, even *Henry IV*, will be a good king.

This is all well and good. But still it begs an obvious question: why does he take so long to get this news across? Why – again – so many words? (And he goes on in similar vein for another 30 or so lines.) Is there anything else in here that our swift summary has omitted to mention?

We might begin by noting a tendency toward overstatement. It may be apt that an archbishop's rhetoric should draw upon images of flagellation and chastisement, but all the same it gives a troubling air of perversion to this latter day saint's virtue. But if this is questionable, it is hardly the only thing here that is. Why the rather creepy Oedipal symmetry whereby Hal's wildness shrivelled and died the moment his father did? Why must 'Consideration' (itself an ambiguous noun that denotes paying one's part in a bargain as much as it does care or love) take the form of 'whipping' out Hal's bond with guilty and suffering humanity ('th'offending Adam')? Should this afford our thanks and relief? What kind of terror is predicted by images of a king enforcing unprecedented 'reformation' in a fault-scouring flood? What hope for the humble in any of this? If the nation is to be diagnosed and tested in this play, then can its leader – supposedly a microcosm of his nation – escape similar scrutiny? After all, a few years later Shakespeare takes a like-sounding intolerant puritan thoroughly to task in *Measure for Measure*: are we to see in King Henry a dry run for the icy Angelo? Indeed the whole speech, as we can see, might be taken as a kind of uncertain question mark.

To 'get' the speech we need to establish its full context: and this context, as so often, includes other moments both in this *and* other plays. More specifically, if the effect is ambiguous, then we may implicitly be asked to recall the clinical finality with which 'sweet Hal' dismisses Falstaff from his affections, patronage, and remembrance ('I know thee not, old man') at the end of *2 Henry IV*. It is a chilling moment of theatre. Falstaff was at this point almost certainly Shakespeare's most popular character. The scene in which Hal rejects him must already have been infamous for its stark opposing of affective sympathies to political necessity. Is Shakespeare making sure that we do not forget this king's capacity for mercilessness? Or is he getting his apologies in first, assuring us that, if he was cruel to Falstaff, the old fat knight was not alone ('With such a heady currence scouring faults'), and that it was all in the interests of kindness to the country? What is certain is that Falstaff is not here forgotten. In a few moments time he will return: but not, crucially, in the flesh. He has indeed been whipped out: it is he above all who is the model or ghost of Hal's 'offending Adam'.

Accordingly, in 2.3 Falstaff is invoked so as to disappear one final time, as we hear Hostess Nell's pathetic account of his gross flesh in its death throes. But there is no simple opposition here of abstract virtue and corporeal vice. As much as Falstaff in his dying fever talks of the 'Whore of Babylon' (2.3.36) and of women as 'devils incarnate', he also plays 'wi'th' flowers' and babbles of 'green fields' (2.3.14–17). We should see, then, that *both* Henry and Falstaff, one in his 'rebirth' and one in his dying, are staging a conflict over the national direction. Both are wracked by a confluence of desire and its prohibition, and by an all but feverish kind of sensuality; both struggle to accommodate God with bodily appetite (''a cried out 'God, God, God!' three or four times. Now I, to comfort him, bid him 'a should not think of God; I hoped there was no need to trouble himself with any such thoughts yet', 2.3.18–21). We should therefore see how the archbishop's speech works in two directions at once. It fills in the recent past; and it looks forward to the later report of Falstaff's dying. In turn, the later scene works backwards to make of the archbishop's speech about the king something different and richer. It is through such techniques that Shakespeare beds down his central themes. As the play shows over and again, there really is no severing of the links between a king and any of his subjects.

We see here how formal rhetoric can often be a channel for ideas or connections that have little specifically to do with the speaker. Invariably, however, the speaker is not a neutral or empty mouthpiece for the play. Henry's archbishop, for instance, is a deeply interested player in the play's unfolding politics. So, before this speech of praise we hear his immediate dilemma. There is a bill being urged by the House of Commons that would confiscate the 'better half' of the church's lands. 'But what prevention?' asks the Bishop of Ely (1.1.21). This is the moment when the archbishop begins his praise of his master: 'The King is full of grace and fair regard...' He goes on, after this speech, to declare his plan. He will recommend to the king invasion and conquest of France. More than a diversion from this unwelcome bill, France might bring to the king's coffers a far greater sum than anything held by England's clergy. A naked material interest thus frames everything the churchman says. Hence, perhaps, the hint of a joke in the Bishop of Ely's two expressions: 'And a true lover of the holy Church' and '*We* are blessed in this change'. He is more than happy to identify virtue when he benefits from it. This context doesn't make his portrait of Henry insincere, but it does add to it one more layer of dubiousness. What if he is being a little bit mischievous? Why, for instance, the curiously repeating 'Never':

> *Never* was such a sudden scholar made,
> *Never* came reformation in a flood...
> Nor *never* Hydra-headed wilfulness
> So soon did lose his seat, and all at once...

Does he really mean *never*? At the speech's end we do at last get the long-delayed release from cynical scepticism – 'As in this king' – but his syntax opens the sense up to the most undermining irony (as does the vehemence of 'Hydra-headed wilfulness').

The same possibilities inform the next scene, when the archbishop is asked by Henry whether or not invasion of France is justified. It is a classic instance of Shakespeare's heavily ironic bombast. So, the archbishop offers the king a justification of no less than 62 lines, his aim presumably being to bore or bewilder the monarch into assent:

> Nor did the French possess the Salic land
> Until four hundred one-and-twenty years
> After defunction of King Pharamond,
> Idly supposed the founder of this law,
> Who died within the year of our redemption
> Four hundred twenty-six, and Charles the Great
> Subdued the Saxons and did seat the French
> Beyond the river Sala in the year
> Eight hundred five. Beside, their writers say...
>
> (1.2.56–64)

And so it goes, on and on, only finally to conclude thus:

> So that, as clear as is the summer's sun,
> King Pepin's title, and Hugh Capet's claim,
> King Louis his satisfaction, all appear
> To hold in right and title of the female.
> So do the kings of France unto this day,
> Howbeit they would hold up this Salic law
> To bar your highness claiming from the female,
> And rather choose to hide them in a net
> Than amply to embare their crooked titles
> Usurped from you and your progenitors.
>
> (1.2.86–95)

Everything about this is parodic (a fact well exploited in Olivier's famous film version): the absurd wealth of precedent, the arcane history and redundant exactitude, the spurious asides and pedantic mastery therein boasted, and the speech's climactic descent into a crabbed and inverted syntax that seems almost wilfully to discard any grammatical object. Accordingly, the king's reply – perhaps bewildered, perhaps irritable, perhaps interrupting – shows just how redundant the archbishop's interminable justifications have been:

> May I with right and conscience make this claim?

Henry himself is not always so brusquely to the point; this question itself reiterates what he had before taken over 20 lines to articulate (1.2.9–32). Clearly, one of the things Shakespeare is playing with – and as so often in the histories the structuring is basically comic – is persuasive rhetoric itself, quite apart from any matter of which the characters are talking. When is it used, how is it used, what does it reveal and what obscure? But still more to the point is the implicit effect of such self-evidently superfluous oratory. For it dramatises (without exactly explaining) the tense ambiguity that pervades the whole play: is the war right, is it worth it, who and what is it for, and how can anyone possibly know either way?

So, this is awful blank verse: long-winded, overcomplicated and confusing. We might think an extreme case of Shakespeare at his most *Shakespearean*. Perhaps: but the 'Shakespearean' bit only really hits home in the comedy. Here this means the comedy of incongruity and contrast: of effective haplessness taking deadly effect. The juxtaposition of meandering verboseness and terse straight talk embodies a principal theme of the play: the decision is for war, and for reasons that have nothing to do with the reasons here laboured so long over. Political language and logic dresses rather than determines the fact. Hence the immediate shift, after these tortuous justifications, to far more thrilling notions of blood-pride and valour: 'The blood and courage that renowned them/Runs in your veins, and my thrice-puissant liege/ Is in the very May-morn of his youth' (1.2.118–20). He will do it because he *can* do it, and the more they all prattle of 'cause' the more we instead recognise 'means, and might' (1.2.125). It is exactly the disparity between gallons of blank verse and barely a thimble of real persuasiveness that makes Shakespeare's point: 'politic' rhetoric is here employed almost entirely ironically.

## EXTRAVAGANT LANGUAGE:
### *ROMEO AND JULIET*

A different kind of over-the-top speech is common in *Romeo and Juliet*. Here, however, extravagant or overdone verse is always designed to be noticed as such. Each scene presents a highly crafted stylistic to and fro: Romeo's lyricism will be countered by Mercutio's obscenity (1.4); young men's bantering idleness is cleared away by the prince's declarative commands (1.1); Juliet's impatient, erotically ingenuous verse is stalled by the Nurse's delaying, erotically cynical prose (2.5); collectively hysterical mourning gives way to the Friar's terse rebuke, which in turn gives way to the musicians' irreverence (4.5). The effect of this is that no single way of speaking ever quite captures the stage. There is always a debunking, redeeming, or otherwise contrasting counterpoint that has just been or is about to be heard. Even the play's most famous scene – the balcony meeting between the lovers – is characterised by very different modes of speaking for each of them: Juliet is much the more simple and plaintive ('But farewell, compliment./Dost thou love me?', 2.2.89–90), suspicious of Romeo's compulsive self-mythologising: *R.* 'What shall I swear by?' *J.* 'Do not swear at all', 2.2.112–13). Romeo's romantic wordiness is repeatedly ironised: 'by yonder blessed moon I vow,/ That tips with silver all these fruit-tree tops', is interrupted by Juliet's 'O swear not by the moon, th'inconstant moon' (2.2.107–9). Similarly, his observation immediately after leaving Juliet, 'The grey-ey'd morn smiles on the frowning night,/ Chequering the eastern clouds with streaks of light' (2.2.188–9) is abruptly echoed and menaced by Friar Laurence's first words, 'Now, ere the sun advance his burning eye/The day to cheer, and night's dank dew to dry' (2.3.1–2). Where Romeo sees the sun's gentle 'smiles' and 'streaks of light', the Friar sees a 'cheer' that is 'burning', its promise one of parching. For the Friar, the sun oversees a world made up equally of 'baleful weeds and precious-juiced flowers' (2.3.4). Any lyricism belongs not so much to Shakespeare as to the characters: it is an expression of desire and perspective.

So, even when the lovers start to speak the same kind of ecstatic verse, full of hyperbolic repetitions and impatient exclamations, they never do so in the same scene. Instead, their mutually echoing verse reflects their new situation: mentally engaged, but physically separated. So, in 3.2 (Juliet), and 3.3 (Romeo), we get basically mirroring speeches. Here is Juliet:

> Tybalt is dead and Romeo – banished.
> That 'banished', that one word 'banished',
> Hath slain ten thousand Tybalts...
> Which modern lamentation might have mov'd?
> But with a rearward following Tybalt's death,
> 'Romeo is banished': to speak that word
> Is father, mother, Tybalt, Romeo, Juliet,
> All slain, all dead. Romeo is banished,
> There is no end, no limit, measure, bound,
> In that word's death. No words can that woe sound.
>
> (3.2.112–26)

And here is Romeo:

> But Romeo may not, he is banished.
> Flies may do this, but I from this must fly.
> They are free men but I am banished.
> And say'st thou yet that exile is not death?
> Hadst thou no poison mix'd, no sharp-ground knife,
> No sudden mean of death, though ne'er so mean,
> But 'banished' to kill me? 'Banished'?
> O Friar, the damned use that word in hell.
> Howling attends it.
>
> (3.3.40–8)

Common theme apart, we get the same obsessive repetitions, nervous internal rhymes, compulsive punning. But the lovers' exuberantly self-circling speeches are then framed by the impatience or pity of their respective older listeners: the Nurse ('Will you speak well of him that kill'd your cousin?', 3.2.96) and the Friar ('Thou fond mad man, hear me a little speak', 'What simpleness is this?', 3.3.52, 77). As the Nurse says when she visits the Friar and witnesses Romeo's all-too familiar misery: 'Even so lies she,/Blubbering and weeping, weeping and blubbering./Stand up, stand up. Stand up and you be a man.... Why should you fall into so deep an O?', 3.3.87–90). These differing registers and framing commentaries give relief from the adolescent hyperbole. Equally, by expressing the necessary 'stylistic' criticism (this is excessive, absurd, repetitive) they free *us* from having to do the same thing. This allows us uninhibitedly – though still with part of our minds detached, worried, judgemental – to experience the intense feeling that generates the 'bad' poetry.

*Romeo and Juliet* teems with the most stylised poetry, with shared sonnets, gauche rhymes, grisly puns, overlong anecdotes; 'bombast' is almost the least of it. But any such styles are there to be noticed. In the most basic sense these styles embody their various speakers' mental and social furnishing. The play's celebrated portrayal of young love depends upon this way of turning style into a kind of allegory.

A typical example is when Romeo and Juliet, after their night together, exchange differing interpretations of the emerging daylight. Romeo's words are highly euphuistic and conceited: 'Look, love, what envious streaks/Do lace the severing clouds in yonder east./Night's candles are burnt out, and jocund day/Stands tiptoe on the misty mountain tops' (3.5.7–10). So, the images concentrate Romeo's anxiety and resentment: his night of joy being spent ('candles are burnt out'), he must now leave; the whole world is against them; a light both 'envious' and 'jocund' neatly conjures Romeo's disdain for a world-order that takes empty joy in foiling others' ardour ('envious' of Juliet's love, on 'tiptoe' like a petty impostor). The lovers then go on to quarrel over the meaning of these signs: 'Yond light is not daylight', 'It is not day', 'It is, it is', before closing with Romeo's climactic pathetic fallacy, 'More light and light: more dark and dark our woes' (3.5.36). Almost everything here derives from lyrical cliché. But such cliché is part of the point: Juliet and Romeo's delighted self-centredness, their astonished sense of suddenly growing into themselves, partly comes from this awareness of having joined a literary tradition of lovers given point and pathos by the outside world's hostility. Their stringing out of the metaphor is not excessive, or even extra to the scene's basic sense: it *is* the scene. Captured at an awful cusp between two 'nows' – the now of *this* and the now of *that* – they possess their moment mainly through knowing that it must pass. Far from being superfluous, the conceit about the light and the lark embodies their very beings.

Throughout the play it is the *recognisable* limitations, corruptions, or second-handedness of the stuff we hear that generates – both prompts, and oddly protects – our feeling and hunger for more ideal forms: this goes for both love and verse. Romeo, for example, experiences through the story his own stylistic alchemy: his initially hackneyed, plagiarised verse is the dross he finally leaves behind, just as later on the hackneyed, plagiarised mourning for the undead Juliet clears the air for the authentic mourning to come. Every scene shows clashing modes of discourse, all imperfect or frustrated. Such collisions are the play's unifying style, and its theme – and the thing that it is always reaching toward overcoming.

## UNUSUAL LYRICISM: HORATIO IN *HAMLET*

Romeo's lyricism is characteristic both of the play and the speaker. But what about this similar evocation of sunrise from Horatio in *Hamlet*:

> But look, the morn in russet mantle clad
> Walks o'er the dew of yon high eastward hill.
>                                   (1.1.171–2)

This is as conventionally 'poetic' as *Hamlet*'s language ever really gets. We have the sentiments of pastoral hope and innocence ('morn', 'dew'), the old-fashioned adjective ('russet' meaning both reddish-brown and a peasant's coarse jacket), the homely provincial noun ('mantle' meaning a woollen cloak), the inverted syntax ('russet mantle clad'), all serving the thankful personification of the sun, a healthy, beaming, and humble yeoman of the countryside, taking a therapeutic early morning constitutional.

But why? Horatio is normally understood as an eminently sensible figure, a humanist rationalist, resistant to flights of fancy and superstition, characterised above all by probity in judgement and balance in expression. As this very speech begins, 'So have

I heard and do in part believe it'. It is the consummate Horatio riposte: the 'in part' suggesting a perfectly equivocal, perfectly respectful dismissing of Marcellus' speculation about the portent of the crowing cock in the Christmas season ('No fairy takes, nor witch hath power to charm,/So hallow'd and so gracious is that time', 1.1.168–9). This then is the immediate context of Horatio's sudden leap into lyricism – and doesn't it explain everything? He has seen a ghost, seen it vanish 'like a guilty thing', and heard himself and his companions start speculating about matters far beyond the normal reach of understanding. It is a situation of mystery, terror, and uncanniness. What could be more natural than to take grateful refuge in the first sign of something that is *not* uncanny or alien, but that instead promises warmth and comfort and routine? For he really does grab at it, as a drowning man might a life-rope (witness the abruptness of 'But look –') A great gush of relief courses through this lyricism; no less than the excited babble about cocks and saviours that succeeds the ghost's sudden disappearance, language here pretends to overcome the stunned dumbness of mystery and self-alienation. The sunrise is more than a return of day: it is a return to daylight logic and its grounded certainties.

Having identified Horatio's particular investment in his trope, further things become clear. So, in blessing the rising sun with this little personified narrative, Horatio is taking some kind of line from Marcellus' talk of the 'bird of dawning' and 'our Saviour's birth'. But he is not about to give up his humanism and wait open-mouthed for grace or fairies or witches to seize the day. Instead, he alerts us and his companions to an alternative source of light and direction: the 'morn in russet mantle clad' evokes a familiar everyman; that he 'walks o'er the dew of yon high eastward hill' suggests that this man, fresh and crisp, is due any moment to enter. Horatio's summons, above all, is to the play's hero; and so now the play for the very first time mentions Hamlet: 'Let us impart what we have seen tonight/Unto young Hamlet; for upon my life/This spirit, dumb to us, will speak to him' 174–6. Horatio's evocation of the 'morn' therefore inaugurates the play's decisive transition, and indeed its ongoing battle, between different kinds of narrative or political agency. Is it a ghost, or providence, or a *man* who will determine the day?

However, even Horatio can never quite speak for this multi-faceted play – and still less for its hero. Accordingly, his faith here may well be misplaced. Of course it is true that the 'young Hamlet' has indeed returned on cue from the east (from Wittenburg). But he is a man for whom the 'dew' is a figure of wishful self-extinction (1.2.130), and who evokes a thoroughly ruined pastoral as one of his most instinctive images of public and private decay (''tis an unweeded garden/That grows to seed', 1.2.135–6, 'Could you on this fair mountain leave to feed/And batten on this moor?, 3.4.66–7). And indeed the world Horatio sees rising – it is tempting to call it an Elizabethan world, redolent of the old romances of ten years earlier, of artisanal solidarity amid pastoral landscapes – is *not* in fact rising at all. The 'young Hamlet', fiercely aristocratic, fiercely private, could never really be akin to anything in 'russet mantle clad'. Just as Hamlet's first speech subverts Horatio's hopes for the 'dew', likewise one of his first puns subverts Horatio's faith in any sort of benign sun: 'I am too much in the sun', says Hamlet (1.2.67). He is too much in the public eye; too much in the gaze of the king. Above all, he is a 'son' twice over, desperate for the shade that could only be provided outside the play, either before it started (when he was a son to only one father) or after its deathly end (when he might be buried). Likewise, the Denmark we witness bears precious little resemblance to the bucolic peace Horatio evokes. This play-world will remain resolutely in darkness, whether that of night, corridor, or closet: when it finally gets back outside it is only to enter a graveyard. Horatio's welcome to 'morn', then, is simultaneously the morning's elegy: it is an entrance into mourning. If he is clearly resisting disappointment or bewilderment, he is equally clearly intuiting just the same.

This can suggest how the 'But look' speech is not only about Denmark, Hamlet, or *Hamlet* – it is about Horatio, too. If we notice some trace of nostalgia and escapism, even some vestige of patriotic special pleading, then it helps give to this terse, rather colourless, but somehow intimate character a rare and surprising tragic colour. We might compare here a similar moment in *Henry V*, when two soldiers express their doubts that the rising sun promises much at all in the way of justice, honour, or escape:

COURT   Brother John Bates, is not that the morning which breaks yonder?

BATES   I think it be; but we have no great cause to desire the approach of day.

(4.1.85–8)

Horatio gestures toward something like the same milieu – home-spun common sense, seeking relief from the battlements – but the difference between his flowery poesy and their unillusioned prose suggests just how self-displacing and wistful Horatio's pathetic fallacy really is. Here, then, is where Horatio's own mini-tragedy is encapsulated: we find it all here, packed into his one moment of linguistic overflow. It prepares for his fate just as much as it prepares for Hamlet's. This fate is roughly of two kinds. First, as the marooned survivor, unwilling to live but pledged to do so, forced to rehearse faiths and hopes that he has long suspected to be a kind of delusion. And second, as Hamlet's closest confidant, the audience's on-stage surrogate, and the voice exactly of a reasonable hope. Accordingly, in some abiding sense 'young Hamlet' does indeed resemble the popular hero after whom Horatio's 'morn' speech yearns. Like Horatio, we wait for this hero to appear, and then continue to wait for him to bring the light and clarity that as the sun/son he should. Horatio's lyrical reaching for hope and solace is certainly overcompensating, and certainly destined for disappointment. But equally it remains powerfully in tune with the romantic longings and expectations that underpin our response to the whole play.

# 5

# WHY RHYME?

*This chapter considers Shakespeare's use of rhyme. We all know that rhymes are easy to hear and to remember, and that they tend to stand out if the rest of the play is in unrhymed prose or blank verse. But what is the dramatic significance of rhyme? When and why does Shakespeare use it? The first section looks at some general attributes of rhyme, particularly its association with ease and order. Examples are taken from* A Midsummer Night's Dream. *The next section considers the rhyming couplet that often closes a long speech of blank verse, and asks what exactly might be speaking through this rhyme. Is a rhyme controlled by its speaker? Or does it speak of some energy or harmony above and beyond the speaker? This leads into a consideration of the comparative importance of genre, dramatic situation, and psychology in explaining rhyme. Here examples are taken from* Othello *and* Macbeth. *The final section is an extended analysis of the use of rhymes in* Richard II. *Can the play's tale of civil war and the transfer of royal authority be traced in its rhymes? We analyse how specific rhyming words complicate assumptions about rhyme's larger associations with harmony and order. We also look at the movement between rhyme and blank verse, and show how the possession of rhyme often corresponds ironically to the possession of power. Finally, we consider the identification of rhyming with closure, and specifically to the endings of both characters and plays. We show how the association of rhyme with termination can work against its associations with fluency and ease. This allows a certain kind of end-stopped rhyme – for example Macbeth's and Bolingbroke's – to embody both stricken fatalism and the longing to escape from it.*

Transitions from one style of address to another are one of Shakespeare's principal means of lending his dialogue variation and accessibility. Without such transitions any reader or auditor would quickly flounder. The most important such shifts are those from verse to prose, and blank verse to rhyme. Each shift from blank verse usually represents a movement into greater lucidity and ease. Both methods can relax an audience: rhyme because of its more sing-song rhythm, its catchiness, and its movement toward definitiveness and finality; prose because of its colloquial directness, familiarity, and humour. For although blank verse supposedly emulates the conversational rhythms of everyday English, it is at the same time estranging: it wrenches familiar patterns of breathing and emphasis out of normal colloquial habits and into unusual constrictions of line, rhythm, syntax, and indeed vocabulary. Here we can compare the much easier feel of rhyme. Always wearing its 'feigning pleasures' on its sleeve, rhyme is usually free from blank verse's more alienating properties.

But only usually: as we will see, rhyme is not as simple and transparent as its reputation might suggest. There are many ways in which particular rhymes might work. Indeed we might potentially read a rhyme in much the same way as we do any other trope, looking out for ways in which the two words relate to or spark off one another. Alexander Pope's well-known formulation, that a rhyme is an 'echo to the sense' is usually true: but then there are many types of echo, from servile to mocking to grandly amplifying. The two words might be antithetical or reinforcing; the second might be the consequence of the first; they might concentrate a narrative, whether of progression, inflation, or deflation; the relationship might be ironic, bathetic, or subversive. The likeness of sound can work to bridge the divide between lines; equally, it can work to emphasise the divide. Similarly, a rhyme can work with or against syntactic or other rhythmic patterns. It can be delayed, or dilated, or omitted entirely. It can surprise equally by its presence or its absence. In other words, a rhyme is more than a neutral prosodic measuring stick; more than an aid to the actor's memory or the auditor's easy comprehension. It is a dramatic-cum-figurative trope, involving two (or sometimes more) words in taut relation to one another. It is as open to play and movement as any other such trope or figure of speech.

Here though I want to look at something other than the specific 'meaning' of particular rhyme-words (as rewarding as such an inquiry would be). For there is another, perhaps more fundamental purpose of dramatic rhyming. That is, rhyme usually suggests a purpose above and beyond the things said: a momentum and self-certainty that the rhyme-form itself conveys, and that is not dictated by the sense of the words. In a way it is not the speaker who rhymes, but rather his speech that 'is' rhymed. It is less to do with the intention of the speaker than the framing mood or orientation of the moment, scene, or genre. An example is the way the potentially catastrophic opening to *Midsummer Night's Dream* is rendered less threatening by the lovers' reversion to rhyme:

> LYSANDER   Helen to you our minds we will unfold:
>     Tomorrow night, when Phoebe doth behold
>     Her silver visage in the wat'ry glass,
>     Decking with liquid pearl the bladed grass
>     (A time that lovers' flights doth still conceal),
>     Through Athens' gates have we devis'd to steal.
> HERMIA   And in the wood, where often you and I
>     Upon faint primrose beads were wont to lie,
>     Emptying our bosoms of their counsels sweet,
>     There my Lysander and myself shall meet;
>     And thence from Athens turn away our eyes,
>     To seek new friends, and stranger companies.
>
>                                             (1.1.208–19)

The rhyming couplets help create the play's distinctively permissive cocoon, one of nostalgia, escapism, and pastoral experimentation. Indeed the forest itself works rather like the rhymes do: suggesting a buoyant serendipity while in fact pre-contracted to comi-magic lore and its conflict dissolving symmetries. More precisely, this dream forest is the site of a battle between a disjunctive blank verse – spoken for instance by Titania and Helena in their powerful speeches of rebuke (2.1.81–117, 3.2.192–244), and in the vicious catfight between Hermia and Helena – and a more magical, passage-smoothing rhyme – overwhelmingly the chosen form of Puck and Oberon, and of the lovers (including Bottom and Titania) in their often confused raptures. It is then telling that once the spell is broken and the lovers awake that they never again speak in rhyme. They speak instead either in blank verse – when they are unsure of their condition and reason, afraid of punishment for thus escaping to the woods – or in prose – when they join with the Duke in ridiculing the mechanics' (rhyming) nuptial play. Rhyme, in this play, is the medium of fantasy, dream, magic, rapture, and transformation. It has its own stubborn and tenacious integrity. Even though the lovers leave it behind, it remains the heartbeat of the play's appeal, transferred at the end into the oddly invincible rhymes of Bottom's play and Puck's magic.

Rhyme usually serves one of two moods: blithe comic confidence or implacable self-resolve. Usually, the 'rhymer' is in accord with the generic mood. This mood speaks through the speaker, but by the same token the speaker rolls happily along with it. A common example is a long speech's closing rhyming couplet. So, Shakespeare usually makes it possible to hear a speech as a single block, determined by its speaker, tone, and situation. We might miss many of its details but still pick up a decisive aura and thrust. Such thrust is often reinforced by the closing couplet, which can approximately sum up what has gone before and clear the decks for the next movement. Particularly in his earlier plays, Shakespeare uses the speech-closing rhyme to lighten and link exchanges of high rhetoric. This supplies a sing-song palatability, a dependable and accessible rhythm to verse that might otherwise seem indistinct or indigestible. The most conspicuous example of this is probably *Richard II*. The first scene alone has 17 such rhymes, either the closing two lines of a longish (usually) blank verse speech, or a shared line between cuer and cued (e.g. '*Rich.* 'Norfolk, throw down we bid, there is no boot.' *Mowbray.* 'Myself I throw, dread sovereign, at thy foot', 1.1.164–5). In cases like these, rhyme presents a kind of appeal beyond the details of the moment: it seems to say that behind present confusions remains some sort of extra-dramatic governing harmony. And it is fundamental to the pleasures of rhyme that we too seem to share in this harmony.

It is not restricted to the world on stage. Rhyme offers an unconscious assurance that *we* are not being held to ransom beyond our will: we are attending someone else's play, but in some basic sense we allow it, endorse it, and survive it.

However, it is exactly this rather uncanny intimacy and ease of rhyme that can make it a vehicle for disturbing complicities. Consider Iago's first two soliloquies. In them he discuss his plans and motives for 22 and 26 lines respectively of unrhymed blank verse, before closing with striking rhyming couplets: 'Hell and night/Must bring this monstrous birth to the world's light' (1.3.401–2), ''Tis here, but yet confused:/Knavery's plain face is never seen, till used' (2.1.308–9). He frames hellishness in a rhyme, which then works rather like 'ironic' quotation marks. The rhymes allow him to exit with a theatrical flourish, nodding to the figure's indebtedness to earlier stage villains and Vices. We can hear the devilry easily enough, too easily. In framing his actions as generically bound craft, the rhyme becomes an ethical anaesthetic.

But surely here we need to pause. For this device is one of any number of audience-lulling seductions that make us complicit in Iago's exercise. We soon enough wish all that Iago has done to be undone. And part of this should involve re-evaluating any (unconscious) permissiveness towards things like ingratiating rhyme. We cannot explain – or allow – rhyme merely by appealing to generic tradition. For Iago himself possesses the rhyme quite as much as any scenic or soliloquial form does. This doesn't mean that Iago knows that he speaks in rhymes, any more than he knows that he often speaks in verse. Rather, there is a fit between Iago's psychology and the conventions that attach to rhyme. Accordingly, the rhyme identifies Iago's specific attributes with those commonly associated with rhyme: a mixture of super-surveying pleasure, irresistible momentum, and agency beyond anyone's rational intervention. The rhyme thus exemplifies rather than euphemises Iago's menace. And it becomes all the more enthralling – in all senses – for being so delicate and self-aware.

In other words, we need always to think about *why* rhyme is being used in any particular case. Such analyses will always bring with them its habitual purposes and effects: the association of rhyme with ease, confidence, familiarity, order, and perhaps above all a comic-romantic cosmic order. But the case of Iago shows that these associations might be present ironically or disjunctively: if we feel concord with the rhymer, then it might just be at our peril. Rhyme can become one more means of representing discrepant perspectives, situational layering, or latent violence.

The example of Iago can remind us of an abiding ambiguity regarding the possession of agency in rhyme. Is the rhyme controlling the speaker, or the speaker controlling the rhyme? Often this ambiguity is not exploited, because the rhyme is so clearly aligned with transitions of scene, theme, or mood. But this is by no means always the case: the ambiguity can become a real focus of dramatic tension. The returning rhythm of Macbeth's rhymes, for example, can seem to beat unerringly upon – or even pulse along with – his palpitations of heart and mind:

> If this which he avouches does appear,
> There is nor flying hence, nor tarrying here.
> I 'gin to be aweary of the sun,
> And wish th'estate o'th' world were now undone.–
> Ring the alarum bell! – Blow, wind! come, wrack!
> At least we'll die with harness on our back.

> (5.5.47–52)

These rhymes are absolutely Macbeth's: because so grimly *chosen* by him; because suspended between mordant awareness and self-denial; because spoken as though with a choking grip upon rising hysteria. But then they are not his at all, because so suggestive of overdetermined impotence. Insofar as the rhymes perform their normal function – recalling playfulness, or invoking escape from harshness or banality – it is mainly a self-subverting joke. The rhyme's repetitious observance of numbered measure is rather like swinging a pendulum over a stopped clock. The use of rhyming couplets in this particular context, then, serves to mimic, even parody, the modes of escape or self-certainty that Macbeth's sentiment invokes. In place of comic impregnability, we get tragic inescapability. Insofar as Macbeth chooses to rhyme, we can hear a sarcastic reminiscence of his 'ambition' (to seize fate and history in his hands); insofar as the speech 'is' rhymed, we can hear his powerlessness before predetermining forms (like the witches). Macbeth's rhymes often work in this sort of fashion, symbolising the play's ongoing battles over agency. In Macbeth's case, this means questioning how much he does is his will, how much an imitation of such will, and how much the pre-emptive ordering of some silently shadowing force. The rhyme-form itself embodies this gathering puzzle.

## RICHARD II

*Richard II* is a good example of the various structural and thematic uses to which Shakespeare often puts rhyme. So, we have mentioned how rhymes often work in the service, or perhaps memory, of some kind of governing harmony. In *Richard II*, however, the rhymes tend to evoke this harmony at the same time as they encapsulate its imminent tearing apart. In a sense the rhyme-scheme works in two ways at once. So, in scenes of unravelling feudal obedience, the rhymes suggest an abiding if threatened allegiance to shared civic values, and to at least an idea of rightful authority. The body of the speeches can be packed with insults and dissent, but in closing with a rhymed couplet there is a recollection of some vestigial order distinguished by shared, 'natural' ethical contraries:

> I do defy him, and I spit at him,
> Call him a slanderous coward, and a villain,
> Which to maintain I would allow him odds,
> And meet him were I tied to run afoot
> Even to the frozen ridges of the Alps,
> Or any other ground inhabitable
> Where ever Englishman durst set his foot.
> Meantime, let this defend my *loyalty* –
> By all my hopes most falsely *doth he lie*.
> (1.1.60–8; my italics)

However, if we look more carefully at the actual rhyme-words we will see how the appeal to order is simultaneously an assertion of violent division: loyalty – doth he lie. The same thing happens again and again. In the first scene of the play alone, we get these speech-ending rhymes: 'full of ire' – 'hasty as fire'; 'not light' – 'unjustly fight'; 'my descent' – 'life be spent'; 'heartily I pray' – 'our trial day'; 'end where it begun' – 'you your son'; 'his heart-blood' – 'must be withstood'; 'let me try' – will I die'; 'do you begin' – 'such deep sin'; 'high disgrace' – 'Mowbray's face', 'officers-at-arms' – 'these home alarms'. We get either directly opposed violence (ire–fire) or directly opposed subversion (begin–deep sin). The scene's final rhyme says it all: the rhyme-scheme scrupulously 'direct[s] these home alarms' (1.1.205). Rhyme here embodies *both* the order and harmony ruined by civil war – symbolised by rhyme's abiding appeal to and derivation from such harmony – and the causes and terms of such ruin – expressed in the specific rhymes' clashing or co-ordinating referents.

The point to hold onto here is the split political 'allegiance' of the rhyme-effect. The rhymes repeatedly concentrate the burgeoning context of conflict and rebellion. But at the same time they evoke some sort of holding on to the order which is being so threatened. This makes sense because no one on either side claims to be doing anything other than fighting for exactly the 'natural' justice that rhyme so effortlessly invokes. The main thing at issue is which individual or what methods are most faithful to the supposedly shared ideals. Hence the division in the rhyme between 'meta-effect' (harmony) and referential content (division): if the story were to be a happy one, then we might expect that in the end there will not only be a return to rhyme, but to rhyme-words whose relationship is harmonious. That this doesn't happen shows how thoroughly Shakespeare makes his rhymes serve and reinforce his themes. For throughout the play we can trace political vicissitudes through its rhymes: their content, certainly, but equally the simple fact of their presence or absence. So, the early scenes are full of rhyming, when allegiance to King Richard is still everybody's public stance. The very fact of rhyme becomes a style of refuge, a holding on to threatened sureties. It is suggestive, however, that perhaps the play's most famous speech – John of Gaunt's elegy for 'this scept'red isle' and prophecy of disorder (2.1.31–68) – is without rhyme. Once rebellion is afoot, the style

completely changes. There are no rhymes at all in the scene that
marks Bolingbroke's return. All is in blank verse apart from the
very final couplet, spoken by York to mark his own abdication of
persuasiveness ('Nor friends, nor foes, to me welcome you are./
Things past redress are now with me past care', 2.3.169–70). It is
one of the principal markers of Bolingbroke's political efficiency
that he abjures rhyme: whether giving orders or justifying his
cause, he works in blank verse. But in these crucial central scenes,
when fates are at a cusp and history uncertain, so too in the main
does Richard. His still-defiant speeches in 3.2 ('I weep for joy/To
stand upon my kingdom once again', 3.2.4–26, 'Let's talk of
graves, of worms, and epitaphs', 3.2.145–77) do not rhyme; nor
does his final, desperate indignation before the rebels, 'We are
amaz'd, and thus long have we stood/To watch the fearful bending
of thy knee,/Because we thought ourself thy lawful king',
3.3.72–100). Blank verse, then, is used in scenes when authority
is up for grabs, and when notions of an inviolable order are not
only in peril but are frankly subordinate to political imperatives.
Richard returns to rhyme, therefore, when he knows that the game
is up:

> Our sighs and they shall lodge the summer corn,
> And make a dearth in this revolting land.
> Or shall we play the wantons with our woes,
> And make some pretty match with shedding tears?
> As thus to drop them still upon one place,
> Till they have fretted us a pair of graves
> Within the earth, and therein laid – there lies
> Two kinsmen digg'd their graves with weeping eyes!
> Would not this ill do well? Well, well, I see
> I talk but idly, and you laugh at me.

> (3.3.162–71)

We get a progression through defeated puns ('revolting', 'fretted',
'well'), to dislocating rhythms ('therein laid – there lies'), to this
aridly rhyming endgame. The subsequent full return to rhyme is
savagely ironical:

> In the base court? Base court, where kings grow base,
> To come at traitors' calls, and do them grace!

In the base court? Come down? Down, court! down, king!
For night-owls shriek where mounting larks should sing.

(3.3.180–3)

Before Richard's fall, the endpoint gestured to by rhyme was something like a divinely buttressed authority. In his fall, however, the only endpoint is the blank mockery of any such preordaining teleology. The rhyme still alludes absolutely to such supervening order. But now framed in the rhythms and repetitions of a nursery rhyme, any such rhyming order doesn't exist *except* as an emptied verbal obedience.

This then is the context for the ironic shifts in the play's final scenes. Richard is in prison and Bolingbroke is king. But now it is Richard who is given the probing dignity of blank verse. We see this in both his long soliloquy ('I have been studying how I may compare/This prison where I live unto the world', 5.5.1–66) and his exchange with the Groom. He has been freed from rhyme as though freed from false obedience or false ideology.

There is, however, one brief but telling exception. It is this, in the middle of Richard's final soliloquy:

> But whate'er I be,
> Nor I, nor any man that but man is,
> With nothing shall be *pleas'd*, till he be *eas'd*
> With being nothing.               [*The music plays*]
>                Music do I hear?
>
> (5.5.38–41; my italics)

The rhyme pretends to be private and fugitive, being secreted within a line. But it in fact draws almost baroque attention to itself. This is partly because the rhyme's narrative of resignation and abdication – here the pleasing surrender of death – is characteristically only half true. He doesn't really want to die at all, and the rhyme asks any who are listening to agree what a pitiable fate it is for any 'man' (let alone a king). But this rhetorical slyness is reinforced by the fact that Richard's rhyme is a quotation from what was in 1595 perhaps the most famous of all theatrical death scenes: the suicide of the revenger, Hieronimo, in Kyd's *The Spanish Tragedy*. There can be no doubt that Shakespeare and his actors knew the moment by heart; hardly less doubt that most in his audience did likewise:

> *Pleased* with their deaths and *eased* with their revenge,
> First take my tongue and afterwards my heart.
>
> (4.4.191–2)

Hieronimo then bites out his tongue and stabs himself. It may well be that the allusion to a suicide scene is a cue for Richard to attempt the same: after all, he knows his days in the Tower are numbered. The music which then intervenes – after the word 'nothing', halfway through the line – can then either interrupt or excuse Richard in this resolve. The artfully suspended rhyme – not given a line-ending finality, yet alluding to contemporary tragedy's most famously self-silencing closure – is a perfect encapsulation of Richard's situation. So, assaulted as he is, the 'heroic' options are varieties of stoicism: basically, patient endurance or noble suicide. But he can manage neither. The rhyme is too furtive and whimsical to suggest patience. But nor can it do more than gesture toward a cleansing suicidal end: it is not a couplet; it does not close the speech. Instead, rhyme, patience, and death are all at once glanced at and then skipped away from.

Bolingbroke, meanwhile, has ascended the throne – and 'descended' into rhyme. The moment he does so is one of meta-prosodic comedy: the Duchess of York enters pleading for her son, and the king suddenly realises just how pre-written his fate has become:

> Our scene is alt'red from a serious thing,
> And now chang'd to 'The Beggar and the King'.
> My dangerous cousin, let your mother in;
> I know she's come to pray for your foul sin.
>
> (5.3.77–80)

From this point on Bolingbroke speaks entirely in rhymed couplets. Richard's final soliloquy and assassination are thus framed by Bolingbroke's transformation into the rhymer. It seems a clear enough signature of political irony: he has 'inherited' the throne, and with it obedience to supposedly necessary but essentially merely nominal forms:

> They love not poison that do poison need,
> Nor do I thee. Though I did wish him dead,
> I hate the murtherer, love him murthered.
> The guilt of conscience take thou for thy labour,
> But neither my good word nor princely favour;
> With Cain go wander thorough shades of night,
> And never show thy head by day nor light.
> Lord, I protest my soul is full of woe
> That blood should sprinkle me to make me grow.
> Come mourn with me for what I do lament,
> And put on sullen black incontinent.

> (5.6.38–48)

We are a long way away here from rhyme's association with lightness and ease. Bolingbroke's closing couplets do recall the link between rhyme and order, but mainly so as to show how strained and coercive this link has become. The rhymes are deadly with finality, each one like a death knell, each returning to the same beginning: to Bolingbroke's hauntedness by sin and darkness. There is therefore a strange uneasiness created by this obedience to rhyme. So, we can't quite forget rhyme's suggestions of a get-out clause, or a certain experiential triteness or lightness: as though to say if it's in rhyme, things can't be too bad. This then connects to a whiff of hypocrisy in the speech, something queasy and even toxic signified by his stylistic conversion. As the incoming king, Bolingbroke is implicitly seeking connection to the play's framing rhetorical architecture: one which links the symmetry and buoyancy of rhyme with a divinely hedged political dispensation. Equally, however, he *knows* that this is a lie: his beckoning after ceremonial forms is merely a hollowed out imitation. From this perspective, the ill fit between rhyme and sentiment illustrates an abiding consciousness of bad faith.

But at the same time Bolingbroke here comes upon his own peculiar stylistic integrity. He inaugurates a type of rhyme, not seen earlier in the play, in which the very hollowness of both form and thought achieves a mode of finality. For the grim immobility of Bolingbroke's words is in a way perfect for rhyme. It becomes the theme of his rhyme, rather than a subversion of it. Rather as Macbeth's do, Bolingbroke's rhymes embody a devastated exhaustion. Each rhyme ends the thought and the sentence, and accentuates the fullness of each stop. Rather than alluding to a cohering socio-cosmic order, the rhymes speak from and break upon a lamentably null and private silence.

The tension of this final speech, then, relates to the struggle it presents over possession of rhyme. Rhyme is *expected* to negotiate the play's passage into closure. Shakespeare pretty much always ends his plays with a rhyme. In the few tragedies where he doesn't (*Hamlet, Timon of Athens, Coriolanus*), he has a rhyming couplet followed by a single flat departing line: 'Take up the bodies. Such a sight as this/Becomes the field, but here shows much amiss./Go, bid the soldiers shoot', *Hamlet*, 5.2.408–10; 'Make war breed peace, make peace stint war, make each/Prescribe to other, as each other's leech./Let our drums strike', *Timon*, 5.4.83–5; 'Which to this hour bewail the injury,/Yet he shall have a noble memory./ Assist', *Coriolanus*, 5.6.152–4). In such cases the effect is to downplay any suggestions of hope or bounty in the tragic end, while simultaneously acknowledging (in the callous way of politics) that public affairs go on. This suggests how rhyme has some implied connection with the more harmonising, mystifying pretensions of romantic, comic, or tragic closure: the hint that we can now stop analysing and accept that things are as they are; stop probing too hard and allow forgetfulness its sway; stop looking forward (say into a marriage's likely happiness) or backward (say into a survivor's collusion in violence) and *allow* the acquiescence and affirmation which the play-end's rhyming finality advertises. In this context it is particularly suggestive that neither of Shakespeare's two late romances, *The Winter's Tale* and *The Tempest*, end the action proper with a rhyme. Clearly Shakespeare is aware of rhymes' associations with closure and mollification; the resistance to rhyme rubs against the romance genre's supposed embrace of reconciliatory appeasement, and suggests how Shakespeare's rhymes – or lack of – can work to question or complicate generic expectations.

The example of Bolingbroke's closing words suggests still another model for exploiting the presuppositions (regarding rhyming closure) attaching to a play's ending. So, he keeps grimly to the rhyme scheme, getting nowhere, circling glumly around his grief and guilt. This suggests a tremendous effort of will, remembered as though by rote and then exercised to keep chaos at bay. But if there is some sense that he 'must' use rhyme – because he is speaking for authoritative closure – the recognition that his actions have severed him from any easy possession of rhyme's harmonising associations means that his decision to use rhyme is, as it were, his own. *He* is speaking, the rhymes are his, and because they are so knowingly severed from organic harmonies they are all the more private and anguished. This effect is reinforced by the subject matter of the rhymes. He displaces his own guilt onto his double the 'murtherer', whom he banishes like Cain into the night; he resolves to go on a pilgrimage to the 'Holy Land' to wash the blood from his 'guilty hand'. He is doubly severed: from his own self, and from spiritual accommodation. His message, then, is that he will now go off and seek the clean slate that is presently impossible. Meanwhile, the rhymes are still partly simulating such closure, doing what they are 'supposed' to do at the end of a play. The impasse between stylistic technique and thematic effect thus subverts, or hollows out, the affected style. Rhyme is transformed from a sign of audible ease, community, and accommodation to one of as-if silent strain, isolation, and alienation. In speakers such as Bolingbroke and Macbeth, rhyme really does harness a rhetoric of the terminal.

# 6

# WHAT DIFFERENCE DOES PROSE MAKE?

*This chapter looks at Shakespeare's use of prose. It begins by showing that prose is often no less mannered or figurative than poetry. It is usually more distinctively individualised than Shakespeare's verse, but it is just as liable to carry a play's themes. Examples used here are Falstaff in* Henry IV *and the comic scenes in* The Tempest. *The next section explores prose's freedom from the poetic line, and above all the choices this gives an actor regarding pauses and emphases. We look at the use of prose pauses both for evoking laughter in comedy, and for embodying pathos in tragedy. Examples include Rosalind, Celia, and Touchstone in* As You Like It, *and Lady Macbeth. The next section examines transitions from prose to verse, or from verse to prose, within a single part. In comedy such transitions are particularly used to mark changes in power relationships, generic setting, or self-possession. Examples here are Rosalind in* As You Like It *and Bottom in* A Midsummer Night's Dream. *In tragedy, the sudden transition from verse to prose conventionally indicates social or mental disintegration. However, an extended analysis of* Othello *shows that Shakespeare uses the movement to and fro between verse and prose to indicate more subtle inward effects. This section shows how Shakespeare's dialogues cannot simply be divided up into slabs of 'verse' and 'prose'. Particularly during sustained passages of emotional intensity, he develops a hybrid of prose and verse that is able uniquely to embody much of the tragic experience. The chapter closes with a close study of Macbeth's ways of speaking. He never once speaks in prose, but his verse is both lexically free and metrically jagged in ways that bring it close to prose. As with Othello, much of Macbeth's tragic effect depends upon a verse-prose hybrid.*

There is for Shakespeare hardly a more basic or indispensable instrument than the *fact* of prose and verse: of prose into verse or verse into prose; of verse 'in' prose or prose 'in' verse. It is a fact to be reckoned with in various material ways: as textual or biblio-graphical fact, in that the part or page is transcribed differently and looks different; as theatrical, elocutionary, rhetorical, and audible fact, in that the words are pronounced and listened to differently; as political fact, in that prose and verse come from broadly disparate ends of the social spectrum; as generic fact, in that prose is comic and verse tragic or historical; as characterological, actorly, or psychological fact, in that transitions in emotion, passion, fortune, or sympathy will be marked by discernible prosodic shifts. The distribution of prose and verse is at once the most broad and most subtle of structuring techniques. There can be neither character nor idea left untouched by its manipulation.

Only Shakespeare's very early 'serious' plays – *1, 2, 3 Henry VI, King John, Richard III, Titus Andronicus, Richard II* – do not feature substantial amounts of prose. Although most of the early comedies use prose fairly sparingly (around 10 to 20 per cent), prose becomes at least as prominent as verse in many plays, both comedies and histories, produced around the middle of his career: *Much Ado About Nothing, As You Like It, Merry Wives of Windsor, Twelfth Night, 1 & 2 Henry IV, All's Well That Ends Well,* and *Henry V* are all at least 40 per cent in prose. Prose takes up about a quarter of the tragedies *Hamlet, Lear, Timon of Athens, Coriolanus*; about the same of the late 'romances' *The Winter's Tale* and *The Tempest*; but less than 10 per cent of *Julius Caesar, Macbeth,* and *Antony and Cleopatra.*

A few basic points can be made. In most of Shakespeare, blank verse is the regular medium, meaning that the audience will become accustomed to hearing its iambic rhythms, and to regulating their listening accordingly. When prose is spoken, it marks a deviation from the norm that is supposed to be *noticed*. Broadly speaking, the switch will signify one of two things: either the entrance of a particular character type (usually comic or common), or the transition within a single part from 'noble' propriety and rectitude to something more disordered (because drunk, mad, or distempered).

There were just as many rules about writing in prose as verse. Indeed the figures and tropes of rhetoric were mainly designed to make public (prose) speech more memorable and persuasive. Broadly speaking there were two models for prose. First was the Ciceronian or 'euphuistic' model, structured around heightened and obvious contrasts, repetitions, and parataxis (lists). Second was a more conversational or consciousness-unfolding model, associated with Seneca or Montaigne. Though no less artful, this attempts to simulate and accentuate the movements of thought, offering more rhythmic variety, short and long sentences, irregular pauses, colloquial vocabulary and perhaps lexical directness. Shakespeare's prose, predictably, absorbs both models, and uses each by turns. He is as likely to produce a parody of one, or a hybrid of the two, as he is a straight version of either. His prose is always thoroughly measured and rhetorical, but never written quite by the book. Partly this is because Shakespeare's prose, far more than his verse, tends to be 'individuated'. Whereas it is often impossible to distinguish one character from another by reference to their particular style of verse, no two prose-speakers ever sound quite alike. Falstaff in *1 & 2 Henry IV* is a supreme example. He speaks in a prose peppered with allusions, quotations, puns, and burlesque. It is always meticulously paced and regulated, but always distinctively his own:

> No, I'll be sworn, I make as good a use of it as many a death's-head, or a *memento mori*. I never see thy face but I think upon hell-fire, and Dives that lived in purple: for there he is in his robes, burning, burning. If thou wert any way given to virtue, I would swear by thy face: my oath should be 'By this fire, that's God's angel!' But thou art altogether given over; and wert indeed, but for the light in thy face, the son of utter darkness.

> (*1 Henry IV*, 3.3.29–37)

We might see from this example that prose needn't eschew thematic seriousness, figurative layering, or metaphoric pregnancy. Falstaff's ebullience betrays the familiar darkness of the jester: a deeply perturbed theology, fear of rejection, anxiety about death. Because his cascades of prose are always meant to entertain some or other audience beyond himself, and because they can seem indiscriminately to jumble together revelry, insult, lying, and playacting, we might miss the confessionary compulsiveness that pulses throughout. But we should invariably hear candour in the gamesmanship, and confessions in the deflections:

> My lord, I was born about three of the clock in the afternoon, with a white head, and something of a round belly. For my voice, I have lost it with hallooing, and singing of anthems.

> A pox of this gout! or a gout of this pox! for the one or the other plays the rogue with my great toe. 'Tis no matter I do halt; I have the wars for my colour, and my pension shall seem the more reasonable. A good wit will make use of anything; I will turn diseases to commodity.
>
> *(2 Henry IV*, 1.3.186–89, 244–49)

Indeed, Falstaff's speech and body – each teeming with appetite, digestion, and overspill – might be seen as metonyms of each other. Hence the following joke, where the enormously fat Falstaff turns the expected 'school of whales' into something equally appropriate:

> I have a whole *school of tongues* in this belly of mine, and not a tongue of them all speaks any word but my name. And I had but a belly of any indifferency, I were simply the most active fellow in Europe: my womb, my womb, my womb undoes me.
>
> *(2 Henry IV*, 4.3.18–22; my italics)

Falstaff's multitudinous 'belly' is also his multi-tongued prose. He feeds upon anything and everything, and is stuffed full with the voices of his age. But there is nothing ad hoc or merely gluttonous about this appetite: it is 'a school of tongues', like any school overflowing with direction, quotation, rehearsal, and rhetoric. Of course, Falstaff is only parodically any kind of tutor (for example to the prince). Much more to the point, he and his prose embody a 'whole school'. They embrace misdirected energy and boundless irreverence as much as learned allusion; they speak the overgrown boy whose precociousness must always refuse maturity. Falstaff is always threatening to overwhelm supposed boundaries of taste, decorum or even (as in the above 'womb' joke) sexual identity. But this excessiveness is no simple festive folly. Like many a lively 'school', he is pitched in-between past and future, imitation and innovation. This is part of the point of his 'womb' joke: if only he were less fat he might be 'the most active fellow in Europe', giving birth to who knows what possibilities. As he later (thrillingly but wrongly) boasts, 'the laws of England are at my commandment' (5.3.136–7). The swelling fertility of Falstaff's prose is an agent and allegory of the part's bracing political challenge.

Even when less colourfully individualised, Shakespeare's prose is always busy. Take our introduction to Trinculo in *The Tempest*. He notices 'another storm brewing' and calls the 'black cloud' a 'foul bombard [bottle/cannon] that would shed his liquor' (2.2.19–21). This links the cloud with various other agencies of power in the play: it recalls Prospero's past and future control of storm, seas, and weather (for instance, the 'deep and dreadful organpipe' of thunder that will 'bass' Alonso's 'trespass', 3.3.98); it anticipates Stephano, the drunken butler about to enter with his own 'colonising' bottle of spirits (2.2.42). The 'foul bombard' then works to facilitate the comparison between the two agents of Caliban's subjugation (Prospero and Stephano, books and booze, and their comparable arsenals of enthralment and violence). In turn, Stephano's bottle, made from 'the bark of a tree', can recall Ariel's imprisonment in a tree (1.2.270–93). This in turn suggests the airy spirit's own recognition that to be 'freed' from one service can be to take up another. These sorts of analogies layer every scene in the play: and they depend absolutely upon the prose not being any kind of forgetful relief from the main 'verse work'.

## THE PAUSE PROSE

Nevertheless, even figuratively overladen prose operates differently from figuratively dense verse. Its meanings might be doubled up, but its semantic and syntactic order almost never is. As we have seen, Shakespeare's verse derives much of its spark from semantic and syntactic disordering: from clauses or lines that work backwards as well as forwards; from 'functional shifts' where nouns act as verbs or verbs as nouns; from chains of metaphor where a subsidiary image takes over as the principal carrier of meaning;

from the apparently surplus, decorative, or illustrative 'vehicle' mutating into the 'tenor'. Generally speaking, Shakespeare's prose does not do these things. The more relaxed, more linear syntax means that referents tend to be heard in a perceptible order. However irregular or idiosyncratic, prose unfolds in a way that is *perceived* both by the speaker and by the audience. This is not to dispute that a prose speaker can express meanings that s/he does not intend or acknowledge. But where there is a covert or surprising meaning, it will usually be held in a pun (e.g. 'How the knave *jowls* it to th' ground, as if 'twere Cain's jawbone', 'Quite *chop*-fallen', *Hamlet*, 5.1.76–7, 190) rather than in destabilising syntactic effects. In prose – of course assuming our vocabulary is adequate – wordplay usually works in fairly straightforward fashion. So, Trinculo's 'foul bombard' gets its significance from two things: the word's inherent polysemy (bombard = bottle/gun/ bassoon), and its consequent links with similar images in other scenes. In this way, prose figuration frequently serves Shakespeare's double plots, parodies, and homologies. Many of Falstaff's jokes about his illness, humours, or the commonwealth of his body, for instance, derive their point from the correspondent illness, corruption, and responsibilities of his rival 'father figure', Henry IV. Verse figuration obviously uses polysemy and scenic echo all the time. However, it adds to them all of the possibilities that attend upon the *poetic line*: ellipses and inversions, compactions and contractions, reversals and recursions. Such techniques are always liable to leave the auditor or reader struggling to keep up. With prose this is almost never the case. The audience keeps pace. This, above all, is the key to how dramatic prose works.

Prose's freedom from strict lineation brings various gifts. For one thing, the actor speaking prose has much more control over pauses and emphases. A typical example is this exchange between Rosalind and Celia in *As You Like It*:

ROSALIND  Nay, but who is it?
CELIA  Is it possible?
ROSALIND  Nay, I prithee now, with most petitionary vehemence, tell me who it is.

CELIA    O wonderful, wonderful! And most wonderful wonderful! And
yet again wonderful! And after that out of all whooping.

(3.2.184–190)

The key here is the way the rhythms shift between arrest and flow.
Celia's teasing echo ('Is it. .?,') of Rosalind's impatient demand
('who is it?') sets up Rosalind's 'Nay, I prithee. . .' sentence. This
repeats the delaying pattern – 'Nay, [indefinite pause], I prithee
now [indefinite pause]' – so as to lay emphasis upon Rosalind's
comically impotent injunction, 'with most *petitionary vehemence*'.
The delay helps emphasise her almost oxymoronic impatience (the
pleading being undermined by the reined-in violence, the violence
by the need to petition) rendering still more bathetic the echoing
demand to 'tell me who it is'. And it is the rhythmic liberty of
prose that keeps the audience so in tune with each movement of
mind. Our apprehension first swells with anticipation, and then
gains release barely a moment after the articulation. Similarly,
Celia's exultant 'wonderful' speech gets its thrilling self-delight
from the way her thought keeps on bubbling over all constraints
or elegance. Indeed the speech is funny largely because in the
course of being spoken it becomes 'about' its own excessiveness:
'and after that out ot all whooping' jokes upon the way
'wonderful' has turned almost onomatopoeic, the pure sound of
joy bursting beyond semantic limits, and all the more joyous for
being absurd. The prose doesn't channel the repetitions into neat
order. Instead, it allows them to be as they are, unpredictable,
self-surprising, standing in for the fact that there are no available
words to express Celia's coiled state of delight, intrigue, and
superior knowledge. The actor can again play the pauses between
repetitions as long or as brief as s/he likes.

Such rhythmic shifts, twists, and returns are not in any sense
difficult. Listeners will pick them up straight away, in a fashion
that Shakespeare's verse very often precludes. Similarly, because
prose is not tied to strict lineation it is more able to absorb
changes of pace and emphasis without undue disruption to
sensory reception or semantic organisation. Again, the ability to
stress, pause, or stop at will is a great boon for the actor seeking
comprehension (or indeed applause).

The individual prose speaker's 'possession' of the pause is particularly useful where an immediate pay-off is required: for instance in comedy that solicits laughter. Here is the fool Touchstone's reply to the courtier Jaques' question 'How did you find the quarrel on the seventh cause?' Possible pauses are marked:

> [*retort to Jaques*] Upon a lie seven times removed. [*change of addressee*] (Bear your body more seeming, Audrey.) [*indefinite pause*] As thus sir. [*indefinite pause*] I did dislike the cut of a certain courtier's beard; [*indefinite pause*] he sent me word, if I said his beard was not well cut, he was in the mind it was; [*indefinite pause*] this is called the Retort Courteous. [*indefinite pause*] If I sent him word again, it was not well cut, [*overt repetition*] he would send me word [*indefinite pause*] he cut it to please himself; [*indefinite pause*] this is called [*indefinite pause*] the Quip Modest. [*indefinite pause*] If again it was not well cut, [*indefinite pause*] he disabled my judgement; [*indefinite pause*] this is called the Reply Churlish. [*indefinite pause*] If again it was not well cut, [*indefinite pause*] he would answer [*indefinite pause*] I spake not true; this is called the Reproof Valiant. [*indefinite pause*] If again it was not well cut, [*indefinite pause*] he would say, [*indefinite pause*] I lie; this is called the Countercheck Quarrelsome. [*indefinite pause*] And so to the Lie Circumstantial [*indefinite pause*] and the [*indefinite pause*] Lie Direct.

(5.4.67–80)

Clearly no actor would observe all of these pauses, or all of the pauses equally. But the point is that the prose *allows* them, and by doing so enables such comic dialogue to do its work. It gives space for the speaker to 'feel' the moment and play the audience; for his fellow actors to fill the gaps or attend the speech's cycles with their own acted responses (boredom, astonishment, impatience, laughter); and for the audience to spend time both anticipating and cherishing specifically loaded phrases and repetitions. As Touchstone himself says earlier, 'This is the very false gallop of verses; why do you infect yourself with them?' (3.2.110–11). He is speaking here about a very particular piece of breathlessly rhyming poesy: but still his implicit comparison is with prose, and its peculiar ability to slow things down, as it were to walking pace, measuring the momentum of speech with a keen alertness to how it will be heard.

Prose pauses can be exaggerated or magnified for clear rhetorical effect. Take Lady Macbeth's final scene, when for the first time in the play she speaks in prose:

> Out, damned spot! out, I say! – One; two: why, then 'tis time to do't. – Hell is murky. – Fie, my Lord, fie! a soldier, and afeard? – What need we fear who knows it, when none can call our power to accompt? – Yet who would have thought the old man to have had so much blood in him?

(5.1.36–41)

In some sense Shakespeare almost has to choose prose here for Lady Macbeth. Decorum decrees that madness should be signalled by exile from the self-control of verse. Nevertheless, such expectation apart, Shakespeare here fully exploits prose's distinctive freedom from the under-rhythms of verse: that onward impelling musicality that keeps the line humming no matter how staccato its sense or its syntax. So, most of the punctuation in the above quotation has been chosen by the modern editor so as to indicate the way he believes the speech should be paced and emphasised. The original Folio punctuation is less fussy, but still it is busy:

> Out damned spot : out I say. One : Two : Why then 'tis time to doo't : Hell is murky. Fye, my Lord, fie, a Souldier, and affear'd? what need we feare? who knows it, when none can call our power to accompt : yet who would have thought the olde man to have had so much blood in him.

It is a mixture of commas, colons, full stops and question marks, all serving two nominal sentences – and about 12 arrested ones – that fall away, return from the dead, stutter ambiguously on as though a syntactical allegory of Lady Macbeth's mental condition. This rhythm of start and stop accentuates the fact of gaps. Each such hiatus becomes charged with a terrific weight of *thought*: of some terrible matter unsaid, or of things suppressed or unspeakable. An actor can make their own choices here. But each punctuation mark might be an eternity, corresponding to the metaphysical vertigo echoing through the Lady's sleepwalk. For instance, the colon (or hyphen in the modernised text) is suspended somewhere between the transitional function of a comma – a pause for breath – and the arresting finality of a full stop – a pause to mark a thought's completion. Accordingly, Lady Macbeth is trapped in just such a space, at once seeking and simulating closure, but haunted by sentences or narratives from the past that simply will not shut down. Indeed the fact of prose itself sustains the speech's doubt and terror. So, what happens *in-between* the Lady's 'One' and her 'Two', or in-between this counting and her statement that "tis time to do't'? How exactly does she go from this to 'Hell is murky'? What relationship is signified by the pause? Is the murkiness what she finds having 'done it'? Or is the murkiness her prompt into deciding to 'do't'? Is she 'in' hell as she counts and resolves? Or does she descend into it having done so? Is she back before her crimes, rehearsing them, girding herself for the dare? Or is she suffering her crimes' inescapable consequences? The prose pause alone does not make such overlapping terror: nonetheless it is 'in' the punctuation that we have to search it out.

## SHIFTS BETWEEN VERSE AND PROSE

Shakespeare's shifts from verse to prose and back usually both serve and signify larger changes. He does not simply apportion prose to one type of character, verse to another, and never the twain shall meet. So, in *As You Like It* Rosalind at first speaks in prose, as befits her confident banter. She continues in prose even with the entrance of the Duke, suggesting both her own aristocratic self-assurance and Duke Frederick's status as a usurper undeserving of deference. Rosalind does shift into verse, however, at the moment the penny drops as to who Orlando really is: the son of her exiled father's dear friend ('My father lov'd Sir Rowland as his soul,/And all the world was of my father's mind./Had I before known this young man his son,/I should have given him tears unto entreaties,/Ere he should thus have ventur'd', 1.2.224–8). The switch to verse therefore marks both Rosalind's tender recollection of her father, and her suddenly sincere affection for Orlando. The verse therefore provides a kind of inward home for *both* character and audience: a space of dependency and authenticity from which all of the prose shenanigans (disguise and so on) spin out and to which they ultimately return.

Another example is Bottom in *A Midsummer Night's Dream*. Being a mere weaver, his dialogue is all either in prose, song or (in the mechanics' play) comically bad verse. This is the case for all except one brief speech, his very final words as the ass. So, adored by the fairy queen ('wilt thou hear some music, my sweet love?', 4.1.27) and courted by servants ('What's your will?', 4.1.21), Bottom is the carnival king. Fittingly for his role as festive interloper, Bottom's every order and response is in prose: or rather all except one. So, tired by the responsibilities of office, Bottom seeks some rest:

> I had rather have a handful or two of dried peas.
> But I pray you, let none of your people stir me:
> I have an exposition of sleep come upon me.
>
> (4.1.36–8)

At last, he speaks 'like' a monarch, or more precisely in verse that burlesques a monarch's dignity ('an exposition of sleep') and peremptoriness ('let none of your people stir me'). But the joke, and the hint of pathos, is that when he wakes from his sleep it will be over. Just as in a dream, the moment of achievement is also the moment of evaporation. Bottom's verse, with all of its erotic charge (there are suggestions in the shift to verse of post coital languor) and political promise, is no more than 'an exposition of sleep'. So, he awakes into a prose that for all of its empirical confusions is a kind of homecoming, both to his theatrical part and his social ease: 'When my cue comes, call me and I will answer' (4.1.199–200). It misses the point to identify this return to prose as a signature of ineradicable buffoonery. For much of Bottom's appeal is rooted in his prose's simple intimacy with an accustomed, body-based self-possession: 'Methinks I have a great desire to a bottle of hay: good hay, sweet hay, hath no fellow' (4.1.32–3). When finally he meets up with his mates again, there can be little doubt that Bottom's distinctively ingenuous, optimistic, swinging prose, all open vowels and airy appeal, is in chord with a vibrant and bracing popular dignity: 'Where are these lads? Where are these hearts?' (4.2.25).

As we have already witnessed with Lady Macbeth's sleepwalking speeches, still more striking effects can come from the sudden switch from verse to prose. This conventionally indicates a 'noble' character's degradation or anguish, and some correspondent loss of status, dignity, and self-certainty. However, as Shakespeare's craft develops, he moves away from schematic formal allegorising (prose equals this, verse equals that). Instead, Shakespeare increasingly develops a mixed mode that within the span of a single part travels from verse, to prose, into a hybrid form that takes something from both. This hybrid form emerges particularly as the tragedy gathers toward emotional climax. Bearing the traces of past dignity (verse based) and the scars of present assault (prose based), the new verse-prose seems specifically designed to suggest the experiential fact of having endured and yet still enduring immense suffering; of radical change that is yet unfinished. In this way, the movement between verse and prose really does encapsulate the basic tragic experience.

## OTHELLO'S VERSE-PROSE

Always the most self-policing, self-regarding of speakers, Othello's verse is from the start a measure both of his worth and its fragility. His blank verse never falls into common or careless patterns, being studied and heightened, lexically ambitious and grand. If we didn't notice just how unlike colloquial banter it is, Othello's persistent harping upon his own 'demerits' as a speaker would alert us quickly enough. All of this makes the great man's sudden capitulation into prose all the more terrible:

> Lie with her? lie on her? We say lie on her when they belie her! Lie with her, zounds, that's fulsome! – Handkerchief! confessions! handkerchief! – To confess, and be hanged for his labour! First to be hanged, and then to confess it: I tremble at it. Nature would not invest herself in such shadowing passion without some instruction. It is not words that shakes me thus. Pish! Noses, ears, and lips. Is't possible? Confess! handkerchief! O devil!

> (4.1.35–43)

– at which Othello faints. Up until now, it is Iago who has been the play's chief prose speaker, but never to Othello, with whom he always speaks blank verse. He uses prose with his lesser dupes, Roderigo, Cassio, and to a degree Desdemona. It is prose, then, which is the vehicle for Iago's most insidious ambitions, perhaps for his frankest confessions (his verse soliloquies are notoriously evasive) and above all for the way he turns others, wittingly or unwittingly, into his agents or his creatures. We have already by now seen Othello's verse become infected by Iago's poison ('O blood, blood, blood', 3.3.454, 'Damn her, lewd minx: O damn her, damn her!', 3.3.478). But the moment when Othello takes 'into himself' Iago's prose in a sense completes this process of being taken possession. So, we can see how Othello's turn to prose is in fact literally dictated by his malevolent guide:

OTHELLO    What? what?
IAGO    Lie.
OTHELLO            With her?
IAGO                                With her, on her, what you will.
OTHELLO    Lie with her? lie on her? We say lie on her when they belie her!

                                                        (4.1.33–6)

Othello has his script – and his obscenely sense-twisting jokes ('belie') – supplied by his 'prose' demon. As so often, Shakespeare's mutations of form meticulously shadow – indeed they create – the mutations of mind and emotion. Here, Othello's collapse out of iambic control prefigures an almost physical dissolving of self, as he chugs and stutters like a dying engine into stasis. The prose does it for him: its grammatical disorder, its staccato rhythms, its ricocheting repetitions, its compulsive resolving into 'untimed' and deathly pauses. The effect is amplified by Iago's contrastive decorum, as he counters his general's prosodic disintegration with unwaveringly ascendant verse:

            Work on,
            My medicine, work! Thus credulous fools are caught,
            And many worthy and chaste dames even thus,
            All guiltless, meet reproach.
                                        (4.1.44–7)

After recovering from his faint, Othello continues to speak mainly in prose for the rest of this long scene (4.1, in which Iago sets him up to witness and misconstrue Cassio's light attitude to the courtesan Bianca):

> I would have him nine years a-killing. A fine woman, a fair woman, a sweet woman!

(4.1.175–6)

This typifies the sorts of repetition distinctive to prose. Shorn of any intricately balanced symmetry, its very directness is at once plaintive (because so 'artless') and thumping (because like a fist or a heart). At the same time the prose is raw with sarcasm: utterly without ironic nuance, and all the more suffering for its rawness. She *was* only moments ago exactly so 'fine' and 'fair' and 'sweet' to him; now the very words are a vicious mockery. The colloquial immediacy of prose ensures that this very primitive balance of opposite emotions is squarely and (to risk an oxymoron) unequivocally communicated. The same words in verse might have cushioned the sheer blow of the thought: poetic forms for such lovelorn thoughts already exist; accordingly, the sentiment of betrayal would tend toward something conventionally mannered and therein *survivable*. Othello cannot and will not survive the opposites he here so feels. The prose ensures that his adjectives ('fine', 'fair', 'sweet') are given the bluntest weight of both perfection *and* its betrayal. Hence, again, the way the prose insists upon the fact (a fact perhaps reinforced by an actor's emphatic enunciation) that each of these simple words of praise has, for Othello, turned treacherously into its subversion. So, 'fine' also invokes subtlety, 'fair' also suggests ethical dishonesty, 'sweet' also refers to the taste on other men's palates. Taken together, she becomes too fine, too sweet, too fair, altogether too worldly and pulchritudinous a creature for the ageing and overreaching Moor.

But if we now look at his next speech, also in prose, we will see the beginnings of something different:

> Ay, let her rot and perish and be damned tonight, for she shall not live. No, my heart is turned to stone: I strike it, and it hurts my

hand. O, the world hath not a sweeter creature: she might lie by an
emperor's side and command him tasks.

(4.1.178–82)

The sentiments here are returning to a delicacy more normally
associated with verse: but not, however, particularly Othello's love
verse, which has until now tended toward the monumental:
'Come, Desdemona, I have but an hour/Of love, of worldly matter
and direction/To spend with thee. We must obey the time'
(1.3.300–2); 'O my soul's joy,/If after every tempest come such
calms/May the winds blow till they have wakened death/ ... for
I fear/My soul hath her content so absolute/That not another
comfort like to this/Succeeds in unknown fate' (2.1.182–91). Here,
even his most private thoughts are spoken as though happening
to someone other, or to one whose self-accounting is the result of
a conscious and rule-bound apparatus of watching:

> I therefore beg it not
> To please the palate of my appetite,
> Nor to comply with heat, the young affects
> In me defunct, and proper satisfaction,
> But to be free and bounteous to her mind.
> ...No, when light-winged toys
> Of feathered Cupid seel with wanton dullness
> My speculative and officed instrument,
> That my disports corrupt and taint my business,
> Let housewives make a skillet of my helm
> And all indign and base adversities
> Make head against my estimation.

(1.3.263–76)

Everything here is structured around large abstractions (speculation, office, indignation, adversity, estimation) that he alienates
from habitual colloquial use into the stiffest and most formal
constructions. The words work like a kind of charm, over both his
audience and, uniquely, his referents. Indeed, the more we probe
Othello's meaning, the more his (and their) body seems to vanish.

Compare this kind of self-speaking with 'my heart is turned to
stone: I strike it, and it hurts my hand' (4.1.179–80). Othello is
declaring, very simply, that feeling is now finished with. His heart
is pure stone. But we should notice that the statement here *begins*

with the physical senses, with the kind of access to flesh and bone that his habitual verse has mystified. In this way the prose attends – in theatrical terms it invents – Othello's pained recognition that even the most acute emotions are in some inescapable way a phenomena of the physical senses. He seems to be recovering this fact as he speaks, rediscovering the terrible fact that misery is found and felt in a body. Paradoxically, therefore, there is the strangest return to feeling here: a casting away of the self-armouring abstractions that have rendered him so aloof from his own experience. This return to the evidence of the senses then feeds into the simple directness of expression. There could hardly be a greater contrast than with Othello's old bombast. We are getting something like a return to a language that is minutely sensitive to the flow and counter-flow of existing: a flow of prose that contains a verselike counter-flow. So, his next thought not only revisits the painful beauty that so 'hurts', but does so in the most plaintive pentameter imaginable: 'O, the world hath not a sweeter creature'.

From this point on in the scene it no longer makes much sense to distinguish Othello's speeches as 'prose' or 'verse'. Instead, Shakespeare merges the available registers into something else. The prose, for instance, is often spaciously iambic ('she will sing the savageness out of a bear', 4.1.185–6), and is repeatedly asked to bear the scene's harrowing pathos. It is not physical coarseness that most distinguishes this prose. Instead, it is the simple repetition of self-intimate words or phrases ('sweet'/'sweeter'): '*Iago.* She's the worse for all this. *Oth.* O, a thousand, a thousand times' (4.1.188–90); 'But yet the pity of it, Iago – O, Iago, the pity of it, Iago' (4.1.192–3). The double repetition in this last example – 'Iago' spoken three times, 'the pity of it' twice – nicely illustrates how prose can reach toward a pathos that has relatively little to do with semantics or vocabulary. Instead, arhythmic repetitions of the sparest referents – his friend's name, his knowledge of loss – indicate the simple inadequacy of language and, concomitantly, a swelling immensity of suffering and need. There is no change in the meaning of the repeated words ('Iago' and 'pity') from one use to the next; there is no accruing of significance through the repetition. Othello pleads for help and understanding, and can get none; he yelps at the fact of tragedy, and can get no further. What emotional or affective accruing there is comes from the bald fact of repetition, and the throbbing impotence it enacts. An actor might take the pauses between clauses as quickly or slowly as seems fit: either way, prose here displays its unique access to a silence and isolation where words cannot reach.

Othello's prose, then, revolves around two kinds of repetition, both of them searching for release from bewilderment and pain, but of contrasting emotional tactility. There is the ineffably delicate kind, traversing the boundary between sensory hunger, nostalgic memory, and metaphysical puzzle. And there is another more brutalised kind, which has Othello dwarfed by the magnitude of betrayal into self-shrivelling role play and set upon dissolution or revenge: 'Get me some poison, Iago, this night.... This night, Iago' (4.1.201–3) 'Good, good, the justice of it pleases, very good! ... Excellent good' (206–10), or this rhyming variation, 'I am *glad* ... to see you *mad*' (237). Far from the life-befuddled lover, he becomes the chuckling villain: part-hysteric, part-Vice – and part of Iago.

All of this is leading up to Othello's full return to blank verse, which breaks back upon him after the shocking violence of striking his wife ('Devil!') at line 239. This brutality ends the prose section, forming a bracket to go with the similar violence of his earlier collapse into prose (marked by fainting). But as much as he now speaks in verse, he has hardly left his 'prose mind' behind:

> Ay, you did wish that I would make her turn.
> Sir, she can turn, and turn, and yet go on
> And turn again. And she can weep, sir, weep.
> And she's obedient: as you say, obedient,
> Very obedient.

> (4.1.252–6)

The repetitions here are not terribly sophisticated: whereas before he took suggestion from Iago ('lie'), here he takes Lodovico's disbelieving defence of Desdemona ('Make her amends, she weeps', 'Truly, an obedient lady ... call her back', 4.1.243, 247–8) and 'turns' it into still more obscene complicity. The repeated words work in much the same way as 'fine', 'fair', and 'sweet' did earlier: 'turn' is a metonym of sexual duplicity and, more than that, precocious sexual facility; 'obedient,/Very obedient' says that she will be pliant before *any* kind of master. Again, Othello fully occupies both sides of his sarcasm, raging mad at how such incompatible things can so easily cohabit. The self-circling, interruptive gracelessness of this return to verse seems almost crassly intent on declaring that Othello's old forms of embodiment and mediation are no more:

> Very obedient. – Proceed you in your tears. –
> Concerning this, sir – O well-painted passion! –
> I am commanded home. – Get you away.
> I'll send for you anon. – Sir, I obey the mandate.
>
> (4.1.256–9)

The speech's final line is the starkest indication of this. It marries decorum and indecorum, courtesy and animality – and of course verse and prose: 'You are welcome, sir, to Cyprus. Goats and monkeys!' (4.1.263).

The point to notice is how comprehensively Othello's discourse draws upon all of its various springs. It then speaks in the fullest sense for the horrors he has felt or feels. But this prose-inflected verse no longer speaks of himself as his old verse did. He no longer sublimates the very possession of flesh in favour of some exemplary public profile. He is instead a sufferer like Job, shamefully and shamelessly *embodied*:

> Had it pleased heaven
> To try me with affliction, had they rained
> All kinds of sores and shames on my bare head,
> Steeped me in poverty to the very lips,
> Given to captivity me and my utmost hopes,
> I should have found in some place of my soul
> A drop of patience...
> But there where I have garnered up my heart,
> Where either I must live or bear no life,
> The fountain from the which my current runs
> Or else dries up – to be discarded thence!
> Or keep it as a cistern for foul toads
> To knot and gender in!
>
> (4.2.48–63)

The magnificence of this is much to do with the way it 'knots and genders' disparate ways of speaking in a single torrent. The image train of rain, drops, fountains, and currents encapsulates how this works. Othello finds all of his past – his faith, trust, courage and hardiness, his solitary stoical masculinity, his pledging of it all for love – rushing together into a great corruptive wash of indictment. Accordingly, the speech itself re-enacts a kind of 'cistern' (appropriately, 'cistern' in the early seventeenth century meant a part of the brain as much as a reservoir for water: *OED*, 'cistern', 4). Othello's subject is the absolute alteration that loving another brings, and the complete mortgaging it effects upon one's being. And the vessel of such awful consequence is equally his *verse* as it is his 'heart' or his brain. For the verse itself bears the symptoms of being filled, then emptied, then left open for further horror to enter, fill, and spill.

This is the context for the distinctive 'verse-prose' that now takes centre stage. For example this:

> O thou weed
> Who art so lovely fair and smell'st so sweet
> That the senses ache at thee, would thou hadst ne'er been born!
>
> (4.1.68–70)

– in which the final line gives up entirely on metrical order. Or the next speech, responding to his wife's question, 'Alas, what ignorant sin have I committed?':

> Was this fair paper, this most goodly book
> Made to write 'whore' upon? What committed!
> Committed? O thou public commoner!
> I should make the very forges of my cheeks
> That would to cinders burn up modesty
> Did I but speak thy deeds. What committed!
> Heaven stops the nose at it, and the moon winks,
> The bawdy wind that kisses all it meets
> Is hushed within the hollow mine of earth
> And will not hear't. What committed!
> Impudent strumpet!
>
> (4.1.72–82)

– which in ten lines of iambic verse spits the metre-splitting 'What committed!' three times, each time three lines apart (4.1.72–82). Or this, haranguing Emilia:

> You! Mistress!
> That have the office opposite to Saint Peter
> And keep the gates of hell – you, you, ay you!
>                                        (4.1.92–4)

The metrical irregularity is itself a signifier of distraction. But equally important is the way Othello's 'verse' keeps open the floodgates from (or to) the substantive *material* sources of his prose. Above all, this means the insult, bewilderment, and self-insurrection of discovering one's mind trapped in a feeling body ('the senses ache at thee'). In this long scene (4.1), Othello mainly expresses this recognition disgustedly, and often disgustingly. But as we have seen, a tender, no less killing nostalgia is always co-present, giving to the violence its suffering. And Othello's prose-like repetitions are the chief bearers of this burden.

So it is that this painful 'prose-verse' builds like a swelling wave into perhaps his most memorable speech of all (and his next speech of any substance):

> It is the cause, it is the cause, my soul!
> Let me not name it to you, you chaste stars,
> It is the cause. Yet I'll not shed her blood
> Nor scar that whiter skin of hers than snow
> And smooth as monumental alabaster:
> Yet she must die, else she'll betray more men.
> Put out the light, and then put out the light!
>                                        (5.2.1–7)

This is of course in blank verse, and spoken in a new tone of hushed concentration. Nonetheless, we will recognise patterns familiar from the prose: most particularly, a pendulum-like lexical repetition. We can then import our memories of Othello's recent repetitions, with their mix of delicacy and fury. Here, all seems to be delicacy ('Let me not name it to you, you chaste stars'). It is as though he is bridling his tongue in deference to the ethical propriety he has vowed to serve. But this lexical withholding is, of course, an evasion. He is advancing to suffocate his sleeping wife. In the barest way this act fulfils the promise of his earlier repetitions: both their delicacy (because he frames the murder as an act of love and sacrifice, because he would not wake her or shed her blood, because he serves 'justice') and their violence (because he is hideously mistaken and savage). The dramatic context therefore helps fill out and explain Othello's strikingly empty noun-phrase ('it is the cause'). But so too does our awareness of exactly how Othello speaks: and therefore how much of his meaning is carried not by strict reference but rather by his speech's stylistic manners. That is, its reliance upon repetition, deferral, evasion, or euphemism. Accordingly, this climactic speech draws together Othello's earlier and later ways of speaking. It both recapitulates and consummates all that has got him to this murderous point. So, his words avoid the body, mystifying the corporeal via imprecise metaphors ('light') or referential impreci-sion ('it'). In this way, his speech suggests a truly tragic continuity between the present murderer and the 'speculative and officed' exemplar of past mastery.

But if he has partially returned to old habits, in other ways he remains far removed. There is nothing here of the old tortuous syntax; no pompous straining after rectitude. Whereas Othello's earlier verse was objectifying and monumental, here his vocabulary is simple, his rhythms slow but measured. There remains in the repetitions an old susceptibility to rhetorical moulds, as though speaking in pre-hewn clauses, chiselled for his and posterity's approbation. But here this wish for order is all part of his present struggle. The sense of strain, accordingly, no longer suggests a man reaching for impressiveness. It expresses a desperate longing to batten down the hatches, to prevent any more madness from finding breath.

We can then hear Othello's nostalgia for order as at once productive of and insanely oblivious to the chaos he is about to enter. All of this knowledge – for we *know* all of the things that he no longer dares to pronounce – is then pouring into Othello's semantic emptiness and evasive repetitions. This is why his insistent clauses, 'it is the cause' and 'put out the light', are so moving. We can hear just how much wish fulfilment is in them, and how much repression. We can feel how much violence is the price for their studied delicacy. And it is the prose that to a large degree insinuates this recognition. Othello's prose rhythms carry in them the knowledge of silent pain. Above all, they embody Othello's stunned rage that 'it', that 'light' – his *or* hers – can neither transcend nor survive embodiment.

## MACBETH

Almost uniquely for a tragic protagonist, Macbeth speaks no prose at all. However, he is also the least facile of verse speakers. His verse-line is from the very beginning an abruptly jagged one, as though always pushing at the edges of metrical permission. Indeed it is almost as though Macbeth's verse starts from the point where Othello's (or Lear's) breaks down. In the most basic sense, the prosody is a metaphor – almost an agent – of Macbeth's spiritual and political agitation.

Macbeth is given various ways of speaking. One is his manner to those he believes are ignorant of his brutality, when he is trying to sound at ease or to ingratiate himself in his office. Shakespeare here supplies Macbeth with a sort of failed oiliness. We get arrested sentiments, unwelcome lists, broken lines, and a distinctively bullying mode of pleading. We get jarring accumulations of synonyms, as though he is struggling to compensate for the echoing insincerity of the immediately previous word:

> The spring, the head, the fountain of your blood
> Is stopp'd; the very source of it is stopp'd.
>
> (2.3.96–7)

Macbeth seems often to hear his own strain. As though forgetting all of the rules of persuasive oratory, he piles up artless and context-free 'evidence' for the perspective he would recommend; or he plunges into impossible rhetorical questions, forcing himself to supply his own answers. This silence in-between question and response then evokes an awful and accusatory inward gnawing:

> Who can be wise, amaz'd, temperate and furious,
> Loyal and neutral, in a moment? No man:
> Th'expedition of my violent love
> Outrun the pauser, reason. – Here lay Duncan,
> His silver skin lac'd with his golden blood...
>
> (2.3.106–10)

We may or may not agree with Coleridge, who thought the last line's mixed metaphor the perfect sign of Macbeth's desperate insincerity. But it seems clear enough that the prosody here – jagged and colliding, rushed and abrupt, diving into dead ends – serves and embodies the meaning. As Macbeth now says of the murdered king, the 'gash'd stabs' look 'like a breach in nature' (2.3.111).

There is no verse in Shakespeare more tinny, less easy on the tongue, more at the very front of the mouth, than King Macbeth's 'public' speaking:

> We should have else desir'd your good advice
> (Which still hath been both grave and prosperous)
> In this day's council; but we'll take tomorrow.
> Is't far you ride?
>
> (3.1.20–4)

If the iambic pentameter is often in Shakespeare a measure of ease and decorum, for Macbeth in such moments it is an awkward barrier to trip upon or stutter over. Each pause and punctuation mark, each clause and sentence, works to freeze out any 'intuitive' obedience to the iambic line. Instead, Macbeth wears this line as uncomfortably as he does the robes of kingship:

> Their cruel parricide, filling their hearers
> With strange invention. But of that tomorrow,
> When, therewithal, we shall have cause of State,
> Craving us jointly. Hie you to horse: adieu,
> Till you return at night. Goes Fleance with you?
>
> (3.1.31–5)

Macbeth's speech is rarely more disturbing than when he is imitating good cheer or heartiness. It reeks of hypocrisy, insincerity, and latent threat. But almost the worst thing is the characteristic Macbethian pauses: the parentheses and cut-off lines which suggest a hopeless private reaching for consolation, or which thunder with the uncompaniable silence of his isolation:

> I wish your horses swift, and sure of foot;
> And so I do commend you to their backs.
> Farewell. – [SILENCE?]                    *Exit Banquo*
> Let every man be master of his time
> Till seven at night; [SILENCE?]

> To make society the sweeter welcome,
> We will keep ourself till supper-time alone: [SILENCE?]
> While then, God be with you.
>
> (3.1.37–44)

Of course, it remains verse: but in the pregnancy, unpredictability, and potential length of its pauses, it draws powerfully upon the liberties of prose.

We see in such examples how Macbeth can never be absorbed or satisfied by the immediacies of conversation or etiquette or even political efficiency. There are always other things to be thought, or other things to be surprised by. Again and again his words don't really seek or even admit of responses from anyone else. This is partly explained as an expression of despotic terror. But, more than that, the metrical abruptness forces Macbeth to 'arrive' at silence. And exactly because these mid-line or short-line silences are beyond answering by anyone supposedly addressed, they work to at once hatch and disclose all sorts of repressed inward content: in Macbeth's case, this means variations upon guilt, anxiety, sin, and despair.

At times, with uncanny appropriateness, the prosodic technique mutates into palpable bodily form. At the Macbeths' ghastly feast, for instance, we get a series of unanswered half-lines and echoing niceties:

> See, they encounter thee with their hearts' thanks.
> Both sides are even: here I'll sit i'th'midst.
> Be large in mirth; anon, we'll drink a measure
> The table round.
>
> (3.4.9–12)

The unease is aching, the mood taut and sickly. And now it is that Macbeth gets what all of his metrical arrests have been casting after: the murderer of Banquo knocks at the door, unbeknown to all eyes but Macbeth's and the audience's (just as Banquo's ghost is moments later, when it too punctuates the festivities):

> Be large in mirth; anon, we'll drink a measure
> The table round. [SILENCE] [*Goes to door*]
> There's blood upon thy face.
>
> (3.4.11–13)

The technique is simple enough. The accumulating, repeating, staccato rhythm – short sentence into general silence, short sentence into general silence – finds some sort of relief or answer – indeed the only kind of 'answer' that Macbeth ever really seeks – in the appearance of the assassin's bloody face. This face, like that of all of Macbeth's agents, is basically a projection of Macbeth's secrets. Here the murderer can embody Macbeth's guilt, just as later the 'cream-fac'd loon' can mirror his rising anxiety and his fear of fear (5.3.10–17). Appropriately, therefore, it is this echo figure who briefly helps Macbeth complete his pentameters and 'escape' from the guilt-ridden arrests of his public speech:

MACBETH   There's blood upon thy face.
I MURDERER                               'Tis Banquo's then.
MACBETH   'Tis better thee without, than he within.
     Is he dispatch'd?
I MURDERER            My Lord, his throat is cut.
     That I did for him.
MACBETH               Thou art the best o'th' cut-throats...
                                            (3.4.13–16)

This metrical sharing is a neat enough symbol of Macbeth's self-division. But equally telling are the disparities between the two speakers. So, the murderer could hardly be more factual and direct: the blood is Banquo's; I cut his throat. Macbeth's lines, by contrast, continue to be agitated by metrical irregularities. He displays an almost baroque decadence, and yet evasive in its very self-consciousness: a jumpy rhyme ('thee without . . . he within'), a euphemism ('dispatch'd'), a self-mocking pastiche of a *Boy's Own* joke ('best o'th' cut-throats').

Let's consider the glib antithesis, 'better thee without, than he within'. He means that the blood is better on the murderer's body than inside Banquo's body. In turning the observation into a rhetorical figure, Macbeth pretends to overleap the very violence that allows his expression's spuriously calming symmetry. He would forget the throat that needs to be cut to remove the blood from inside to outside; forget the unutterable difference between something visible but dead (the blood on the face) and something invisible but alive (the blood in the body). At the same time – and characteristically – Macbeth's knowingly fake evasion houses the most pressing self-perception. So, 'better thee without, than he within' refers most fundamentally not to Banquo's inwardness, but to Macbeth's. He is saying that it is better to experience his own agency and culpability in the self-mirroring face of the assassin – at least Macbeth can see it, order it about, dismiss it – than in his restless fears of a spectral Banquo somehow inside him. Macbeth's nervy language thus seems to intuit how Banquo functions both as Macbeth's double (valiant soldier, witness to the witches, royal ambitions) and his foil (for the same reasons). Stylistic choice, therefore, is here all about Macbeth avoiding perception of what he at the same time so baldly sees before him: criminal enormity, self-alienation, absolute loss.

The metrical form, then, is tracing and encasing Macbeth's movements of mind. He desperately wants to be 'Whole as the marble, founded as the rock' (3.4.21): a 'perfect' pentameter to frame his longing for certainty and harmony. We know he never can be, and the knowledge is reinforced by the combination of metrical asymmetry and lexical unease. We see it with 'Thou art the best o'th' cut-throats'. The previous two exchanges with the murderer complete taut ten-liners. Here, the line has 12 feet, leaving Macbeth's grisly joke to hang out like a nearly severed limb. He now learns that Banquo's son is not dead. Accordingly, his hopes for 'perfection' swiftly decline from wistful metrical completeness to the flailing, claustrophobic, overlong list making that repeatedly marks his apprehension of inescapable un-freedom:

> Then comes my fit again: I had else been perfect;
> Whole as the marble, founded as the rock,
> As broad and general as the casing air:
> But now, I am cabin'd, cribb'd, confin'd, bound in
> To saucy doubts and fears. – But Banquo's safe?
>
> (3.4.20–4)

Typically, this 'cabin'd...' example itself suggests the point: the line's fourth successive participle ('bound in') ruins alliterative snap and metrical ease. What could have been emphatic assertion is transfigured into anguished meta-poetic paralysis. And again, the discourse chosen for tragic suffering is a verse barely worth the name: a verse by turns stretched and contracted by prose.

Of course, Macbeth's dark murmurings are often lit by sudden and extraordinarily memorable poetry. So, in the midst of the (metrically/lexically) ugly dissonance of his lies, Macbeth is confessing all kinds of searing truths in (metrically/lexically) arresting poetry: 'the wine of life is drawn', 'ruin's wasteful entrance', 'into the sere, the yellow leaf', and so on. But these treasures can only take their effect in a chest full of the most varied – and often stolen – discursive wares. So, the gravest sentiments are punctuated, almost cognitively structured, by 'silently' detonating jokes or bathetic puns: 'his gash'd stabs look'd like a *breach* in nature . . . their daggers/Unmannerly *breech'd* with gore' (2.3. 111–14). As Macbeth plummets deeper into barely communicable isolation, one manner of speaking increasingly merges into or is overtaken by the other. This is particularly noticeable when he speaks to 'himself', or to those who are under the illusion that they know all of his secrets (wife, murderers, overt enemies). On the one hand, his words have an aura of piercing gravity. On the other hand, they display an array of 'comic' manners. In turn, these comic manners are taken hostage and – as though from the 'back' of his mouth – forced to at once serve and ameliorate his terror. We get grim wit ('what purgative drug,/Would *scour* these English hence', 5.3.55–6); mirthless puns (*'Cow'd* my better part of man', 5.8.18); ribald hyperbole ('had I three ears. . .', 4.1.78); fake-joyous incantations ('The mind I sway by, and the heart I bear,/Shall never sag with doubt, nor shake with fear', 5.3.9–10); childish insults ('Where gott'st thou that goose look?', 5.3.12); fairy-tale magic charms ('But swords I smile at, weapons laugh to scorn,/Brandish'd by man that's of a woman born', 5.7.12–13). Shakespeare develops for his great usurper a multiply sourced stylistic 'heteroglossia'. It is at once folksy and forbidding, and from the start is refusing many of the traditional prerogatives of 'noble' metred verse. Like the final verse forms of Othello, Macbeth's most characteristic poetry is always a prosodic, generic, and lexical hybrid.

Verse is never only the speaker's doing. It is a communal rather than individual construct; a creature of custom and precedent more than momentary improvisation. Other momentums than the speaker's are always working through it. The verse will always more or less resemble a pattern heard before: it carries 'inside' it the terms upon which it might be assessed. But in the case of Macbeth, such resemblance to known patterns is increasingly less and less, as he complicates or interrupts expectations with all kinds of untoward innovations. We can interpret this prosodic licentiousness as another sign of his wilfulness, his overreaching, or his violence; or we can interpret it as his helplessness, as a sign of his failure to rest easy in the modes he would appropriate; or of course we can identify something of each.

There is an enormous advance here upon merely indicating 'character' through verbal idiosyncrasy: things like hyperbole, malapropism, or excessive conceitedness. Such things need not be a conscious choice of the speaker. But they are rhetorically declared, publicly audible, and heard via easily shareable codes of meaning or decorum. In cases like Macbeth's, there is no such code: no such judgemental immediacy is given to the reader or auditor. It is at once more lurking and more permeating. We might sense the verse-prose's discomfort in its own skin, but struggle to locate any lexical or metrical reasons for it. But such reasons are there all the same, and involve not *quite* observing the forms we expect, inherit, or desire – an iambic pentameter, a lucid trope, a suitably noble *imitatio*. The crucial development, then, is to give individuated shape to the very moulds in which meaning seeks form. This in turn means that the verse-prose form itself bears experiential and metaphysical significance. Form is not a mere vessel or vehicle of meaning. Instead, poetic form operates both in alliance with semantic content and *as* such allegorised content. Prosody is more than merely an echo to the sense. It literally makes sense: without it there can never be the same externalising of the mentalities active in any particular dramatic moment.

# 7

# WHY ALL OF THESE PUNS?

*This chapter explores Shakespeare's wordplay. The first section looks at puns in comedy, taking examples from various plays, including* The Taming of the Shrew, All's Well That Ends Well, Much Ado About Nothing, *and* Twelfth Night. *These comic puns are usually explicitly performed: that is, spoken so as to be noticed by the audience. This both focuses and limits their significance. The limitations of wordplay, however, are basically those of its generic context: if the genre is expansive, then so too is its puns. The pun becomes a fundamental tool for structuring genre and character, and for organising emotional response. A discussion of the brothel in* Pericles *shows how puns can lay the groundwork for a genre's political ideas (in this case romance). The next section looks at the functions of the clown, a figure who seems almost to embody the performed quibble. However, we see how clown functions in Shakespeare are not limited to his licensed fools, but are instead diffused throughout all sorts of figures and places. The following section explores puns that are not overtly displayed to the audience. Particularly in tragedy, they are often latent or subdued. The second half of the chapter thus explores examples of tragic puns. First is an analysis of Mercutio in* Romeo and Juliet. *This shows how puns can be a crucial means of expressing inwardness, and so a basic vehicle of characterisation. Then comes a discussion of how Hamlet's puns concentrate his particular tragic self-awareness. The final section on* Macbeth *brings together many of the techniques and possibilities discussed throughout the chapter. It shows how wordplay concentrates the energies of the dramatic moment, and contributes to tragedy's most powerful ethical responses.*

The pun is a rhetorical device. But it is importantly distinct from most other types of repetition or emphasis because it is usually understood to have little to do with the moving of emotion or persuasion. At times a pun might suggest nervousness or anxiety, but invariably it is understood as a frivolous sideshow or merely intellectual satisfaction, with little if anything to do with the main games of comic love tension, political conflict, or tragic pathos. Why then does Shakespeare keep on punning?

For it is almost impossible to talk meaningfully about Shakespeare's figurative language, or more broadly about the difficulties (and often the frustrations) of his language, without coming upon the problem of his punning. Indeed the two are almost the same thing: Shakespeare is almost never figurative without also punning. This need not at all mean that he is trying to be funny: merely that more than one arc of meaning is set in motion by the nominally single word unit.

There was nothing unique about Shakespeare's devotion to double meanings. So, to recover something of the classical Roman fondness for puns (found for instance in Virgil and Ovid) was a thoroughly humanist thing to do: such verbal sensitivity and fluidity was seen as a corrective to the rigidities of medieval scholasticism. Heraldic mottos often pun; so too – as new translations were revealing – do many moments in the Bible. And in popular literature punning never ceased being in currency. Chaucer is often arch or subtle with quibbles; the medieval morality plays are rife with puns; and it remained a popular device in songs, ballads, broadsides, prose pamphlets both fictive and controversial – and of course the public theatre. George Puttenham's mid-Elizabethan survey, *Art of English Poesie*, celebrates a vernacular teeming with semantically doubling or turning figures of speech. Perhaps less predictably, the pun is also constantly used in supposedly more erudite Elizabethan productions such as Spenser's *Faerie Queene*, Sidney's *Arcadia* (indeed even his classically inspired *Apology for Poetry*), and Donne's poetry. Even Milton, who disdained anything silly or showy, thoroughly saturates his verse with learned wordplay. This is not to say that puns were entirely respectable. There was an ancient tradition that recognised the popularity of puns but sought to limit their use. The Roman rhetorical tradition (influential in Shakespeare's period through the works of Horace, Cicero, and Quintilian) advertises a 'masculine' kind of linguistic restraint. These writers did not forbid wordplay, indeed used it often enough themselves: but any disciplined punning will be philologically erudite and thematically suggestive.

The main charge against puns is pointless showing off: just the sort of indulgent triviality that has long been identified in Shakespeare. So, his contemporary, Ben Jonson, deplored Shakespeare's too easy fluidity and ridiculed his weakness for fatuous paradox. John Dryden, writing much later in the seventeenth century, discerns an almost childish lack of reserve: 'his comic wit degenerating into clenches [i.e. punning], his serious swelling into bombast'. In Dryden's preface to his rewriting of *Troilus and Cressida* he speaks of Shakespeare's 'stile' as being 'so pester'd with Figurative expressions, that it is as affected as it is obscure'. Samuel Johnson's eighteenth-century judgement is the most memorable (and most often quoted):

> A quibble is to Shakespeare what luminous vapors are to the traveller: he follows it at all adventures; it is sure to lead him out of his way, and sure to engulf him in the mire ... he was content to purchase it by the sacrifice of reason, propriety, and truth. A quibble was to him the fatal Cleopatra for which he lost the world, and was content to lose it.

Nineteenth-century romantic critics such as Hazlitt often praise Shakespeare's electric 'combinations' of word and image, but in doing so quite transcend the specific referents of his wordplay. And indeed it remains the most usual response to Shakespeare's puns to sigh (in comedy) or avert the eyes (in tragedy). Rarely is a creative link perceived between the specifics of Shakespeare's punning, and his fabled comi-tragic vision.

However, if we want to come to terms with Shakespeare's language use, then we really need to reassemble some such creative link. This doesn't mean laboriously defining all of Shakespeare's punning exchanges. But we do need to see how much he enjoys puns, is magnetised by them, and how he never ceases to think 'through' them. In a sense this becomes all the more so as his work develops. This is partly to agree with Johnson when he claims that Shakespeare follows a quibble 'at all adventures': it is decisively to disagree with Johnson when he sees this fascination as wasteful and barren. The quibbles of Shakespeare can be tiresome, and can seem the reflex of a mind too fluid and uncritical. But there is no Shakespeare without them. The sweep and intimacy of the work is rooted in hyper-allergic linguistic sensitivity.

## PUNS IN COMEDY

Shakespeare's wordplay works in all sorts of ways, but roughly speaking we can divide it up into two types. First is *performed* wordplay: that is, spoken so as to be recognised and enjoyed as a verbal quibble. Second is subdued or latent wordplay: that is, not appealing directly to an audience (on-stage or off-stage), and therefore heard as though we are listening in to something private or concealed. Again broadly speaking, the first is associated with comedy, the second with tragedy. Here we will look at both types of pun in turn. First, however, a brief word about the pun in the history plays (discussed in greater detail in Chapters 4 and 10). Despite the histories' supposed seriousness, they use performed puns much more than subdued puns. This is partly because the histories are 'early' Shakespeare, in which the puns are always asking to be noticed. But it is also because the occasion of such puns always presupposes a present and *interested* audience. Importantly, this audience is both the crowd at a theatre and the English populace for whom the battles are (supposedly) fought. Accordingly, puns in the histories invariably serve – rather than subvert – the rhetorical purpose. They are used to spice up high-flown oratory (as in the speeches from *Henry V* and *Henry VI* discussed in Chapter 4), or to ingratiate the politician with a sceptical or eager crowd (as in the opening soliloquy of Gloucester in *Richard III*, discussed in Chapter 10). The puns may well reveal private appetites or private sarcasm. But they take effect in public, with very public consequences (again see the analysis of Gloucester's 'winter of our discontent' speech). Puns always work in context, and crucial here is the generic context.

The use of performed puns in comedy is likewise framed by the basic orientation of the genre. Such comedy is always packed with social codes and commentaries, and often carries some political edge or satiric ambition. So, it targets fusty authority, idiotic time-servers, fashion victims, and the like. But even so, it appeals to those who join in such intelligent indignation. The audience is presumed to share with the ironists a bedrock of good sense and non-pedantic values. It might mock or jolt conventional forms, but allegiance to these forms remains the boundary beyond which the wit will rarely reach. Accordingly, the mockery is often of the unwitty. For example, those who imitate the stratagems of wit – the unusual contrast, the unlikely conceit – but fail because they are not swift enough or because they lurch into absurdity (Malvolio in *Twelfth Night*, Costard, Armado, et al. in *Love's Labour's Lost*). Consequently, the punning wit familiar in Shakespeare's comedies rarely works in a self-revelatory way. It rarely attempts any radical reconstitution of social values or ethical possibility.

This is not to deny that Shakespeare frequently unsettles any complacency about the easy possession of decorum. Indeed he often makes the jokers themselves breach the rules they supposedly possess. For example, gleeful victimising goes too far, and our gaze turns uncomfortably upon the mockers. Hence the discomfort, the sense of ugly comic plumbing suddenly on show, in witnessing the ganging up that so humbles Shylock in *Merchant*, Malvolio in *Twelfth Night*, Helena in *Midsummer Night's Dream*, and Hero in *Much Ado*. Nonetheless, the first audience for comic wit is invariably (to risk circularity) the theatre audience. And this audience is assumed to be at one with whichever speaker is the most in control. A pun may have a coincident purpose in a power game or courtship. But its first and most necessary cause is to be heard and understood by us: to identify who's in and who's out; to accord with generic expectation; to trace the by-ways and about-turns of comic recognition. There are few secrets, and any 'surprises' are those of a familiar plot unfolding. In other words, this kind of wit requires a fully grounded sense of what is appropriate. It invariably knows its audience, knows how far to take things, knows what can be acceptably surprising as opposed to unacceptably shocking or disturbing. Doing so, it assures all who are with them that their assumptions are fundamentally sound.

Comic punning, then, is usually a fairly straightforward vehicle of whatever is at stake in the scene. Obviously enough, what is often at stake will be audience pleasure: for example, the humour of derision, as the puns are used to manipulate misunderstandings or incongruities and so identify a victim of laughter:

GRUMIO   First know my horse is tired, my master and mistress fallen out.
CURTIS   How?
GRUMIO   Out of their saddles into the dirt, and thereby hangs a tale.
CURTIS   Let's ha't, good Grumio.
GRUMIO   Lend thine ear.
CURTIS   Here.
GRUMIO   There. [*Strikes him.*]
CURTIS   This 'tis to feel a tale, not to hear a tale.
GRUMIO   And therefore 'tis called a sensible tale...

(*The Taming of the Shrew*, 4.1.48–58)

Words here are almost like physical agents, serving the response they work toward achieving. There is a corresponding limit as to how precisely the specific referents of particular puns bear upon speaker or situation:

CELIA   Here comes Monsieur Le Beau.
   *Enter* Le Beau.
ROSALIND   With his mouth full of news.
CELIA   Which he will put on us, as pigeons feed their young.
ROSALIND   Then we shall be news-crammed.
CELIA   All the better; we shall be the more marketable. *Bonjour* Monsieur
   Le Beau. What's the news?
LE BEAU   Fair Princess, you have lost much good sport.
CELIA   Sport? Of what colour?
LE BEAU   What colour madam? How shall I answer you?
ROSALIND   As wit and fortune will.
TOUCHSTONE   Or as the Destinies decrees.
CELIA   Well said! That was laid on with a trowel.
TOUCHSTONE   Nay, if I keep not my rank –
ROSALIND   Thou losest thy old smell.

(*As You Like It*, 1.2.88–102)

The jokes here invoke pigeons, smells, mouths, news, and so on, but none of these things really matter in themselves. The terms that allow the witticisms are essentially accidental: they are cues for the ascendant trio's improvisation. We see here how this kind of comic-ironic wit is usually remote from any imperilled or ambiguous inner life. It doesn't work to question or remould the speaker. Of course, it can ridicule a character's possession by various all too familiar tyrannies (career, acquisitiveness, sexual slavery, children). But when the puns do speak something more personal – for instance Celia's 'marketable' alludes to her defining status as marriageable – it offers a release from rather than reinforcement of social pressure. There can be oxygen in self-derision: in surviving it we gain strength and vigour. This kind of punning is about a meeting of minds (the speaker's and the audience's) much more than a splitting or clashing.

Of course, comic puns are not always so comfortably possessed. With *Much Ado*'s Beatrice and Benedick, for instance, the reliance upon wit is a way of avoiding candour. So, Beatrice turns past hurts into armour, and uses quibbles as a weapon (*Don Pedro*. 'You have put him [Benedick] down, lady, you have put him down.' *Beatrice*. 'So I would not he should do me, my lord, lest I should prove the mother of fools', *Much Ado*, 2.1.265–8). The wit here does seem to bear some deeper inward reference: the 'fool' that Beatrice fears spawning might be recapitulate her past folly (as the disappointed love dupe of Benedick), as much as joke about Benedick's folly ('the Prince's jester, a very dull fool', 2.1.129). But even in the case of *Much Ado*, where there is this undercurrent of unspoken feeling, it is attitude and circumstance rather than witty reference per se that carries any latent emotion. The quality of the punning repartee will work to summarise a character's function and reputation (of course such things might shift during the play, and along with it the style of wit, as happens with the principals in *Much Ado*). But the question is mainly whether the puns work in harmony with courtly or courting purposes. For in comedy the punning energy – rather like rhyme – does not entirely belong to the punner. The puns get their force and permission (or lack of) from their relation to social and aesthetic values that precede this particular example.

This is not to say that comic puns are all about flattery or anaesthetics. Punning is always partly concerned with the possession of interpretive power: who says what is right and true, on what basis, according to whose criteria? This means that both the occasion and the specific referents of wordplay can epitomise ongoing power games. *The Taming of the Shrew* is built around just such games. Here, for example, the battle of wits works as both instrument and metaphor of the play's pervasive erotic and political wrestle:

PETRUCHIO   Myself am mov'd to woo thee for my wife.
KATHERINA   Mov'd, in good time! Let him that mov'd you hither
  Remove you hence. I knew you at the first
  You were a movable.
PETRUCHIO                              Why, what's a movable?
KATHERINA   A joint-stool.
PETRUCHIO                    Thou hast hit it. Come, sit on me.
KATHERINA   Asses are made to bear, and so are you.
PETRUCHIO   Women are made to bear, and so are you.
KATHERINA   No such jade as you, if me you mean.
PETRUCHIO   Alas, good Kate, I will not burden thee!

                          (*The Taming of the Shrew*, 2.1.195–203)

Once again the content of the jokes is generally less important than the energies they enact. But – as with Celia's 'marketable' – we might notice a more pregnant social and psychological sense inside the exuberance. So, Shakespeare strings together a sequence of quibbles that are relatively incidental. However, they are leading up to one particular pun that will carry a predictive, more powerfully metaphorical connotation. Here, that word is 'bear': the 'burden' of the whole story being whether or on what terms Katherina must do so.

It is important, therefore, not to be too absolute. There is no sure-fire rule that puns in comedy work only on the surface, or that comic wit is situational rather than subjective. A fairly mature comedy like *Twelfth Night* is full of both types of wit. The double meanings of Viola work simultaneously outward and inward, as evidenced by the fact that her addressee rarely realises that any joke is being spoken at all:

OLIVIA   Are you a comedian?
VIOLA   No, my profound heart: and yet, by the very fangs of malice
   I swear, I am not that I play.

(1.5.177–9)

We are a long way here from any glib identification of comic puns with an appeal for laughter. But still – even though the secrecy of such wit is a chief vehicle of *Twelfth Night*'s power to be so moving as well as so funny – the ambiguities of Viola require an audience. If *we* don't recognise them for what they are then the play cannot really work. And in this appeal to the audience there is also a recognition that the cause and terms of the joke will be escaped. We take responsibility for the violence or confusion behind the joke; the comic genre allows release.

   It is this soliciting of an audience that defines the possibilities of comic puns. The 'home' of wit is not the speaker at all. It is the hearer. As Rosaline in *Love's Labour's Lost* has it: 'A jest's prosperity lies in the ear/Of him that hears it, never in the tongue/Of him that makes it' (5.2.852–4). For if we permit the jest, then we have somehow got there first. This implies a fundamental limitation to the affective and ethical power of such wit. Above all, these limits of comic wit are the limits of more or less 'straight' comedy. After all, comedy is supposed to give pleasure, and a crucial part of this pleasure is self-forgetfulness. But by the same token this need not imply any intrinsic limit to the experiential, emotional, or ethical reach of wordplay. It is simply a question of the *context* of any wordplay. The second half of Shakespeare's career – one in which he never again attempts a 'straight' comedy – can also be seen as a sustained experiment in the dramatic potential of the humble pun.

## THE BROTHEL IN *PERICLES*

Traditionally, a pun is exhausted in the act of speaking and hearing it. It might contribute to the scene's mood or to the delineation of character; it might even get a laugh. But the pun is, almost by definition, momentary. However, Shakespeare's puns often do not work so briefly. For instance, his quibbles contribute to the play's larger generic design, and consequently – as is always the case with questions of genre – to its political orientation.

The case of the brothel in *Pericles* is a good example. The puns spoken by the brothel workers have their own almost unique manner. So, the common delight of wit is simply irrelevant. There is no pleasure in the speaking or surprise in any recognition. Instead, degradation and cynicism are simply achieved and on display. Like some over-ripe fig, the pun is already and always split, already and always seedily open to view. Rather like the brothel itself, the depths have risen to the surface, and repressed meaning has taken over as daily reality. This means a strange dispossessing of the potency of doubling language. The degrading pun is not funny and not surprising, because it is so overwhelmingly in line with trading assumptions:

BAWD   Well, well; as for him, he brought his disease hither: here he does but *repair* it.

(4.2.108–9)

The Bawd is speaking here of the knight's 'disease'. The joke is that the supposedly primary meaning of 'repair' (to get better) is irrelevant. It doesn't even get a look in. The only 'repair' here imaginable is a *return* to the infected source. Or consider this from the Pandar: 'Therefore let's have fresh ones, whate'er we pay for them. If there be not a *conscience* to be *us'd* in every trade, we shall never *prosper*' (4.2.10–12). The word 'conscience' will normally suggest something like moral sensibility. But here the Pandar doesn't admit the meaning, doesn't even see it (even if we do). His 'conscience' is defined entirely by its verb: it is to be 'us'd', a thing of merciless material increase and sexual exploitation ('us'd' includes usury, the sin of deriving a profit from 'nothing', here the vaporised whores). Accordingly, 'conscience' excludes its normal referent and comes to mean simply shrewdly applied intelligence.

Or consider this: 'O, our *credit* comes not in like the *commodity*, nor the commodity wages not with the danger. . . Besides, the *sore terms* we *stand upon* with the gods will be *strong with us* for giving o'er' (4.2.28–33). The sense here is of genuine worry, close to self-disgust, and of recoil from his own 'meaner air'. But he has no language but that of his trade in which to speak. So, the idea of 'terms' evokes a contract with God, with the approach to salvation broadly Roman Catholic. But the 'sore'-ness here is beyond transubstantiation: it speaks of penis and vagina. It is the whores and their 'continual action' (4.2.8), or it is the 'roasted' clients, turned on a rotisserie of disease. '[W]e stand upon' continues the mirthless phallic sense: man here is nothing but a fallen maypole.

However, we might also see how the particular employment of the puns is helping to bed down the play's larger generic patterns. So, the language use simply denies the supposed priorities of pastoral romance. It evokes thoroughgoing entrapment, or stale beings soaked like logs in a poisonous pond. But although very close to bitterness and cynicism, and lacking any jester's panache, the language is still working toward its enabling 'romance' context. So, it is part of the brothel scenes' ambivalence that we can never quite dismiss the workers as contemptible; they are not irrelevant to the terms through which the heroine Marina might bring to the play-world more general 'repair'. The examples of both Boult and the whores should provoke us to ask difficult questions. We should be aware of both material compulsion (do they have a choice?) and possible transformation (is anything really irredeemable?). In turn, some of the sentiments of the brothel workers do *try* to look beyond present entrapment. Their puns often foreshadow surrounding possibilities, or throw out hypothetical lifelines that luckier others – like the governor Lysimachus – might soon grab on to.

A good example is the Bawd's comment about her 'Creatures': 'they can do no more then they can do' (4.2.7–8). She appears to speak a very simple, proverbial tautology, invoking a shared form of compassion and understanding: of course, you can only do your best. But we need to recall who is here speaking. Compassion is remote from the Bawd's function. She keeps her eye on the main game, and no one is more than a counter in her capitalist arithmetic. Accordingly, what she means is very bald indeed. There is nothing generalised or sentimental about 'do': it means to have sex. The girls can have sex no more than they can have sex: the 'no more' signifies not so much the weight of their duties than the clicking accumulation of customers, and therefore money. The thing at issue is not the energy or exhaustion of an individual, but numbers of paying patrons.

However, the distinctive thing is that the Bawd is oblivious to any suggestion of wit. She speaks a pun, but *she* is not punning. She and her confederates are in fact closer to speaking malapropisms than to wittiness. Hers is a peculiarly serious, deadly focused kind of linguistic blindness – but a blindness to which we can bring light. That is, we see more in 'do' than she needs to. Like the entire brothel, the pun here evokes ruin as both a thing in shreds and pieces *and* as the full things lost from view. The images then work rather like crushed bicycle wheels, a mangle that recalls a perfect circle. The 'better' meaning is invisible to the Bawd, but this makes it easier to be possessed or even cherished by us. The Bawd's callousness can serve 'romance' by evoking a focus of mourning and a hope for differently sourced 'repair'.

The example of puns in *Pericles'* brothel scenes shows that intricate verbal affects do not work in conceited isolation from all of the things that a worthwhile play will be doing. Puns operate in tandem with all sorts of other communicative structures. Some of these are 'macro', some 'micro', but all work toward giving the story emotional, ethical, and political punch. It is easy to miss the extent to which precise linguistic details are necessary to the creation of these broader satisfactions: the 'big' things simply do not exist without the 'little'.

## CLOWNS

Before we look at puns in tragedies, it might be useful to trace a figure whose own mutations through the plays suggest the movement of Shakespeare's quibbling from primarily public display to private concealment. This is the figure of the licensed Fool or Clown.

Of course the Clown is not only about quibbles: he offers extravagant physical comedy, bawdy innuendo, and fantastical simulations; he mediates the action to an audience, speaking indulgently of virtue and ridiculing pomposity or hypocrisy; he presents his own scrapes as transparent parodies of the main action. But still the puns of a jester do just about encapsulate the basic remit and limits both of the role and more generally of a performed (as distinct from a learned) wordplay. So, their quibbles have two main purposes: to get a laugh; and to use the cover of laughter to express otherwise forbidden criticism or mockery. Of course many of their jokes are no more than for the moment, popping like corn for an audience to savour:

PANTHINO   Come; come away, man, I was sent to call thee.
LAUNCE   Sir, call me what thou dar'st.

(*The Two Gentleman of Verona*, 2.3.54–5)

But even here the Clown's joke bears upon this play's larger patterns of identity confusion and casual male violence. However irrelevant a Clown's jokes seem to be, they invariably allude to the follies displayed – or perhaps hidden – in the central action. It is common for a single joke to be incidental, but rare for an entire dialogue not to be working toward some kind of parody or critique. This exchange between Parolles and the Clown (Lavatch) in *All's Well That Ends Well* is typical:

PAROLLES   Away! Th'art a knave.
CLOWN   You should have said, sir, 'Before a knave th'art a knave'; that's 'Before me, th'art a knave'. This had been truth, sir.
PAROLLES   Go to, thou art a witty fool; I have found thee.
CLOWN   Did you find me in your self, sir, or were you taught to find me? .... The search, sir, was profitable; and much fool may you find in you, even to the world's pleasure and the increase of laughter.

(2.4.28–36)

The jokes play upon the unrecognised identity between the official fool (Clown) and the actual fool (Parolles). The purpose of Shakespeare's quibbling Clowns is always some variation upon Lavatch's question here: 'Did you find me in your self, sir, or were you taught to find me?' There is here no real difference between the individual pun and the role itself; both are distorted mirrors in which the 'courtly' might do well to recognise themselves.

Here, however, we should see how even the declared, comic quibble may do more than offer marginal commentary or fleeting amusement. It might substantially contribute to the very identity of those at the centre. Shakespeare is here developing a long popular tradition. In some morality plays, for example, buffoonery takes centre stage, becoming a crucial limb of a compositely constructed 'Everyman'. The clowning may not be performed by the central figure, but it is an allegorised part or possibility of that individual. This relationship was crucial to the development of character in the Elizabeth theatre. So, in Marlowe's *Dr Faustus*, Faustus's temptations are counter-pointed by low-life puns and clowning. Importantly, however, Faustus himself engages in a fair amount of slapstick buffoonery. The Fool – and the pun – is coming closer to a frank inhabiting of the plays' central consciousness.

Shakespeare accelerates this process of inclusiveness. So, neither the function nor the discourse of his licensed jesters is securely stratified. Feste in *Twelfth Night* has been unexplainably away from Olivia's court, has to battle jealously for preferment, and is in some sense on trial throughout as potentially inadequate or redundant. So, his first scene is set up so that we should judge his wit. Whether we allow it to just about pass muster, as Olivia does, or reject it as tired and dull, as Malvolio does, there is no way that the Clown can retain here the slightest situational transcendence. His wit is at best one voice in a medley. Similarly, Touchstone in *As You Like It* is far from the court. He shadows the 'courtly copulatives' rather than serves them, and turns licensed folly into a subject for others' contemplation and even envy. The Fool in *Lear* has likewise kept away from his master, as though generating or nursing some inward hurt; his 'all-licens'd' insolence then stands for a general pattern of knightly (rather than clownish) misrule. He gets exiled with the king into the storm and hovel and then unaccountably vanishes – or unaccountably unless we assume that his role gets taken up into that of Poor Tom, the mad Lear, and the 'poor fool' Cordelia. All of these Clowns to some extent do what Fools should do. But more pertinent is a sense of either straining at the leash, or hanging for dear life onto it.

Indeed from the beginning of Shakespeare's career we find Clown functions taken up by others than the licensed jester. The most obvious are generic 'Clowns' such as the policemen Dogberry and Verges in *Much Ado*, the 'simple constable' Elbow and pimp Pompey in *Measure for Measure*, the Porter in *Macbeth*, the Shepherd in *The Winter's Tale*. None of these are court jesters, but they are all recognisably Clowns. The main difference from the licensed Fool is that none of them *intend* to mock, parody, or criticise the powerful. Such witty critique is no longer their profession; their puns are instead often accidental, or malapropising (where they get the word wrong). But more than anything this suggests a diffusion of the potential of punning throughout the playtext: rather than the possession of a specific typecast role (the jester) it is part of a play's central nervous system. Similarly, such satiric punning is spread throughout different social roles and public places. Shakespeare's performed puns are from the start leaking beyond courtly permission.

In the first half of his career (before *Hamlet*) the characters that most decisively 'live' the function of Fool are not the licensed motley wearers at all: they are the upper-class figures of Mercutio in *Romeo and Juliet* and Falstaff in *Henry IV*. On a lesser scale we see Clown functions adopted by a gallery of gardeners, minstrels, drinkers, vagrants, fishermen, and rebels; sundry variations upon the floating witness or footloose courtier; and, perhaps above all, by the heroines, young aristocratic women in their invariably semi-disguised travels. Increasingly, punning language is simply indistinguishable from what we now see as definitively 'Shakespearean'. So, if we wanted to list some of Shakespeare's most overtly riddling speakers we might think of Cressida, Viola, or Lear. If we seek for his greatest improvisers, we find Richard III, Helena in *All's Well*, Edgar. If we look for characters defined by play-acting or ventriloquism, we might think (again) of Edgar, Cleopatra, the Duke in *Measure*, and most of the romantic heroines. If we search out Shakespeare's most compulsive punners, we might well settle upon perhaps his very darkest couple, the Macbeths. And all of these categories would have to be topped by the most 'Shakespearean' discoursers of all: Mercutio, Falstaff, Hamlet, and Iago.

## PUNS IN TRAGEDY: MERCUTIO

If there is one particular character that embodies the shift from a frivolous to a tragic wit then it is Mercutio in *Romeo and Juliet*. His murder famously marks the point where the play swerves from apparently comic redeemability to tragic inescapability. But we might also identify it as a moment where Shakespeare's art itself makes a decisive transition: that is, from jokes that can be escaped from (comic) to jokes that in some basic sense come true (tragic). We see this simply enough in jests such as Mercutio's 'Come between us, good Benvolio, my wits faints' (2.4.67–8) or Romeo's 'He jests at scars that never felt a wound' (2.2.1), both of which anticipate Mercutio's fatally accidental stabbing. More profoundly, the whole of Mercutio's part can be seen as an experiment in pushing puns beyond their normal possibilities.

From the start of the play punning wit lacks its normal unaccountability. Instead it is smugly, almost indolently close to the enacting of violence. The play's tetchy opening scene establishes that quibbling manners are somehow compulsory, a kind of low-level common fever:

SAMPSON    [W]hen I have fought with the men I will be civil with the maids, I will cut off their heads.

GREGORY    The heads of the maids?

SAMPSON    Ay, the heads of the maids, or their maidenheads; take in what sense thou wilt.

GREGORY    They must take it in sense that feel it.

(1.1.21–7)

The ponderous way that the jokes are explained suggests that this 'witty' compulsion is so much masculine ennui, sub-militaristic prattle, a kind of legionnaire's disease. But if even these slowly unfolding puns promise violence, then what of Mercutio's? For where the underlings' wit is all painting-by-numbers, Mercutio's is like a mind on fire:

ROMEO    The game was ne'er so fair, and I am done.

MERCUTIO    Tut, dun's the mouse, the constable's own word.

If thou art dun, we'll draw thee from the mire

> Of – save your reverence – love, wherein thou stickest
> Up to the ears. Come, we burn daylight, ho.
>
> (1.4.39–43)

There could hardly be a swifter, more mercurial speaker than
Mercutio. The act of speaking is one of compulsive play: he takes
what is abstract and makes it physical; what is innocent and makes
it obscene; what is single and divides or multiplies it. And he does
it all as a performance for his listeners:

MERCUTIO  Signor Romeo, bonjour. There's a French salutation to your
French slop. You gave us the counterfeit fairly last night.
ROMEO  Good morrow to you both. What counterfeit did I give you?
MERCUTIO  The slip sir, the slip. Can you not conceive?

(2.4.44–9)

Because his puns are so clearly performed, we might identify
Mercutio with Shakespeare's familiar 'witty' comedy. In turn, we
might assume his audiences' basic comfort with this wit. But
although such comforts are appealed to, they are both violated
and inadequate. For Mercutio's wit is often *not* directed at any
audience; or it is directed to himself, as though his own
compulsive pleasure ('A gentleman, Nurse, that loves to hear
himself talk, and will speak more in a minute than he will stand to
in a month', 2.4.146–8). Time and again it flies beyond the needs
of the moment and the comprehension of his hearers. On-stage
and off-stage, his audiences are always leaving him, or wishing
that they could do so. Consider Romeo's dismissal, 'He jests at
scars that never felt a wound' (2.2.1), or his battle to close down
Mercutio's Queen Mab fantasy, 'Peace, peace, Mercutio, peace./
Thou talk'st of nothing' (1.4.95–6). Later there is Benvolio's
bewildered response to a comic tour de force, 'The what?' (2.4.28),
and his exasperated interruption, 'Stop there, stop there' (2.4.94).
Mercutio sets out to mock or shame others, or to gather allies in
such shaming. But again and again his allies are only ambiguously
or nervously with him. They resist his seductions even as they trail
in his wake. Repeatedly Mercutio's wit cannot carry the moment.
What this basically means is that it cannot quite fit into any genre
on offer. It rubs uncomfortably against the priorities of a fatal love

story. But then it bounces beyond the permission of conventional ironic wit. From whichever perspective Mercutio is heard – tragedy or comedy – he exceeds agreed measure, decorum, or appropriateness.

His wit can be discomforting for it, but so too can his role. We wonder why he talks so much; we wish he might rein it in, for all of our sakes. The effect can be one of a ricocheting sort of embarrassment. The shaming is turned back upon Mercutio: as pity that such gifts should be so squandered, or that neediness should be so deflected by clowning.

Shakespeare is doing something new here with Mercutio. We are getting both an entrance *and* a resistance to tragic inwardness. The key here is exactly what cannot be easily accommodated: the sheer surplus of his language. Through this surplus Mercutio constructs parallel or alternative worlds. He does this most famously in his Queen Mab tour de force, but all of his fantasies and improvisations do something similar. He seems to do so for barely coherent reasons. But this is the point: we have to search the extravagant playfulness to discover them. For Mercutio's reasons are there to see: only not in the way that bantering wit usually possesses, where we find the purpose in the occasion rather than in the precise referents. With Mercutio, we have to locate his rationale precisely in and as his semiotic material. His consciousness *is* his jokes. Let's take just one example from many:

MERCUTIO  Sure wit, follow me this jest now, till thou hast worn out thy pump, that when the single sole of it is worn, the jest may remain after the wearing solely singular.

(2.4.61–4)

Mercutio is here responding to Romeo's joke about his well-flowered 'pump' (meaning both slipper and penis). His response takes its place in a friendly combat of wits. Even so, it is a challenge. It is a test of masculinity: as in the opening scene, the context suggests heat, boredom, and an itchiness to fight; once again, a pseudo-knightly violence finds frustrated expression in puns. Whether or not Romeo wants to play (having met Juliet, he now has other things on his mind), Mercutio is keen to prove himself. Consequently, the 'sure wit' he addresses might equally be Romeo himself, or some presiding deity of 'wit' whom Mercutio imagines observing the competition. The further context is that Romeo has just returned from lovemaking: Mercutio thinks with the now rejected Rosaline; we know with Juliet. Mercutio obscurely resents Romeo's preoccupation, and wants to draw him back into the gang.

With this context in mind, we can interpret Mercutio's basic joke. So, Mercutio alludes to Romeo's chasing (on his pumps/slippers) after a random woman; he urges him to have sex until he can do no more ('worn out thy pump'); but then he advocates something even better and more authentic than sex, which is the amusing stories that can be told about it ('the jest may remain after the wearing'). In other words, Mercutio speaks like a typical male friend, jealous of his power, anxious to neuter and exclude women. He will do so through peer-group mockery and laughter: Romeo can enjoy his new idolatry, but the true god is male bonding and the jests that sustain it. But of course Mercutio is not talking primarily about Romeo, or for his gang. He is talking of and for himself. There is furthermore a note of wistful pleading (a recurring tone, often understood as latently homoerotic). The thing at issue is less Romeo's singularity – the boy who leaves the group – than Mercutio's abiding solitariness. Mercutio so resents Romeo's independence because of how it bears upon his own: a reminder, a mockery, and, worst of all, a transcendence of Mercutio's 'sole-singular' world. What then is the home truth that succeeds Romeo's sexual diversion? What 'remains' as Mercutio's 'singular' recommendation? It is Mercutio's own lonely sexuality: one emptied like a 'pump' into friend-tiring jokes, and left abandoned at the close of play to whatever auto-satisfactions memory can muster ('the jest may remain after the wearing solely singular').

This layered inward reference can suggest that arguments for a *primarily* sexual meaning might need modifying. After all, we should not assume that such ribbing jokes between men must always be fundamentally 'for' the obscene pay-off. Instead, we might see Mercutio's ribaldry as a camouflage for his speech's more primary intensities. We may notice, for instance, that the thing that Mercutio again and again harps upon is 'the jest'. It is as though this, above all, is the primary thing. Everything he says both continues *and* analyses the joke: the jest for him really has a defining significance. If sex is a jest, then a jest is sex: both can be everything and nothing. So, the 'pump' is a slipper, appropriate for dancing, courtly games, seduction; this suggests both a condom and a cock. In turn, 'pump' is a verb as much as a noun. It is both full and self-emptying; both conical force and effluent swill. In this it fits a sexualised penis, moving from inflation to deflation. But it equally fits Mercutio's wit – tragically ditto.

For Mercutio, a jest would be both proof *and* proxy of his masculinity. But then the joke is that one must take from the other: if his manhood is a joke then it can hardly count. This suggests how we can take Mercutio's puns almost alarmingly literally. His 'follow me this jest' speech literally identifies his own possibilities with the passage of his jests. So, he recommends a self-mutation into a 'solely singular' joke. It might be understood as a call to arms, a challenge directed precisely to his conceited imagination. It is then almost a kind of secret soliloquy. Can I go still further? Can I take wittiness so far that nothing will be left standing except this murderous joke? Mercutio wants to strain meaning so fine that no one else can get it. But he doesn't so much survive his joke as he becomes it. Mercutio's thought is therefore strangely self-dissolving: certainly it anticipates the way he dies through (and as) a 'grave' sort of joke gone wrong. Hence the further pun on 'pump', which in Mercutio's projection is worn down to a 'sole': that is, to a single layer of material that he then equates with a human soul. To be 'worn' also means to be worn out: Mercutio is then imagining a life run dry, or a frayed 'soul' that has nothing left to it but the earth into which it is dissolving.

The point to notice is how thoroughly identified Mercutio is with his wit. Without it he is nothing: but it is leading him all the time exactly into 'nothing' (1.4.96). This proposes a basic paradox about the part. The fact that Mercutio is so completely wrapped up in his jokes means that he is 'essentially' impenetrable. He is a semiotic force field 'as thin of substance as the air' (1.4.99)

– or as a single sole of a slipper. So, his death might mark the play's shift into tragedy: but his character lacks the substance for this death to be 'tragic'. For as a sympathetic character Mercutio suffers from exactly the same limitations as the pun (his *literally* constitutive verbal material). Because they lack rhetorical immediacy, neither can move an audience to emotion or action. Instead, we witness the fireworks in a kind of stunned and recoiling awe. But this dramatic withholding – and Shakespeare is very clearly holding things back, very clearly blocking Mercutio's channels to the audience – at the same time nurtures something secretive and pregnant. For if in one sense Shakespeare is holding things back with Mercutio, in another he has all his guns blazing. The sheer verbal energy must contain something; it must screen something. As the nineteenth-century philosopher Nietzsche said of Shakespeare: how much suffering, to be so much the buffoon!

This is to suggest that Mercutio is for Shakespeare a formal experiment in characterisation. Everything about him is described, enacted, and essentially limited by jests. So, in his very first scene, about to go the masked ball, Mercutio puts on a 'visage':

> Give me a case to put my visage in:
> A visor for a visor. What care I
> What curious eye doth quote deformities?
> Here are the beetle brows shall blush for me.
>
> (1.4.29–32)

Can we find 'Mercutio' in this, the real thing beneath all of the seeming? In a sense no: because we will only ever come upon one more strategy of self-dissociation. All he describes is both he and his mask. Even the 'blush' is performed by a false agent. He is always both inside and outside himself; always watching himself and aware of others watching him; always performing and always performed. The manic, almost autistic rhymes tell their own narrative: *visor – visor – I – eye – deformities – blush for me*. They are all his and all him; equally, they are all displacements or deflections of any self-identity. But this very elusiveness can then suggest a certain psychology. We can identify a self-narrative precisely in the puns. So, Mercutio here is deep brewed in the shame of inelegance and, consequently, of concealment. The mask is a 'visor' for his ugliness: it protects Mercutio from seeing others see him. At the same time, it *is* his ugliness. The mask repeats what lies beneath. And exactly the same goes for his jokes and puns.

Some such self-consciousness, at once buried and displayed, generates many of his jokes. For example, 'this drivelling love is like a great natural [an imbecile] that runs lolling up and down to hide his bauble in a hole' (2.4.91–2). Moments earlier he conflated his wit and his sex in the image of a 'pump'. Here he compounds phallus (bauble) and chatter (babble) in a single image of dignity subverting protuberance: the idiot's toy, all the more grotesquely self-identifying because the fun of its possession is all directed to its hiding. Tellingly, however, the fool's hidey-'hole' leads to the plumbing of Mercutio's depths. It is both the channel to it *and* the flushing of it: like the 'pump' of his wit, it is a source at once of self-gathering and self-drainage. The 'drivelling love' works similarly. So, the 'drivelling' of the natural comes from his protruding (phallic) tongue and his uncontrollable saliva; the 'drivelling' of Mercutio comes from *his* protruding tongue (likewise an agent of frustrated conquest or invasion) and its uncontrollable aspirations. His entire, compulsive role seems accountable once we identify the insistent theme of his jokes: a mind perverted with desire and a body monstrously undesirable. 'Prick love for pricking, and you beat love down' (1.4.28) is Mercutio's first advice for Romeo, a bit of wisdom drawn from the master's own experience. We hear the bitter instruction to revenge love for being cruel, to beat violence with violence, and to do so on one's own. Typically, 'you beat love down' seems like an advertisement for masturbation (cf 'worn out thy pump ... wearing solely singular').

The recurring feature of Mercutio's jokes is this sheer concentration of reference. And the more precisely it is defined, the more it seems to express a mono-maniacal, tunnel-like psychology. An example is Mercutio's grim joke upon Romeo's entrance in the 'pump' scene: 'Here comes Romeo, here comes Romeo!' shouts Benvolio: 'Without his roe, like a dried herring', replies Mercutio (2.4.37–8). The 'dried herring' refers to Romeo's spent sexuality ('roe' is sperm): he has lusted himself dry, thinks Mercutio, and turned thoroughly 'fishified' (2.4.39). But there is more to Mercutio's joke than fishy-phallic puns. So, 'Without his roe' asks us to subtract 'Roe' from 'Romeo'. We are left with 'me-o'. Mercutio is commenting tartly upon Romeo's lovelorn solipsism, as he walks around all by himself, 'groaning' for love. For Mercutio, to be in love is to be alone: it is to be hung out to dry like a salted 'herring'. But then merely to be a 'me' is itself a condition of emptied or gutted lamentation ('o'). The more we allow it, the more the pun seems fierce and bitter; and the more we consider its simple concentration of meanings, the more it seems to be a self-echo. That is, the 'me-o' Mercutio recognises is no less than himself: *Me*[rcuti]*o*. Again, Mercutio is hiding his bauble/babble in his own hole ('o').

With Mercutio, this hole leads, literally, to nothing. Shakespeare is not here interested in making this hole a channel into experiential or dramatic depths. It is no accident that Mercutio's speeches almost always lack the situational clarity or dramatic immediacy that comes from being cued by unfolding conflict. In a sense, he is the very epitome of Shakespearean surplus. Each referent is 'essentially' arbitrary and circumstantially unnecessary. But it is because of this peculiar redundancy that it speaks so suggestively of self-concealment and self-revelation. If his teem of wit wasn't so optional, it could not speak so powerfully of compulsion. Mercutio emerges as identical with his jokes' meanings, no more, but no less. He personifies his 'jests' as though they are beings separate from his observing consciousness. But they are this consciousness, and their dizziness is his own. At the same time this sense of a teeming vacuum is immensely suggestive for future formal innovations. Shakespeare is experimenting here with a new kind of verbal wit, one characterised by an intense pressure of repression, as it were drilling down toward reservoirs of inwardness. In later plays this sort of verbal wit – no less 'private', but tied crucially in with political and emotional movement – becomes almost the signature of Shakespeare's tragic protagonists.

## PUNS IN TRAGEDY

Shakespeare's tragedies are full of puns that neither seek nor get laughter. In his tragedies he rarely dwells on a pun in the way he so often does in the comedies; nor does he unfold his puns overtly. It often seems as though the tragic pun is not addressed directly to the audience at all. We are not *asked* to listen, and still less forced to. But if this suggests secrecy, then it is a peculiar fact that these puns can often seem semi-secret to the character as well. They can seem unaware of the punning, or unwilling to face its implications front-on. Puns can then evoke a discourse of privacy, self-delusion, or unconsciousness; or they can be vehicles for a critique of character, as the puns present perspectives, judgements or consequences unacknowledged by the speaker. In one sense the pun becomes increasingly internalised. In another sense, however, it becomes externalised, as microcosms containing or suggesting much larger patterns of theme, story, or characterisation. Consider the basic architecture of a pun: it is multiple, folded, or at cross-purposes; things lurk or move at angles; it beckons toward different pasts and possibilities; it evokes alternatives within predetermination, a 'virtuality' to rival actuality, perhaps a consciousness of waste. All of this makes the pun peculiarly able to concentrate, intensify, and unfold a moment's situational and psychic layers. Shakespeare's punning becomes almost the *least* dispensable of his techniques.

Still, there are often difficulties in deciding how seriously to take Shakespeare's wordplay, particularly when it is not the clearly directed wordplay of barbed wit or quibbling clown. How literally should it be understood? The answer is that we should habitually take Shakespeare's puns very literally. If we unfold each aspect of the pun then the impact and significance of the moment is almost always enhanced. To argue this is to maintain a simple but powerful premise: rather like a gifted ball-player, Shakespeare 'sees' things early, finds space where others cannot. This gives him time to play, and therefore his delivery is at once more complete and more substantial. It means that the most common arguments against wordplay – that it is trivial and self-indulgent – are pre-empted. For Shakespeare's most characteristic wordplay is not about dazzling display. It is simply about the spoken moment bearing multiple lines of possible unfurling.

This implies a series of simple but profound things: that we can say one thing while thinking something else; that the mind can hold more than one option at a time; that the addressor and addressee may agree on a meaning that a third party – the overhearing reader or audience – may not agree on; that a word, however carefully chosen by its speaker, may be simultaneously possessed or redirected by alternative forces of energy. We should therefore recognise a broad and deep potential in punning: it may bear the freight at once of the speaker's sense of a situation and something like the 'objective' situation; it may communicate both the speaker and the circumstances that (acknowledged or not) carry the speaker along; it may plot how intention gets complicated by happenstance, accident, or history.

There can still be a difficulty, however, in knowing quite how to prioritise the different sign systems going on at any single moment. This is particularly the case with the latent or subdued puns that pepper Shakespeare's mature work. For the basic point of a subdued pun — one that doesn't draw obvious attention to itself – is that it is fundamentally anti-rhetorical. It does not appeal to the audience or ask for a particular response; it doesn't guide us into any specific mental or emotional movement. But at the same time the subdued pun is usually working within a speech that is enacting just such a rhetorical function. The 'speech-block' will usually convey a definable emotion or attitude: the pun, however, may be working at odds with any such definition. A potentially interesting relationship develops between overt rhetoric and covert pun. The effect depends upon the distribution of irony: that is, who exactly *knows* about the subdued pun? A speech that secretes or 'hides' its own wordplay becomes at some level self-oblivious, unaware of certain parts within it; alternatively, the speaker might be cherishing the pun specifically because the addressee doesn't get it. Clearly, there can be no hard and fast rule about how we interpret such elusive material. The pun may modify or subvert the rhetoric. It may allude back to circumstances that the rhetorical attitude is pretending to forget or simplify. It may be precisely in the wordplay that Shakespeare is plotting a particular play's working architecture, the connecting points 'beneath' the various characters and crises. Puns are thus a prime example of our need to negotiate between relative obscurity and dramatic immediacy. As always, each will inform and alter the other.

Of course, there is one other interpretive option: if a pun seems unnecessary or accidental, then ignore it. This may be a tempting response in cases where the pun seems beyond the intention of the speaker, or if its sense seems destructive to the clear lines of the speech-block, or to a character as we like to understand them. Such a response is no doubt tempting – but also probably self-deluding. For the evidence is overwhelming that Shakespeare was not in any final way to be surprised by the words he chose. When a surprise came along he took it as a cue for improvisation. There are hundreds of examples where he picks up the suggestion of an apparently irrelevant metaphor from a line or two earlier and, via further tributary punning, turns it into the main vehicle of the sense. It seems highly unlikely that we could show Shakespeare a pun that he hadn't seen for himself. If the sonnets are any guide to his most private ways of thinking and composing, then we might think rather the opposite.

We have already seen how puns can be an essential medium of characterisation (Mercutio) and how they can be a vehicle for a genre's politics (the brothel in *Pericles*). Let us now look at two more examples where Shakespeare's puns work as more than an immediate verbal 'hit'. First, as particularly suited to concentrating tragic self-awareness (*Hamlet*). Second – and combining all of the above – as a means of concentrating the energies of the dramatic moment, and helping to furnish tragedy's most powerful ethical responses (*Macbeth*).

## HAMLET

Often it seems that tragedy itself generates puns. A typical example is Hamlet's wry comment in the graveyard, spoken of and to a 'chopless' skull: 'Did these bones cost no more the breeding but to play at loggets with 'em? Mine ache to think on't' (5.1.91–3). The crucial word is 'ache'. It expresses his absolute identity with the skeleton, and his anguish at this identity; his hopeless sympathy for himself and for all who have died or must die. At the same time it is a joke. So, Hamlet moves from the thought of 'breeding' to the thought of 'bone-ache'. The joke is that bone-ache is slang for the pox, transmitted by the act of breeding, and so the torturous cause of death. The pun upon 'ache' thereby concentrates the narrative progressions that obsess Hamlet: flesh is always on the turn; the body is a death sentence; desire is disease. This sort of joke doesn't seek anyone's laughter. It barely seeks an audience at all. Instead, the pun is mainly 'for' Hamlet. It allows a pleasing click of release: but the fact that this release is so frankly impotent reinforces how trapped he is.

From the start of the play Hamlet's puns concentrate his tragedy. In particular, his more highly charged words embody the give and take between external provocation and inward self-accounting. A typical example is when the as-yet silent Ghost is leading Hamlet into unknown spaces. As Hamlet follows, Horatio warns him of the peril:

HORATIO   What if it tempt you toward the flood, my lord,
    Or to the dreadful summit of the cliff ...
    And draw you into madness? Think of it.
    The very place puts toys of desperation,
    Without more motive, into every brain
    That looks so many fathoms to the sea
    And hears it roar beneath.
HAMLET                                      It *waves me still*.
                                    (1.4.69–78; my italics)

Let's consider Hamlet's response: 'It waves me still'. This is a reference to the Ghost's 'waving' arm ('It beckons you to go away with it', 1.4.58). In turn, Hamlet seems blankly to ignore Horatio's terrifying vision of mortal despair and metaphysical vertigo. However, far from ignoring it, Hamlet absorbs the vision: he makes it his own. This is suggested by the way he completes Horatio's line – 'And hears it roar beneath./It waves me still' – but more particularly by the fact that Hamlet's response is a pun. So, 'waves' refers both to the Ghost's gesture *and* to Horatio's roaring sea. The effect is to dissolve distinctions between the two visions. Horatio speaks truer than he knows. His fearful geography is in Hamlet's mind already the province of the Ghost: it is the mental space into which the Ghost has led the hero. In turn, the phrase 'waves me' doesn't only mean 'wave to me'. It means that Hamlet is himself being 'waved' like a sea. The geography is internalised: it is Hamlet who is 'many fathoms' deep, and Hamlet whose unplumbed depths are 'roar'-ing.

If 'waves' can be a transitive verb, then it opens up a further pun upon 'still'. That is, he continues to ('still') wave me; he is waving me into 'stillness'. The pun becomes a more general comment about Hamlet's condition. So, the Ghost's movement causes Hamlet's own paralysis ('still'). Simultaneously, the Ghost's movement becomes Hamlet's: the *still*-ness suggests a morphing between the two, whereby Hamlet mutates into his father's phantom. In this way the pun is also a prediction of what is to come. It foretells how Hamlet will *not* effortlessly pick up his father's mantle; how he will *not* easily take on the role of armoured avenger. In place of the avenging hero, we get this oddly neurotic joke and its unmistakable air of infantile melancholy. We hear a son paralysed by the father's example and instruction: *still* paralysed. For there is in Hamlet's humour a wry sense that this kind of instruction has been going on all his life: 'still', he seems to say, I am the man-child, dwarfed or frozen by the great precursor and following half-meekly and self-mockingly in his footsteps.

In this fashion, the surplus of meaning in 'still' holds in poise Hamlet's dilemma. It presses, ever so gently, upon his private doubts and his suddenly alarmed sense of challenge. It revives the guilt of inadequacy: the father's command and urgency, the son's meekness and impotence. It intimates Hamlet's 'move'-ment into the Ghost, and so into a mode of secular purgatory, or into a condition marked by between-ness or boundary-lessness. Taken together, the puns upon 'wave' and 'still' perfectly capture the young prince's present condition: a mingled fear and exaltation that boundaries have evaporated; that there is no distinction between self and other, subject and object, mind and matter, movement and inertia. Everything is captive to a paranoid semiotics; everything is uncanny. The wordplay thus foreshadows Hamlet's preoccupation with – indeed his occupation of – a space of imaginative self-erasure. Tremendous nervous energy is compacted into these 'jokes', pressing for release.

## MACBETH

I want now to look at a brief example that shows how wordplay can serve the fundamental material of drama. It can articulate mental activity, embody action, express and move emotion. It can be at once shouted and silent, action and meditation. It can work both 'in' its spoken moment and in relation to earlier or later moments. Accordingly, we will see how a punning expression can work instantaneously in violently opposite but psychologically and situationally coordinate directions.

Here are some of Macbeth's words as the army against him closes in: 'They have tied me to a stake: I cannot fly,/But, bear-like, I must fight the course' (5.7.1 2). The words come as the action approaches climax, and they have an appropriately immediate effect. So, Macbeth is saying something like, 'I'm trapped, there's no way out, but I will fight to the end'. But how far does such a paraphrase actually get us? What is he trapped *by*? What does it mean to fight? Above all, where exactly do we locate Macbeth in these observations and resolutions? What is his (mental/spiritual) attitude to the (martial/physical) 'attitude' he here adopts?

The basic image is of a tied bear being baited by dogs: a popular entertainment in Shakespeare's day. But to grasp the image is not necessarily to place it. Indeed a series of questions propose themselves. Exactly what sort of thing is the 'bear'? Is it noble, bestial, sacrificial, ridiculous, doomed? If it brings to mind a spectator sport, should we – the spectators – be feeling with the victim or the witnesses? Should we emphasise the cruelty or its pleasures? Does Macbeth's 'bear' begin and end in this circus? Or is his chained vulnerability a sad defilement of a once great indigenous virility? Is there some nostalgic allusion to an uncut forest, proper home to the bear before these mocking days of walking woods? Or does he allude to a heraldic coat of arms, casting back to his abandoned status as loyal and worthy thane? Is the image insulting, or gloating, or consoling? Is he wallowing in his degradation? Or perhaps cheering himself up?

Clearly, 'bear' as a noun is a referential battlefield. But flanking puns reinforce this multiplicity. So, 'bear' can be a verb, meaning to endure, or to undress. If we take this to be the sense, then Macbeth is imagining himself as an authentic tragic survivor, experiencing the limits of existence like an Oedipus or Lear. In turn, 'stake' means more than the post to which the bear is tied. It also refers to the money laid on the game by the eager crowd: Macbeth here is the contemptible object of public entertainment. But then 'stake' can equally evoke crucifixion: perhaps Macbeth briefly (irreverently, consolingly, sarcastically?) identifies with a very different kind of tragic martyr. Similarly, the word 'course' can be the predestined end, the rabbit hunted by the dogs, or the dead 'corse' or corpse at which the game aims (his enemies' or his own). With punning referents shooting out at all angles, the speech proffers all sorts of Macbeth-bodies or Macbeth-attitudes in one: it is like a battle, as his words animate his inward alternatives and situational antagonisms. To add to the difficulty, the basic intent of Macbeth's speech-act is paralysed with ambiguity. 'I cannot fly' might equally express pride, panic, fear, boastfulness, fatalism, or even strategic military logic.

How do we make sense of all of this? The bear-baiting will invoke the Bankside theatres, and we might well see Macbeth as rehearsing 'tragic' solutions, even epiphanies, familiar from Shakespeare's earlier tragedies. So, he might be a stoic in defeat (like Brutus), a hopeful self-mythologiser (like Othello), a sacrifice to history's dark symmetries (like Lear), or an accident of mocking providence (like Hamlet). But of course all of these identifications are illegitimate. He is not finally or decisively any of these things, even though he touches upon all of them. Any notions of manly transcendence are subverted by images of public humiliation.

And, importantly, Macbeth sees it all. This is where his puns come in: they tell us that he knows himself to be a sort of fraud. In other words, Macbeth's words are looking two ways at once: with a defiant sort of stare, out to the audience or over the battlements, he invokes splendid if suicidal bravery; but in the same motion he 'peeps' back into himself, and sees something like a contemptible clown, caught in flagrante in a stolen bearskin.

What we need to see is how the single line is sparking with the simultaneity of the moment. Macbeth's words act the necessary action, at once concealing, revealing, and commenting upon the mind at odds within it. Every referent carries a life-thought, as memory or projection, or as mordant, wistful, or enraged observation. In a different context, Macbeth's figure might have been a more or less dead cliché: I am tied to a stake. That it is instead so intensely alive is due to Shakespeare's insistence that every constituent of the speech here signifies. Far from trivialising meaning, the punning here grounds the words with an existential authenticity. This sort of language really does concentrate all that is at stake.

In a sense this is simply to say that the words are responsible for their own possible meanings: they are planted and plotted; they can be held (as it were) to account. And part of the proof that the puns are thoroughly intended is the way that they pick up or look ahead to moments in other scenes. So, it is no accident that Macbeth here seems to collect into himself the judgements of those who loathe him. Consider this comment of Angus, a few moments earlier: 'now does he feel his title/Hang loose about him, like a giant's robe/Upon a dwarfish thief' (5.2.20–2). As we have seen, just such a sentiment animates much of the internal division in Macbeth's simile of 'bear-like'. And indeed the more we look, the more we should see how Macbeth's furiously splitting language *includes* the preceding judgements of others:

> Some say he's mad; others, that lesser hate him,
> Do call it valiant fury: but, for certain,
> He cannot buckle his distemper'd cause
> Within the belt of rule.

(5.2.13–16)

Here his enemy, Cathness, offers an assessment of Macbeth. When he speaks of 'rule' he means primarily 'the rule of law': Macbeth is a tyrant; his path to power and his methods in power have been corrupt and violent; all he does is implicitly unlawful; he can 'rule' nobody's hearts and would rule nobody's actions except through the 'belt of rule'. Here Cathness puns upon corporal punishment (the belt) so as neatly to evoke the childish petulance within Macbeth's martial terror ('hang those that talk of fear', and so on). But the metaphors are doing still more. So, the image-train of 'buckle', 'distemper'd', and 'belt' evokes – like the 'bear' speech – Macbeth's own ragged and flailing body. Macbeth's 'constitution' at once symbolises, causes, and absorbs all else (just as the 'tragedy' is his as much as Scotland's). In offering alternative judgements about Macbeth, Cathness prepares us to look carefully at the tyranny when next he appears. So, is he mad, vicious, pitiful, valiant, suffering? However, there are still further implications of Cathness's 'He cannot buckle his distemper'd cause/Within the belt of rule'. Insofar as Macbeth is 'embodied', he will exceed all 'rule', burst beyond measure and decorum. Of course this is true of his behaviour: but it is equally true of his language. That is, Cathness suggests how Macbeth's own words will struggle to contain all of these warring extremities. For it is his words that – far more than the actor's clothes or physique – more scrupulously enact whatever Macbeth is becoming. Cathness's 'choric' speech thus prepares us for the real focus of the play's climactic scenes: that is, Macbeth's own take upon his condition, exemplified in conceits such as 'bear-like'.

There is nothing undramatic about this kind of wordplay. It is absolutely in the service of evoking and moving the most basic emotions. That is, we should see how linguistically grafted, how thoroughly worked into the play's rhythms and echoes, is the strange magnetism of the hero. For it can be puzzling to think that Macbeth retains our sympathy: it's rather like feeling for Stalin in his murderous paranoia. There are lots of reasons why the play achieves this effect, but one of them is here apparent. It relates to the simple fact that Macbeth's language is so layered. It is the speech of a split consciousness, and a split conscience. So, we might hear a devastating frankness inside his self-delusion; we might sense his residual hold upon other buried versions of himself; glimpse in his 'virtual' self-projections a faith that given different accidents an entirely different 'Macbeth' was possible (and so on). This is to say that Macbeth's wistfulness and regret, his shame, guilt, and humiliation, his knowledge that everything has been bartered for *nothing*, are in some sense shared by us as they are recognised. And part of this sharing is founded in the way Macbeth takes into himself the judgements expressed by Angus and Cathness. These judgements are more or less allowed by us. Macbeth has not been privy to them. But once he too speaks them, it is as though he alone has generated them, or he alone is responsible for them. He takes from us as from his enemies any distinctive prestige in thinking such things about him. We are not in such judgements superior to him, nor indeed detached. Instead, we are absorbed into his plenty.

Even when a character's judgement of Macbeth is unequivocally insulting or jeering, its terms will often move beyond the speaker's control and into Macbeth's. Consider Macduff's final challenge: 'yield thee, coward,/And live to be the show and gaze o'th' time:/We'll have thee, as our rarer monsters are,/Painted upon a pole, and underwrit,/'Here may you see the tyrant'' (5.8.23–6). The bald insults – 'coward', 'monster', 'tyrant' – are less important than Macduff's framing conceit of a carnival grotesque. Macduff here directly echoes Macbeth's own recent self-vision as a contemptible fairground entertainment and burlesque saviour: the bear tied to a stake.

It is difficult to pin down the effect of the fact that Macbeth has got there first with the taunt. It doesn't neuter Macduff's words, or make them less effective or final. In a way it adds to their decisiveness, because it can make the specific terms of Macduff's final challenge seem prophesied (all prophecies have uncanny truth-making power in *Macbeth*) and necessary. But alongside this sense of necessity is the feeling that Macbeth somehow *knows* that this will be his fate; that Macduff is little more than Macbeth's own medium; and that Macbeth has already claimed responsibility for the leering abuse that he faces. In having glimpsed the picture already, and then having to bury the awareness, Macbeth becomes strangely and pathetically intimate to us. Perhaps it is because he has (once again) peered in upon his 'future instant', and become his own unwilling audience; perhaps it is because in his and Macduff's shared projection he has become the mocked victim. Either way, in being thus *acted upon* – a very dark paradox – he very simply and surprisingly elicits our pity. The feelings that this play evokes are often complicated, even murky. The techniques which create the effects are correspondingly insidious, tentacle-like, even secret. But we need to recognise how the coalescence between Macbeth's punning self-fashioning and Macduff's tangible prediction for him meticulously furnishes the most basic tragic emotions.

Of course, we might not recognise such interconnections as we experience the play. Similarly, we might not consciously decipher the puns that pepper the tyrant's fall. But it is of the essence of the play that many effects work cumulatively, through echo and murmur, as much as through self-aware inference. It is part of Shakespeare's dramatic immediacy that we can feel things without identifying all of the feeling's sources. Tragic puns are rife with echo and allusion. As such, they are a classic instance of the crucial theatrical coalition of immediacy and withholding: of withholding *as* felt and troubling immediacy.

# Part II

# CHARACTERS

# 8

# WHAT ARE THESE SPEAKING THINGS?

*This chapter considers different approaches to the question of character. It begins by recognising some of the resistances to character studies in recent literary criticism. We all think we know what a character is, but do we really? How can we talk about characters in a way that isn't merely anecdotal, and that is attentive to the basic differences between dramatic personae and real people? As a way of going back to basics, and trying to think about character from first principles, the chapter goes on to explore the implications of a series of terms used to refer to a play's 'speaking things'. These terms are 'inwardness', 'subject', 'role', 'part', and finally 'character' itself. Each section draws out something of the word's complexity, its place in history or its relation to theatrical practice, showing how these different shades of meaning suggest different possibilities for characterisation. Our critical terminology is not neutral, but implies many things about the figure being referred to. The chapter closes with an extended discussion of how the word 'character' bears upon Angelo in* Measure for Measure. *We see here how Shakespeare's use of the word 'character' itself concentrates and comments upon his broader developments in characterisation.*

There are no plays without characters. It is the most basic theatrical fact, the very first thing for actor and audience alike. It may also have often been the first thing for the playwright. Shakespeare wrote many of his parts for particular actors, shaping them to fit his colleagues' type or temperament. But if Shakespeare's personae had some kind of life of their own even in their first conditions of production, the subsequent history of these works has borne out the fact many times over. Four hundred years of responses to Shakespeare's plays have again and again seen his characters spoken about as though they have inward thoughts, private passions, unspoken desires or regrets. Impossibly, they can seem to have a past before the play, or to enjoy some kind of life or vitality beyond it. When Shakespeare's lead actor Richard Burbage died, it was imagined that his most famous roles might die with him. Shakespeare's characters had already generated an imaginative currency outside of the stories that supposedly house them. As the seventeenth century went on, much of Shakespeare's fame was generated by spin-offs that often took the favourite scenes of favourite characters and built a fresh entertainment around them. Once Shakespeare became the pre-eminent English classic, it was his characters that for centuries dominated critical discourse. And it remains undeniable that Shakespeare's plays depend upon the joys and tensions of affective response: fearing this, desiring that, wanting to know more than the playtext presents to us.

But how can we treat of such things in serious academic criticism? It is one thing to feel fiercely with or against a character if all we are doing is enjoying the material or talking about it with friends. It can seem another if our job is to place and explain these things in a responsible scholarly context. So, even if the scholar/student's cherished responses to a play are all products of a sympathetic imagination – 'poor Hamlet!', 'stupid boy!', 'what do I care about Duncan?', 'I just love Cleopatra!' – these are likely to play little part in what that same person writes about the play. This is understandable: there is a generally predictable range of such responses to any character, and we do not need endless pen-portraits offering paraphrases of their main characteristics. Accordingly, there is a strong current of opinion which holds that the very category of character is falsely naturalising: because it assumes that 'characteristics' (if not social position) are individual and self-generated; and because it ignores the political scripting, all of the semi-hidden systems of oppression and persuasion, that underscore any self-constructs that we like to cherish. There is no authentic being before or beyond all interpretations, or one who survives all attempts at possession (where could this real thing possibly be located?)

Take the example of Cleopatra. For centuries she was written about almost entirely in terms of her feminine arts or attractions. She is a 'tinsel pattern of vanity and female cunning' or a queen with 'greatness of soul', or some mixture of the two. Ethical appraisal leads to verdicts of the kind of character she 'is'. More recent criticism, by contrast, is likely to see her actions as symptoms of forces largely outside her control. Either that, or it will concentrate attention upon all the different sorts of judgement that she attracts – both during the play and in the critical history of responses to the play – and analyse these judgements in terms of *their* politics. It becomes increasingly unusual to identify character as any kind of endpoint of contemplation. A character contains things or suggests things; a character exemplifies things; a character is a symptom or an effect of other things. What a character is not is any kind of free agent. This tends to mean that enjoyment or analysis of a character needs to be justified by attachment to some larger dignifying discourse. For instance, if we 'approve' of Cleopatra then it might be because she has to work within (or against) specific geopolitical or masculinist agendas. What were once merely 'feminine wiles' become 'discursive strategies', rhetorical manipulations designed to locate some space of agency. Cleopatra becomes a screen or vessel for other concerns: ones that neither start nor finish with *Antony and Cleopatra*.

In thinking broadly along such lines, a lot of literary criticism of the last 20 years or so resists the almost instinctive identification we make between a staged body and a correspondent individuality. We assume that the characters contain some sort of self-consciousness; we posit a unified individual 'behind' the words spoken and acts performed; and we use such an assumption of unity to correct discontinuities, inconsistencies, or absences in the character's presentation. In this fashion, we project our own presupposed idea of selfhood – our intuitive trust in a self-present 'I' – onto dramatic personae. The danger here, clearly, is a form of self-fulfilling experience of the plays: broadly lacking the power to surprise; broadly filled with the shapes we expect to find and taking the shape that we bring to it. But the alternative danger is no less: that we deflect the emotional power of these plays, or ignore the fundamental centring of political and ethical effect in the experience – in *our* experience – of characters.

For while it is right that we should resist over-predictable, generalised, character-centric responses, this resistance should not be to character per se. Rather, we have to be careful about falling for glib or pre-assumed notions of what makes a character. We have to think scrupulously about exactly where characters come from: their sources, their reach, their limits. Perhaps such things are not quite so simple, so given, as we can at times assume. And to do this means – at least as part of our response – that we really do need to 'denaturalise' the way we think about characters. After all, the twenty-first century is not the sixteenth century; on-stage characters are simply different from off-stage persons. Very simply, to acknowledge such difference implies an abiding attention to our own models of thinking. Of course, to think about the methods we use in our reading can seem unnatural: but it is also (paradoxically) probably the surest way to repossessing the plays' freshness and immediacy.

## WHAT SHOULD WE CALL THIS SPEAKING THING?

What term should be used to denote the personages in a Shakespeare play? Many have been tried: actors, parts, players, persons, personalities, people, men/women, characters, figures, shadows, subjects, agents, subjectivities, individuals, types, roles, identities, inwardness, interiority. Roughly speaking, we can divide these up into four categories. First, there are those that emphasise the debt specifically to theatre as the enabling medium: *actor*, *part*, *player*, *role*, *shadow* (and perhaps even 'person', which derives from the idea of impersonating). Second are those which might apply to any mode of literature and which emphasise the debt to textuality: *character*, *figure*, *type*. Third are those that identify a basically straightforward human equivalence with the world outside the theatre: *him/her*, *man/woman*, *individual*. And finally there are those that because they are not habitually used in discussions of 'real life', tend to reinforce the argument that we cannot simply assume that we know what we are talking about when we invoke those who act and speak in a play: *subject, inwardness, agent, interiority.*

This last category, it will come as no surprise, is the most recent, and the only one that is pretty much peculiar to scholars. It is as rare for actors or audiences to speak of Othello or Portia as 'subjects' or 'interiorities' as it would be for them to refer to their friends or sisters in such a way. But this is the point. It is not really that professional academics want to cherish their very own private language, hostile or impenetrable to all intruders. It is that a certain distancing effect is needed if we are to see straight – or, perhaps more pertinently, if we are to see with appropriate angularity or reflexiveness. Whatever terms we prefer, our choice assumes certain historical or theatrical contexts, and suggests particular preferences and exclusions. To recover these things can help refresh our practices and, consequently, help refresh the sorts of plays that we find. Let's consider a few examples.

## INWARDNESS

The word 'inwardness' gets particular impetus from the Protestant stress upon inward faith and its attendant relation to the word of scripture – silent prayer, silent reading, silently listening to preaching. The idea here is that the only relationship that matters is the private one between the believer and God. Both a cause and consequence of the Protestant Reformation was a rejection of what we might see as the more theatrical elements of faith: not only its art, music, pageants, images, icons, but also the mediating power of priests and the cleansing facility of rituals. In place of public theatre, we get the private book. The term 'inwardness' then helps us focus very clearly upon this question of finding a way to channel or communicate the most intimate movements of the soul (Shakespeare seven times refers to the 'inward' soul or mind). But then to use the term – partly because it is so awkward sounding – can also be to bring into question the very thing it invokes. If truth is inward, how can it find public expression? Won't such public expression necessarily bastardise any integrity? How can definitively inward truth get embodied before thousands of people at a public theatre? These challenges are difficult to refute, but thinking carefully about our own language can help. For there was another common use of 'inward' in early modern England: it referred to the bodily organs, and more precisely the entrails or bowels. Things inward become inseparable from early modern 'humoral' psychology; body and mind are of an ever-changing but absolutely linked temper (as Iago has it, 'For that I do suspect the lusty Moor/Hath leaped into my seat, the thought whereof/Doth like a poisonous mineral gnaw my *inwards*', *Othello*, 2.1.292–4; my italics). Shakespearean inwardness (like Shakespeare's language) is always moving between physicality and abstraction. Our use of the term can keep us both historically *and* linguistically sensitive.

## SUBJECT

Another term often used in recent criticism is the 'subject'. This word too carries interestingly divided meanings. It is much used in philosophy to mean the generating mind or consciousness, implying a faith in the self as the abiding home and director of meaning. In grammar, the subject is similarly the moving or doing agent (e.g. 'I' in 'By God, *I* cannot flatter', *1 Henry IV*, 4.1.6). However, if it is transferred to individuals, this grammatical use can suggest almost the opposite: the subject 'I' becomes an effect of language, a thing scripturally and textually overdetermined. This application of the word (drawing upon structural linguistics) can in turn shade into the most prevalent early modern resonance of 'subject': a person under the dominion of another, and so one who owes obedience and allegiance to a ruling power ('When I do stare, see how the *subject* quakes', *Lear*, 4.6.107). The word invoked feudal obligations. It described a status of subjection and inferiority: hence Richard II's mordant joke, 'I live with bread like you, feel want,/Taste grief, need friends – *subjected* thus,/How can you say to me, I am a king?' (3.2.175–7). In other words, a 'subject' is defined by what s/he is subjected to. To use the term in this way is to focus upon the systems – political, legal, economic, ideological – that ensure this subjection, prescribe its customs, and delineate any liberties. Accordingly, when literary critics refer to the 'subject', it is most often a mutation partly from this legal denotation and partly from structural linguistics. That is, a thing made up out of the particular discourses in which that subject is situated. This 'subject' is explicitly not the same in all times and all places.

Consequently, we might recognise a potential tension between 'subject' as a free-thinking agent (as in *subjective*) and 'subject' as a thing over whom rights are exercised or to whom discourses are dictated (as in *subjected*). We can give the word a specifically political or legalistic reference, and mean by it a particular subject condition – with accordant rights, duties, and so on – that will vary depending upon whichever society is at issue. We can mean by it something much closer to freestanding selfhood. Or we can allude specifically to the 'anti-essentialist' construct favoured by post-structuralist or materialist thinking. Best of all when reading Shakespeare, perhaps, might be to recognise that this ongoing wrestle in the word's history concentrates something akin to the unresolved conflicts staged in Shakespeare: conflicts which find a locus in many of his most interesting 'subjects'.

## ROLE AND PART

The terms 'part' and 'role' remind us that the persona is at base a performed one. Shakespeare is almost always writing roles for very specific actors; an actor duly allows and makes the part; we allow the actor. The role is not a transparent window onto some 'real person': to use the terms can be to stress just how mediated this imitation person really is. But this in turn influences the very fibre of Shakespeare's characterisations. It is not always only the playwright, actors and audience who know that each personage is an impersonation. It is often the case that the 'person' being played seems similarly to know that what s/he does is a role. To use the words part or role, then, invokes one of Shakespeare's favourite tropes: existence as role playing, and therefore meta-dramatic characterisation.

There is no playwright contemporary to Shakespeare who so often reaches for impersonation to solve (or indeed create) a problem. There is barely a plot that doesn't hinge upon one or another kind of cloak or visage. But more than this, his characters are compelled to talk about acting. They do so at any time, in any circumstances. They do so playfully, describing how disguise and deception will help them foil a rival or elicit a laugh. And they do so tragically, almost as *the* tragic conceit. So, Hamlet's very first speech of mourning sees him scorn the truth of anything 'played', and yet he is soon investing his fiercest hopes exactly in theatre's power to reveal hidden things. Cleopatra is horrified at the prospect of being turned into a pantomime 'queen', but then finds her apotheosis through dressing up on a great stage-like monument. Coriolanus defines his integrity as opposite to all dissimulation, and then acts out the consequences through namelessness and disguise. Even Macbeth, who locates as his ultimate example of nihilism a 'poor player', expresses his despair less in straight confession than in all kinds of 'actorly' ploys – rhyme, pastiche, bathetic role play – as though his 'inwardness' involves the concentrated internalising of theatrical exchange. 'All the world's a stage' is no idle conceit for Shakespeare. As has long been recognised, acting is Shakespeare's working metaphor, almost his instinctive existential trope: playing a part is like life; life is like playing a series of parts.

However, the terms 'part' and role' evoke more than an actor's pretend persona. They share a very precise physical reference: both (although 'part' was the more commonly used) refer to the pasted together scroll, listing in order a specific part's cues and speeches, which the actor would receive and from which he would learn his role. It may seem obvious enough how this specifically physical reference gave way to the much more open senses of 'role' and 'part' familiar today. But still it might be useful to dwell more particularly upon this physical part, and to consider what it might suggest about the characters it scripts.

So, how might we picture this part? Perhaps as a tightly rolled cylinder, in its own way perfect and entire: in this construction, the roll might suggest an idea of 'essential' character, correspondent to the infinite potentiality of a pre-embodied text. Alternatively, we might picture the roll as an almost empty collection of material: pasted sheets, in a cylindrical bundle, with a defining hollowness in the inner chamber. What it 'is' is just rolled paper on the outside and, on the inside, infinite air. Understood in this way, the roll becomes a blank symbol of 'character' as nothing more than its material or textual traces. Anything more – anything humanising or fleshed out – is either an actor-at-work or our own projection. Or again, we may think of the roll as a thing to be unrolled, serving a preordained individuating design: the roll is as long as the role; it is a story to be opened, harbouring a gradual movement into clarity and finality.

But again we might propose an alternative: after all, it is unlikely that in rehearsal a long part like Falstaff or Richard III would have been unrolled, like some ceremonial carpet, every time the actor had to parse a line or scribble down some direction. Perhaps at the start, as the actors were getting a feel for the whole role, they might have got on a floor together and literally unrolled their parts into flatness, checking length, the kinds of address, the broad movement between the verse and prose. But the real creative use of the part/roll must often have been much less measured and ordered. As the actor learns his lines, recognises the cross-references, the part will likely have been folded this way and that, become a thing of creases and intersections. There will be different bits within the part that need to be consulted simultaneously, and folded or torn in such a way as to allow such cross-reference. The simple physicality of a major part will therein be altered; it will change from a 'two-dimensional' single sheet into something uniquely three-dimensional.

This physical geometry might then trace developments in both character and characterisation. That is, both the physical part and the imaginary persona might undergo a movement similar to the conventional distinction between two- and three-dimensional characters. As the physical part is worked by the actor, so too is the simulated part worked out. The imitation figure follows a comparable process of psychological development: so, something smooth or even generically anonymous (the perfectly rolled scroll, the character 'type') develops roughness, folds, distinctiveness.

Something similar to such materially grounded methods of characterisation is exemplified by a dialogue between Orsino and Viola/Cesario early in *Twelfth Night*. Here the Duke wants Cesario to get 'audience' with Olivia and plead his love:

> Cesario,
> Thou know'st no less but all: I have unclasp'd
> To thee the *book* even of my secret soul.
> Therefore, good youth, *address* thy gait unto her,
> Be not denied access, stand at her doors,
> And tell them, there thy *fixed foot* shall grow
> Till thou have *audience*. . . .
> . . .*unfold the passion* of my love,
> Surprise her with *discourse* of my dear faith;
> It shall become thee well to *act my woes*:
> She will *attend* it better in thy youth. . .
> . . .Diana's lip
> Is not more smooth and rubious: thy small pipe
> Is as the maiden's organ, shrill and sound,
> And all is *semblative a woman's part*.
>
> (1.4.12–34; my italics)

Orsino often makes reference to books, acting or music in expressing his humours, and here he outlines an intimate connection between theatrical artefacts and passionate inwardness. So, a secret soul is a 'book', 'unclasp'd' in the act of confession. The passion is to be 'unfold'-ed, and the unfolding is a mix of 'discourse' and 'acting'. The ensuing 'act' will be a mixture of 'smooth' sight and 'shrill' sound, spoken in 'fixed foot' (regular meter) that demands an 'audience'. The passage in Orsino's stage directions to his servant – from printed 'book', to 'unfolded' passion, to enacted 'part' – repeats that of any actor's part as it moves from the playwright, to the player, to the audience.

The whole play seems to spool out from this way of conceiving of self-truth as a product of script and acting. In *Twelfth Night*, both comedy and pathos are built around acts of 'pretend' that are at one glance false and at a second unerringly true. Hence the basic joke of the consequent scene between Viola and Olivia (1.5).

Disguised as Cesario, Viola 'acts' as her master bids and does his courting for him. Her discourse in this scene then has about four main registers: she frames what she is to say on Orsino's behalf as the 'studied' work of an actor on 'commission' (1.5.184); she speaks the part she has learned, faithful to the awful poetry of her writer ('I am very comptible, even to the least sinister usage', 1.5.170–1); she talks about her own suffering in the guise of sticking rigidly to her 'text' ('Where lies your text?' 'In Orsino's bosom', 'In his bosom? In what chapter of his bosom?', 'To answer by the method, in the first of his heart', 1.5.217–21); or she turns her text into double entendre by making it speak both the part Orsino wishes her to act and her own secret feelings ('My lord and master loves you: O, such love/Could be but recompens'd, though you were crown'd/The nonpareil of beauty!', 1.5.246–8). There is here no escape from part playing, or from parts 'conned' (learnt) in private, in 'great pains'. Viola's twice-spoken joke ('it is excellently well penned, I have taken great pains to con it', 'Alas, I took great pains to study it, and 'tis poetical', 1.5.168–9, 189–90), in which her 'pains' can allude both to her reluctance to play this part and to her patron's turgid script, is also (of course) a more aching secret confession.

We might identify on display here something like the basic 'technology' that goes toward Shakespearean characterisation. It is not only that the 'woman's part' (as inward truth, outward beauty, and so on) proceeds via playing various parts. It is that the 'folded' truths that are coming to define psychological veracity or emotional worthiness are pictured in, and in some basic sense derive from, the material and technological processes of theatre. This early scene is probably the one where Viola's character is most fully presented: before it we take on trust her vivacity, wit, and pain; afterwards, we trust it. And this intimacy is achieved through various almost physical planes of self-representation. We might picture her character as different folds of a page, different 'parts' of a part, with each one nestling beneath or folding into the other.

Consequently, identity can be imagined here not so much in terms of the regular turning of a page, recto to verso and back; nor as the unrolling of a scroll. Rather, it is represented as something much more irregular, a superimposition of parts that are at once separable and connected. As Shakespeare's craft develops, he displays a growing interest in a model of individuality that we might see resembles the actor's experience of working with a textual part. Increasingly, any 'planes' get internalised, and we get the remarkable parts-*within*-parts that are so characteristic of Shakespeare's most celebrated characters. In other words, the psychic architecture of Shakespeare's characters begins to be shaped rather like a much rehearsed – but never quite done with – actor's part.

## CHARACTER

Shakespeare never uses the word 'character' to denote a theatrical player, nor to describe a simulated person. This is not quite to say that the word could not mean something close to these things at the time – because as we shall see it probably could. But the primary meaning of 'character' was still very close to its etymological roots: it meant a brand, stamp, or other graphic sign, and consequently was most often used to mean either written 'characters' (e.g. letters of the alphabet) or writing style. How might we explain the movement from a graphic symbol to a personality invested with distinctive attributes and qualities?

There is a simple enough historical explanation. Before there developed the common usage of 'character' to mean writing or letters, it meant a stamp: an impress, engraving, or cutting, such as we might find on a coin or, at the other end of the social scale, on a bond-slave's forehead. It is a small step from 'character' meaning the idea of such a graven symbol, and it meaning this symbol's content: the 'character' of the leader is true coined in noble profile; the 'character' of the slave is tattooed in full-frontal, low-browed, bodily ignominy. The physical fact of a 'character' is made to freeze (or perhaps burn) a particular symbolics of type. So, leaders are distinctively 'this', slaves distinctively 'that'. 'Character' then begins to mean something like an essential trait or feature marking one class of person apart from another. Each such 'character' might then provoke its own pithy auto-narrative, a little pen-portrait describing the typical henpecked husband or pretentious courtier. Indeed Shakespeare's career coincided with the development of the literary sub-genre called 'The Character', which involves compiling just such colourfully detailed, often satirical single paragraphs about particular recognisable 'types': puritan, lover, chambermaid. These sketches fit neatly into a humours-based understanding of psychology and physiology: it is no coincidence that Ben Jonson, the foremost dramatist of the humours, was one of the first to use the term 'characterism' to help describe dramatis personae (in his play *The New Inn*).

It does not, however, quite explain Shakespeare's most distinctive or important characters. Of course his characters always bear some relation to stock types. But the fit is almost never comfortable, or free from all kinds of irony, splitting and combining. For instance, however much the comic heroines are quickly established in our minds as virtuous, witty, eligible young ladies, all of them briskly peel away from any such type into role play that bears little relation to their supposedly originating type – apart perhaps from attesting to that type's frustrations, and to the questing after possibility that both social and generic pigeon-holing can provoke. Similarly, Hamlet is a 'malcontent', Caliban a 'monster', Iago a 'Vice', but the remit of such familiar types can hardly define their reach or functions. Certainly Shakespeare's characterisations are indebted to the notion of 'character' as a brand: but they have all sorts of surplus beyond this debt. Let us see whether Shakespeare's use of the word 'character' can help us trace how he brings this more complex individuation to the stock idea.

At first glance, 'character' in Shakespeare means a form of writing. However, Shakespeare hardly ever uses the word without wanting it to mean both a graphic sign *and* the thing this sign is attempting to signify. In this way we can identify in Shakespeare's use of the word something like the decisive transition in its function. Initially denoting just a style of handwriting or stamped impress, it opens up to mean something much closer to a personally distinctive inwardness.

A typical example is in *King Lear*. Gloucester is shown a letter purporting to be in the hand of his legitimate son, Edgar. He asks of his bastard son Edmund, 'You know the *character* to be your brother's?' (1.2.62; my italics). In the next scene between the two, Edmund quotes a speech of treachery and defiance which he pretends his brother has spoken:

> Thou unpossessing bastard, dost thou think,
> If I would stand against thee, would the reposal
> Of any trust, virtue or worth in thee
> Make thy words faithed? No, what I should deny,
> As this I would, [ay,] though thou didst produce
> My very *character*, I'd turn it all
> To thy suggestion, plot and damned practice...
>
> (2.1.67–73; my italics)

On both occasions the word 'character' refers most immediately to Edgar's handwriting. Much more importantly, however, the handwriting is asked to stand for something true and essential about the person. *If* it is his 'character' – his hand – then it must describe his hidden mind and motives: that is, his true 'character'. One type of 'character' (as a graphic sign) is serving a much more potent notion of 'character' as inherent vice or virtue. Hence the loaded emphasis of my 'very character': it is not handwriting per se which here deserves the emphasis, but its origin.

It might seem that scenes like this are proposing a fairly straightforward sort of allegory between one type of 'character' and another. So, implicit in Edmund's lie is the idea that 'character' (handwriting) *should* supply evidence of something like self-presence. However, explicit in his lie is the fact that it very easily does not. Edmund knows how easily 'character' – writing as the true stamp or brand of the writer – can be confused by 'suggestion, plot and damned practice': that is, we might say, by the improvisatory arts of theatre. And Shakespeare, of course, knows exactly the same thing. Writing is neither fixed nor transparent: nor, consequently, is self-identity. If 'character' as self is a kind of mutation out of 'character' as letter, then we can expect Shakespeare's persons to be as shifting and multiform as language itself.

Accordingly, the 'character' here at issue really is Edgar: not so much his handwriting, but much more profoundly the question who or where he is. We have no idea, other than a basic assumption (inferred from little but his absence from the plot woven by Edmund) that he is not evil. In all other essentials, this early plot sets him up to be at once exiled and, pretty much literally, erased. His 'character' is unwritten. Insofar as Edgar is concerned, a basic job for the rest of the play is to locate some sign or stamp that *does* in fact, unlike Edmund's 'character', coincide with his mind and body. Of course, as Edgar's descent into Poor Tom suggests, this might be as difficult to arrive at for him as to accept by us. But this early play upon 'character' – questioning the meaning of resemblance, subverting the identity of signifier (writing) and signified (writer/written) – establishes the terms of his subsequent characterisation (see Chapter 9).

'Character' becomes equally the materials of dramatic art and its central subject. Shakespeare does a similar thing with Polonius's advice to Laertes: 'these few precepts in thy memory/Look thou *character*', (*Hamlet*, 1.3.58–9), and again here with Orlando in *As You Like It*:

> O Rosalind, these trees shall be my books,
> And in their barks my thoughts I'll character,
> That every eye which in this forest looks,
> Shall see thy virtue witness'd everywhere.
>
> (3.2.5–8)

Once more we see a transference between the graphic mark – the letters here cut in the bark – and inward truth: in this case a conflation of Orlando's 'thoughts' and Rosalind's 'virtues'. The world gets to 'witness' these twin interiorities only through the medium of Orlando's 'character'. Or perhaps more accurately, his 'charactering': for we see here a typical example of Shakespeare using a supposed noun as a verb (*OED* gives Shakespeare as the first to do so with 'character'). A much greater force is thereby given to the word: 'character' becomes the most intimate of making words, and the most intimate of possessions. The word in such cases harnesses perhaps the most basic Shakespearean capability: the movement from thought to body; the simultaneity of consciousness and embodiment. The poetic conceit both shadows and suggests the magical materiality of drama.

## ANGELO IN *MEASURE FOR MEASURE*

Let's conclude with an extended discussion of a moment in *Measure for Measure* which epitomises the interconnectedness of Shakespeare's word use and his techniques of characterisation. This scene sets up the basic challenge facing Angelo: are you as virtuous as everyone thinks? The Duke begins the challenge like this:

ANGELO    There is a kind of *character* in thy life
        That to th'observer doth thy history
        Fully unfold.

                    (1.1.27–9; my italics)

The crucial word is 'character', but what we need to notice is just how overloaded, almost nervous with potential, the term seems to have become. There is a working analogy here between the idea that a person can be 'read' in a single 'character' (as written figure) and the idea that truth and virtue can be read in the fixed 'letter of the law'. 'Character' and 'government' are always each other's allegories in this play, and here we can see how the word 'character', with its inherited fixities and its incipient movement, is a testing ground for *Measure*'s exploration of human justice and desire. Linked to this is a certain charge in the word, intuited or conscious, of historical change: as though the two-dimensional 'brand' is coming to three-dimensional life.

So, the Duke says 'a kind of character', and the effect of 'a kind of' is to qualify the self-certainty of 'character' at the same time as place the word upon a syntactic pedestal. Shakespeare is at once pressing hard upon the word *and* oddly skirting around it. His use of the word generates an aura of self-awareness, as though declaring that whatever is animated within it – the battles that the word contains – will also be the things that the rest of the play must go on to dramatise. The 'character' suggests something like the sign or image that Angelo presents to the world: not the full story. To the extent that 'character' as 'brand' is a metonym of 'character' as personality, we get a presentiment of radical self-division. (This idea of a self made of different parts, and therefore not effortlessly and coherently self-present, is twice repeated in the next few lines: 'Thyself and thy belongings' and 'to waste/ Thyself upon thy virtues', 1.1.29–31.)

Shakespeare is exploiting the contradictions inherent in the basic physical referent of 'character'. It appears single and absolute, but whether a coin, a tattoo on the forehead, or handwriting, the fixity is more a sign of violence and power than it is a proof of the likeness between the pictured thing and the real thing that it supposedly brands. Indeed Angelo hints at just this as soon as the Duke allows him to respond:

> Now, good my lord,
> Let there be some more test made of my metal,
> Before so noble and so great a figure
> Be stamp'd upon it.

> (1.1.47–50)

In speaking of a 'figure' being 'stamp'd' upon 'my metal', Angelo invokes the most standard of all definitions of 'character'. But as much as he recognises the Duke's figure (metal–mettle/coin–true coined), he also makes it problematic. He needs to be 'test'-ed: to be put through fire, to be beaten, and so to be strengthened or broken by extremity. Angelo, that is, would place himself back in the furnace. Rather than forged, finished, and true coined, Angelo is in his own eyes materially impure. It would be pleasing to be a true fixed coin, to embody the letter of the law, to be exactly what the Duke requires. Angelo knows the satisfactions of very simply being a product of the 'means of production'. But even as he looks forward to the time when he might indeed be such a finished brand – 'Before so noble and so great a figure/Be stamp'd upon it' – the attempt at humility is dwarfed by a feeling for humiliation. There is a certain rapture here that is little short of masochistic. So, 'stamp'd' obviously continues the figurative train of 'character' and 'metal'. But as much as Angelo is desperate to *be* just such a functionary – a living embodiment of the ducal seal or the book of law – he is also a man, with 'organs' (1.1.20) of his own. A 'character' is a material sign *and* an inferable inwardness; this is likewise true of metonyms of 'character' such as 'metal' and 'stamp'd'. So, 'stamp'd' will also evoke more frankly human agency. It becomes something like the boots of the great Duke, pressing down upon his grateful subordinate; or Angelo is in a mortar, beaten to pulp by the Duke's pestle. True to the play, we hear the violence of power, the abjection of sexuality, and the repression that protects and warps desire. Angelo's inwardness extends and contracts with the words that 'character' him.

But if the metaphors are here doing most of the psychological work, they are equally the main bearers of historical and political movement. So, the Duke tries to symbolise Angelo through a simple enough material artefact. He chooses a single graphic image ('character'): but this single thing is at the same time supposed to be 'unfold'-ed. It represents not so much a mixed metaphor as a colliding one: and one that concentrates exactly the history of 'character' that we are here exploring. So, in becoming 'unfolded', the material artefact makes way for a material *process*; any single character must contribute to the many leaves of a book; in turn, character moves from a flat plane to something folded. The Duke pretends that merely to see Angelo's image is to 'fully unfold' his book, thereby hoping to reconcile the two metaphor clusters that his basic figure of 'character' lets loose. But this is impossible. (We really cannot judge a book by its cover.) The fact is that the two versions of 'character' that the Duke evokes posit opposite relations to history. One is a graven brand; the other is a 'folded' story. This evokes not only increasingly sophisticated technologies, but also an increasingly sophisticated medium for narrative.

The point is that 'history' cannot be condemned to the past: accordingly, 'doth thy history fully unfold' points as much to what may be done as to what has been done. Of course the Duke here presumes a power of clairvoyance: he thinks that the past is the truest guide to the future, and that Angelo is an 'open book' telling a foreseeable and exemplary tale. In other words, the Duke interprets Angelo's character in terms of customary generic type. But there is hardly a play less comfortably fitted with its generic antecedents than this one. Angelo will indeed 'unfold', but in a way that is faithful to the 'folds' in words like 'character' and 'figure' rather than in any way that the Duke appears to expect. A rather different inference then appeals. This 'history' will 'unfold' as the play does; we are 'th'observer'; *Measure for Measure* is this book.

And so it is that the same image returns to herald the play's final scene – which also happens to be the next time that the Duke and Angelo meet face to face:

> O, but your desert speaks loud, and I should wrong it
> To lock it in the wards of covert bosom,
> When it deserves with *characters* of brass
> A forted residence 'gainst the tooth of time
> And razure of oblivion. Give we our hand,
> And let the subject see, to make them know
> That outward courtesies would fain proclaim
> Favours that keep within.

(5.1.10–17; my italics)

The Duke is speaking with heavy irony here – he knows what has been kept 'within' his deputy – but this serves to reinforce the ironic charge in the word 'character'. The word implies 'outward', but merely to use it is to beg questions about what 'keep[s] within'. Shakespeare's familiar interest in matters of appearance and deception serves to make his dramatic techniques almost like his insistent subject: 'outward courtesies would fain proclaim/ Favours that keep within'. This is one of the great tasks of his work, and once more it is 'characters', in all of their internally divided ironies, that are both medium and symbol of this larger story of suppression and revelation. But we should always try to keep somewhere in mind – as Shakespeare clearly does – the derivation of 'character' in writing, figuration, and types. Not only Shakespeare's characters, but also his characterising materials, are forever in a kind of furnace, and being subjected to their own testing, smelting, and reshaping.

# 9

# WHERE IS A CHARACTER?

*This chapter is about the construction and location of character. A dramatic character is never simply present and complete. It is always in process, being formed out of all sorts of textual and theatrical effects. A character doesn't only act and react in particular contexts. It is made up out of these contexts: both the society and relationships represented in the play, and the techniques and structures of playwright and playhouse. What we take to be a character's inwardness is invariably inferred from particular external phenomena. The chapter begins by surveying some of these things: stock types, popular sources, haunting ghosts or 'others', scenic organisation. It then gives a short analysis of a scene in* King Lear *that shows how even the most delicate inward changes in characters are signalled through external appeal (to the audience) and allusion (to another character), and by the scenic placement of speech-acts. Shakespearean characterisation does not always revolve around the single, self-responsible body. Instead, individual experience is often represented through shared or conflated bodies. Similarly, allegorical functions often work in tandem with more 'lifelike' psychological patterns. Two long sections then explore these questions: the first on disguise (focusing on Edgar in* Lear*), the second on doubling (analysing Cloten and Posthumus, Pericles, and Macduff and Macbeth). Both techniques complicate the presence of a single, self-identical character, and raise questions about the limits of self-responsibility or the security of self-identity. Equally, both can powerfully regenerate and reorganise a play's emotional, ethical, and political charge.*

190

The study of character should be faithful both to the responses they generate and the techniques that make them. This means being wary of falsely normalising assumptions about what characters are, how they work, or where they are located. The way to avoid this is to stay sensitive to the numerous dramatic phenomena that can embody characters. Of course it is our experience of a play that allows any character to 'be'. But this experience is found and grounded in the *forms* of the play: its words, scenic shifts, storylines, costumes, and so on. Crucially, these forms are diffuse and multicentred. For we cannot decisively identify and locate character in that character's words and actions, as though to say s/he is whatever s/he does or says, or is to be discovered only there. Clearly these things are indispensable. But it is to mistake drama for mime or monologue to think that these are the only phenomena that we draw upon (even in uncritical ignorance or complacence) when we put together our sense of a particular character. Just as the 'personality' of music – embodying pathos, excitement, melancholy – often works by anticipation and echo, meaning that we 'hear' things that are not actually present, so too the personality of a dramatic character is a compound of present *and* absent stimuli. It is fundamental to Shakespeare's orchestrations that characters can be built as much from forms that move from the 'outside' in as from the 'inside' out.

The theatre uses multiple media, and all might contribute to the phenomena that we perceive or intuit as filling out the dramatic person. The most obvious of all is the simple fact that – before any speech or story – we see them. The body on stage always means things before and beyond anything that the actor's voice speaks. The most culturally 'straight' appearance is packed full of codes and signals to do with place, status, wealth, function, decorum, gender, and so on. The very power of customary appearance makes it easy to use the unusually dressed or differently fleshed body for comic or political purposes. We might think of Malvolio's yellow cross-garters, Othello's blackness, or Caliban's category confusing oddness. Clearly a production of the play will often be decisive here: our basic sense of Cleopatra, for instance, can radically change according to how 'African' or

'Arabic' her hair, how alluring her dress, how 'strumpet-like' her manners.

The apparently simple idea of character in fact involves a number of interpenetrating considerations. It can include a notion of 'essential' inwardness (although with many minor characters no such inferences come into play), as we reach after what sort of person so and so 'really' is. But this in turn is tied up with questions of function, and of the particular place of the character in relation to things like audience desire and generic orientation. Are we on their side? Do we laugh with or at them? Are they working with or against any larger movement toward resolution? Often these questions are answered simply enough (Don John in *Much Ado* is hostile to the audience, hostile to comedy, and so a 'hostile' character): but equally often they are not. It is frequently the case in Shakespeare's comedies, for example, that the script on its own leaves open the question of a character's power to command either the audience's gaze or the generic momentum. Consider this from *Merchant of Venice*; it is when Portia, dressed as a young lawyer, first arrives at the trial scene:

PORTIA   I am informed throughly of the cause, –
    Which is the merchant here? and which the Jew?
DUKE   Antonio and old Shylock, both stand forth.
PORTIA   Is your name Shylock?
SHYLOCK                        Shylock is my name.
                                  (4.1.171–4)

This might seem a simple enough introduction, but in fact the exchange is riddled with ambiguities. Most of these hinge upon two things: the extent to which Portia is in control and therefore playing to the audience; and the extent to which Shylock's physical appearance marks him out as a Jew. If Shylock is dressed as a typical stage Jew – perhaps with a 'Jew mask' on – then Portia's question becomes ridiculous. Everyone knows who the Jew is; it is all too obvious: the question becomes a bald joke, lightly ridiculing lawyerly claims to impartiality, but more forcibly laughing at the Jew as irrevocably alien and different. In such a case, Shylock can be little more than a comic butt, as the scene stages further jokes about false misidentity ('Is your name

Shylock?' Portia asks Antonio). His appearance as the stage Jew already marks him out as a caricature, and Portia's game reinforces the idea that Shylock's character does not exceed such a type. Everything is different, however, if Portia's question is a genuine one. The uncertainty and the mistakes are real; the deadly opposites are also insidiously identical; Shylock carries the fullest weight of Venice's and the play's divisions. Like so much in this play, the moment teeters between cruelly complacent slapstick and implosive tragedy: the characters are almost entirely shaped by how they fit, or fail to fit, into the generic package. Of course the genre is as up for grabs as the character here. The pressure of redefinition goes in both directions: it is one of the crucial distinctions of characters to exceed or embarrass their supposed type and thereby to make a play exceed or embarrass its own.

Such moments show just how much inference is necessary to fill out dramatic character. This is particularly the case if we are reading the play. Productions on stage reduce the need for inference – principally by turning its guesswork into bodily fact. But 'character' here is as open as comedy itself: both can be radically different things in the same moment. A production can make choices, but cannot resolve matters with any further finality. We are not dealing here with essentially knowable characters, consistently given and dependably locatable whatever the reader or audience.

Much of what we take to be a particular character will be represented with apparent sensory directness, as we watch the character in action or attend to their speech. But significant elements need not be. What can seem the most immediate – that is, direct and unmediated – responses are often in fact constructed through highly subtle processes of allusion and comparison. This is particularly the case with the various sources that lie behind or shadow specific characters. If a character is not drawing upon one or another stock type (magician, clown, Vice, pastoral maiden, puritan, malcontent, wild man), then they are likely to represent either a familiar historical personage (Caesar, Cleopatra, the various kings) or a figure whose story is well known from myth, ballads, or other literature. The majority of Shakespeare's primary sources for his characters are hardly obscure – Plutarch, Boccacio, Ovid, Chaucer, Homer, Holinshed, and various popular Elizabethan romances or earlier Elizabethan plays – and we can assume that many in his first audiences would have been measuring the 'name' on stage against the same name read or heard about in other contexts. Even those characters that seem most uniquely 'Shakespearean' – Hamlet, Lear, Caliban – carry from the very start something like their own hinterland of potential associations and memories. So, Hamlet is not only a 'revenger', but also one whose story had been seen on the London stage less than ten years before Shakespeare's version. Something similar goes for Lear: his story is there to be read in the chronicles, and it was staged as a broadly Christian tragi-comedy around the same time as the earlier *Hamlet*.

Caliban is certainly unique, but he will also evoke images of other pastoral beasts and misfits: one of the most popular of all contemporary plays, *Mucedorus*, featured just such a monster in the figure of one Bremo. It is not that any of these characters is remotely explained by such precursors, or that they decisively owe their being to them. But they don't come from nothing, or work in their own allusion-free bubbles. Unconsciously or not, all sorts of contexts and associations go toward any audience's construction of a character.

Furthermore, we need to be attuned to the characterising potential of a host of formal devices. We have explored some of these in earlier chapters: things like single images or clauses that at once contain and conceal alternative self-narratives; speeches that construct virtual biographies with as much reality as the most instrumental dialogue; the festive space of a joke or pun, whereby daring or unsustainable options can be played out and yet survived. We are used to such micro-effects in Shakespeare, where small details are packed with content. But his is equally an art of the macro, in which the larger structures of scene or setting represent a particular consciousness. Shakespeare's characters would be composed very differently were they were not presented in sequences of scenes: soliloquy, for instance, would be far less important; so too the doubled scene or personae; so too the need to infer motive or alteration in physical absence. The abrupt transition from one scene to the next and back ensures that we can always be aware of things that the character is not. We can both invest in the scene before us and keep some organising power aloof. This means that the basic substance of any character before us is always being augmented or adjusted by memories or expectations of neighbouring scenes.

So, a suffering psyche might be organised scenically: *Pericles*, for example, moves from place to place, each scene presenting a basically similar setting: layered out one after another in this fashion, the scenes work as though the horizontal unfolding of Pericles' mental trauma. Or we might think of *Macbeth*'s highly charged geography. Its heaths, caverns, castles, doorways, skies, ditches, and so on serve to externalise the characters' most secret places, as crime or anxiety find expression in uncanny mutations of place. The same kind of thing can be collected in a single scenic snapshot: Edgar's invented vision of the 'dizzy' Dover cliff in *Lear* encapsulates the similarly dizzy minds of both the suicidal father and the self-exiled son.

Another common example is the shifting identity between a character and a ghost (Hamlet, Brutus, Richard III), or soothsayer (Macbeth, Cleopatra), or fiends (Edgar's 'foul fiend', Alonso and company in *The Tempest*). Sometimes this extra-rational thing is clearly distinct from the figure being possessed; sometimes it is an emanation of the mind; sometimes it could be either. There is often the doubt or fear that the character has made up this thing themselves, as though coming upon it exactly as their private language or symbol. In turn these semi-separate entities can bear various relations to the supposedly organising consciousness. They might be proto-divine, proto-diabolical, proto-parental, or proto-selves (or all of these things at once, as with *Hamlet*'s Ghost). They can bear various relations – cause, effect, commentary, self-shadow – to whatever draws them into being. There are relatively simple cases such as the ghosts that haunt Richard III or Brutus, which work as expressions of guilt, doubt, or retribution. But then there are much more doubtful cases such as Macbeth's witches or Edgar/Poor Tom's 'foul fiend'. In these cases it is perilously difficult to pin down just where possession ends, or independence begins, or indeed who is acting in or for what. These haunting 'others' partly work as external prompts, as cues for action or thought. Equally, they work as symbolical explosions of inward struggle. In this way, they contribute to the very substance of this emerging individual.

Shakespeare isn't at all tied to the idea of a self-contained body: all of these ghostly self-shadows help to body forth characters often radically at odds with themselves and their surroundings. In turn, it is the very primitivism of the technique – a hangover from the morality plays with their cast of allegorised tempters and fiends – that allows Shakespeare to explore so methodically the folded layers of consciousness.

## EXTERNALLY CONSTRUCTED INWARDNESS: LEAR

To say the obvious: characters are built up through spoken words, framed in scenes marking a particular place and moment, played before an audience. To see how this can work let's look at a famous moment in *King Lear*. It is during the storm scene, when Lear resists the repeated requests of the disguised Kent to enter the hovel, and instead stays behind to speak a prayer for and to the houseless:

> Poor naked wretches, whereso'er you are,
> That bide the pelting of this pitiless storm,
> How shall your houseless heads and unfed sides,
> Your looped and windowed raggedness, defend you
> From seasons such as these? O, I have ta'en
> Too little care of this. Take physic, pomp,
> Expose thyself to feel what wretches feel,
> That thou mayst shake the superflux to them
> And show the heavens more just.
>
> (3.4.28–36)

The speech is often interpreted in terms of Lear's state of mind. So, these are his final sentiments before the entrance of Poor Tom and the unbridled onset of madness. As such they intimate the wisdom that his madness similarly if distractedly articulates, and work as a pledge to be taken up when his full mind returns. But as much as Lear is the first focus of attention, the intensive pathos of the speech in fact only partially arises from the speech's confessionary aspect ('O, I have ta'en/Too little care...). Instead, the effects come from the way the speech goes *outside* Lear for its substance, appeal, and referents. And these external things are the basic stuff of theatrical exchange: the present audience; other characters; self-embodying words.

The appeal to the audience is exemplified in Lear's phrase, 'whereso'er you are'. The 'you' he is addressing is supposedly the 'poor naked wretches', cowering in their holes or freezing under hedges: decidedly not the enfranchised clients of the theatre. But at the same time the audience – themselves out in the open air – is indeed directly appealed to by the speech's invitation to 'expose thyself'. This appeal is centred in the feminine openness of the phrase, 'whereso'er you are'. It is all vowel, almost all air (as the thrice-repeated 'air' sound reinforces). It is therefore multiply addressed: spoken directly to the audience, *and* to each member within it, *and* beyond their heads into some space of speculative possibility where they might conceivably find either themselves or a suffering compatriot. Lear is positing more than a brief episode of slumming it. He is praying for an exposure to feeling – both one's own and others'. The socio-political message – that we have all taken too little care of the suffering that we can safely ignore – is an instruction to look and listen more sensitively. We need to attend to whispers and murmurs, to that which is not staring us in the face.

In other words, as much as it is an appeal to repair 'houseless poverty' and share wealth around, it is equally a vindication of the urgency and relevance of theatre: and, more particularly, of theatre's mixture of inclusiveness and sudden, surprising, novel self-accountability. This accounts for the simple situational immediacy of 'expose thyself'. Lear is saying something like 'you here, now, *feel it*': but it is a message that needs theatre for its realisation. A lone reader is likely to be protected from such doubt or surprise. It needs the open air and at least the threat of bad weather; it needs the one in a thousand, and so the recognition that it may be but not must be 'me' that is addressed; it is being present in a body, with sore feet and cold hands, which enables the effect. Lear's call to attend is a call to look and listen: if we feel close to Lear here, it is because we are sharing in his own surprising exposure. Equally, if we get a fuller sense of the king's compassionate inwardness, it might be because we are filling it up with our own too-neglected capacity for such care: a profound recognition of oneself in others and others in oneself.

But here there is an imminent shift. For these naked wretches will very soon be the most immediate of physical presences. Within minutes the stage will be dominated by two of them, as the naked Poor Tom, cued by this speech, in turn cues Lear to take off his own 'lendings'. Here is the second way in which the speech typifies theatre's externalising methods of constructing feeling and inwardness: Lear's mindscape mutates from word into bodily form. Another character seems to owe his presence to Lear's conjuring. Whether or not Poor Tom has other reasons for being exactly here, exactly now, is to this extent irrelevant. For the play here 'gives birth' to Poor Tom as the embodiment of Lear's prayer, as the externalising of his thought, and as the necessary agent of his newly magnetised political and ethical imagination. Of course Edgar/Tom is more than this: but the 'character' of Lear, as embodied in this moment, is filled out partly through this transference from his speech to another's body.

Lear's prayer and Lear's character as embodied in it are given further dimensions by subdued puns. So, Lear's 'bide the pelting of this pitiless storm' contains at least two jokes: 'bide' means both endure and live within; 'pelting' means the hammering of the rain but also clothing (pelt). The joke is that the stinging rain is all the clothes those poor phantoms have. The 'pelting' is the suffering *and* the nakedness: they have to wear the storm; it becomes part of them, their 'pelt' being nakedness beneath all weathers. This in turn evokes the challenges of this storm: its invitation at once to undress and re-dress. The pun on 'pelting' allows the speech to escape from its material immediacies – getting drenched, feeling miserable, thinking about all the other poor sods suffering the same – and dimly promise some kind of safety and regeneration. If Lear intends the pun, he sees this; if he does not, it is still a promise that his 'character' will in due course grow into. As much as he is to be pitied, he is also for the first time taking up the challenge of care appropriate to a king, father, or companion. As with the co-presence of the audience and other characters in the speech, the puns add another plane, another dimension, to what we here understand as Lear. We might compare such effects to an atomic compound in which different particle bubbles weld to each other. Through such connections Lear's distinctive properties – what we take to be his inwardness – are finding composition.

It should be clear that we cannot account for how Shakespeare's characters work if we stick with an idea of clearly stratified, singular, psychologically coherent individuals. He sometimes writes characters like this: but it is often the case that a character that we are prone to recognise as being thus singular is *also* working in parallel networks that suggest a quite different construction of character. Shakespeare is always thinking in terms of echoes and shadows, of anti-types and doubles; he likes to mix in allegorical allusions with more naturalistic methods, natural with supernatural. He is always moving back and forth between individual and environment, making one the screen or projection of the other. All of this means that character might exist in a virtual space, or through almost telepathic connections that are no more – but no less – concrete than language.

## DISGUISE

Many of Shakespeare's plays involve characters in disguise. Usually a disguise is a way for that character to act out otherwise impossible things. The romantic heroines, for example, invariably dress up as young men and do what women normally cannot. Clearly such disguised agency can have all sorts of political implications. But so too can a disguise make it difficult to judge exactly where a particular character begins and ends. Is the disguise an expression of the person behind the mask? Or does the disguise develop its own distinct identity? Rosalind in *As You Like It*, for example, remains identifiably herself throughout her performance as Ganymede: we hear the same wit, the same preoccupations, the same confident asides to friend or audience. The disguise of Portia in *Merchant of Venice*, however, is perhaps less continuous with her undisguised persona. She prepares us for her role as a young lawyer by joking about how she will mimic a 'manly stride', tell 'puny lies', and practise 'a thousand raw tricks of these bragging Jacks' (3.4.63–77). But when she soon appears 'accoutered' like a man at Shylock and Antonio's trial, the simple gravity of the scene seems entirely to take over. Unlike Rosalind as Ganymede, there are no asides gesturing to her hidden identity. Indeed nothing in her trial script bears any relation to the boastful heartbreaker she prepares us to enjoy. Her role as Balthazar can of course be acted in a 'bragging' fashion; similarly it is possible that Portia/Balathazar's notoriously swift transition from talk of 'mercy' to insistence upon 'law' might be faithful to her declared intention to act in a wilfully whimsical manner ('tell quaint lies ... Which I denying ... then I'll repent'). But we can only find this residual playacting 'Portia' inside the lawyer at the expense of the trial scene's menace and pathos. Its urgency is ironised, its tension deflated: the scene turns into Portia's winking, cross-dressing tour de force. Clearly, we have to allow for a basic discontinuity here between the disguise and the disguised. This is not to say that Balthazar has 'his' own distinct inwardness or self-responsibility. But if Balthazar remains part of Portia, then this Portia is not adequately explained or controlled by the earlier one. Portia performs a function for the play: but a character's function may not always bear upon that character's 'interiority', or what we take to be that character's emotional or psychic infrastructure. Disguise can provide the permission for a character to more fully realise their possibilities, and more faithfully express their 'true selves'; equally, the simple usefulness of disguise (for plotting and comedy) can make it a challenge to the very idea of coherent individuality.

## EDGAR'S DISGUISES

Usually the fact of disguise is announced: but not always. Shakespeare's most extreme employer of disguise, Edgar in *King*

*Lear*, for instance, describes his first incarnation in baroque detail, but thereafter switches personae with bewildering and often unacknowledged swiftness. The effect is to unbalance the supposed hierarchy of character/disguise. The disguise can take over or become to all intents a separate character.

If Edgar's disguises are exceptionally substantial, it is partly because Edgar 'himself' is not. Indeed this is the premise of his entire role. So, Edgar's brother has framed him and his father wants him dead. Edgar is running for his life. But if this is the case in terms of plot, it is equally the case in terms of the type of character he is and the functions it has to perform. For when Edgar is 'himself', before becoming a fugitive, he is almost entirely without colour or substance. He is given no words at all to give him distinctiveness. The passage is instead into faintness and extinction: 'How now brother Edmund, what serious contemplation are you in?', 'Do you busy yourself with that?', 'Why, the night gone by', 'Ay, two hours together', 'None at all', 'Some villain hath done me wrong', 'Armed, brother?', 'Shall I hear from you anon? *Exit*' (1.3.138–75). Considering that Edgar's brother has just told him that his father wants him dead, the sheer absence in Edgar's response is almost lobotomal. The Folio gets rid of the only hint of a mind or irony ('How long have you been a sectary astronomical?'). This authorial cut is telling. Shakespeare is presenting Edgar as 'essentially' nothing ('Edgar I nothing am', 2.2.195). He will henceforth gain value principally by what happens to frame him: the accidents and people he meets, and the disguises he thereby happens upon.

Accordingly, the role has long been understood as allegorical, shadowing or counterpointing the travails of others. So, Poor Tom gives Lear a body and a script for his own suffering; or Edgar philosophises the implications of Lear's misery; or Edgar's fake madness sets off and highlights the reality of Lear's; or Edgar acts as both good and bad angel to his suicidal father, leading him to temptation and ministering to him in his abjection. More broadly, Edgar's disguises embody a wider world in misery, straddling histories, places, genres, and even species. Taken separately, each picture in the Edgar panorama is a single life: but cumulatively too they might picture a single life. The sum effect is of a modern everyman, collecting in miniature something close to the complete arc of existence.

His first disguise is also the most complete: Poor Tom. Edgar enters his disguise as a self-confessed 'nothing', and from this ground zero simulates almost a Darwinian ascent through biological and social possibility. Poor Tom himself pops out – as though half from the 'straw' (3.4.44) and half from the depths ('fathom and half: Poor Tom!' 3.4.37) – like a foetal amoeba. As he speaks he seems a beggar or madman, but this is merely the latest in a frenzy of incarnations. So, Poor Tom's autobiography rehearses the rites and temptations of any human soul, distilling tales of probation, perdition, or redemption ('Whom the foul fiend hath led through fire ... hath laid knives under his pillow...', 3.4.51–3). He immediately starts to narrate his own passage through existence, taking in pond life, the lower beasts, and gradations of service, courtliness, and vice. In some ways it resembles a microcosm of evolution: a rough passage through embryonic concealment (in the 'happy hollow' of the tree), newborn nakedness ('grumbling' in the 'straw', 3.4.43–4), childlike neediness ('Poor Tom's a-cold'), serviceable villainy (3.4.84–7), and various types of youthful waste and luxury ('Wine loved I deeply, dice dearly; and, in woman, out-paramoured the Turk', 3.4.89–91).

But it is nothing like as safe or ordered as the notion of a progress through social stages suggests. In this disguise, nothing is static, and least of all the mutating body. So, Edgar's ventriloquism produces a radically metamorphic body, one that takes into itself all that he describes: twigs, thorns, brambles, puddles, scum. At times it can seem like a process of demonic osmosis, as Poor Tom comes to absorb and reproduce his environment, even his diet: 'through fire and through flame, through ford and whirlpool, o'er bog and quagmire', 'Poor Tom, that eats the swimming frog, the toad, the tadpole, the wall-newt and the water –; that in the fury of his heart, when the foul fiend rages, eats cow-dung for salads; swallows the old rat and the ditch-dog; drinks the green mantle of the standing pool' (3.4.51–2, 126–31). Far more than any cosy exemplary progression, Poor Tom's body and biography represent a torturing, hurly-burly simultaneity: he has been everything, he has been anything, and he might be anything again at any moment.

Edgar's disguises are in part an extravagant example of how the body itself can be an overdetermined text. It is undeniable that Poor Tom's words are hard to absorb in one go, such is the torrent in which they fall: and of course Shakespeare knows it. This is why he concentrates into his physicality alone such layered and vehement articulacy. His words are packed with reference, but one of the prime effects is to anticipate, to pack in, a terrible significance in the visible physicality itself. It is the fact that we are seeing it, at times as though in a mime, which lends these scenes their rare power of allegory-driven pathos. So, Edgar describes scrupulously how he will make himself look (2.2. 175–95). We await this appearance, and when finally it happens ('Fathom and half, fathom and half: Poor Tom!', 3.4.37–8) the effect is like a rabbit in the headlights. Everything freezes for a split-second; all eyes stop upon the object; the storm scene's accelerating violence collects in a single image of its victim, both a moment before the crush and (as it were) in the fact of this crushing. Frozen in this way, the simple visual image – the disguise – gathers into itself a highly layered allegorical immediacy. The effect is to freeze Poor Tom in and as his pain and fear. It petrifies and magnifies the figure as an exemplary tableau. His mortified flesh declares something like a communal genealogy: the muddy past we thought we'd left behind, suddenly arisen from the swamps as the threatened new future.

Accordingly, we seem to catch Tom in the spokes of a purgatorial wheel. Tempted and chased by the 'fiend', forced to relive his past, he has to rehearse and purge its viciousness. However, when he repeats his necessary ethical lessons, we find him doing so at the behest of the devil: 'Take heed o'the foul fiend; obey thy parents, keep thy word justly, swear not...' (3.4.79–80). If the disguise (and the word is hopelessly inadequate for the persona's intensity) bears a moral message, it is definitively unfinished, its conclusions uncertain. As the breathless rhythms suggest, there is no relaxation from a spinning vortex of desire.

Most immediately, Poor Tom embodies sudden, almost vertiginous possibility. In this he is a perfect specimen of the larger play.

Poor Tom's accelerated CV then feeds into Edgar's larger role as it unfolds. Partly this is repetition, as his subsequent disguises embody a similar range of social potential; partly it is repair, as these disguises tentatively reclaim the prosperity lost by Tom. He begins as the madman leading the blind, but soon turns into a 'better spoken' guide (4.6.10), a moneyed friend (28–30), a 'bold peasant' (228), a gracious 'sir' (5.2), an avenging knight, a returned son and brother, an inheriting earl and, perhaps, the heir apparent (5.3). As with Poor Tom, the key to all of these incarnations is that they are both in the past *and* an immediately returnable possibility. Edgar's disguises, that is, embody the world that has been blown aside or forgotten by the violence at the centre. Each mutation represents something else that has been lost: but also something that necessarily if precariously survives (sometimes miserably, sometimes with stoic fortitude). In this, again, he embodies the play.

However, none of this is to say that Edgar only exists for others, or for allegorical purposes. We must never forget that 'he' is in there. His disguises do much of their work in relation to those who witness them: but one such witness is Edgar himself, and the suffering he simulates always bears some oblique relation to whatever Edgar might be. As he explains, 'While I may scape/I will preserve myself ... And with presented nakedness outface/The winds and persecutions of the sky' (2.2.179–86). It is a *'presented nakedness'*: at once self-consciously performed and astonishingly raw. Hence the pun, *'preserve* myself': it means both protect and remain. He will maintain his self in safekeeping: equally, every mutation of his disguise is this self in action. Disguise alone opens up for Edgar the possibility of discovering something more authentically and distinctively his own: as we have seen, he was never so anonymous as when 'himself', the noble, well-dressed imbecile. His disguises therefore propose a semi-identity, a kind of leasing of the self into alternative lines of becoming. Consequently, Edgar bears various simultaneous relations to his 'presented' performance: his disguises are the only self he has; they are a means of hiding from self-recognition; they are the whirlpool that allows Edgar, secreted in the centre, his saving self-collection and concentration; they are a masked projection of his hidden self, as in the multiple layers of pretence he gets revealed all the more starkly. His body becomes a rehearsal space and laboratory of both world *and* self. As theatre director Peter Brook says of the mask:

> This is the fundamental paradox that exists in all acting: that because you are in safety, you can go into danger. It is very strange, but all theatre is based on that. Because there is greater security, you can take greater risks; and because here it is *not* you, and therefore everything about you is hidden, you can let yourself appear.
>
> (Brook 1995, 231)

Accordingly, and allegories aside, we always know that at some level it is simply Edgar. This is so even with Poor Tom. We know that he has been surprised in his hiding place; that another accident has befallen him; and that he now has to confront his king and father in their appalling miseries. His amazing improvisations are a way of dealing with the surprises he suffers, giving him the physical freedom and mental space to do so. But the terrible intimacy of these surprises suggests that his improvisations will be moving ever closer to the self 'lurking' inside them (3.6.113). Indeed the word 'disguise' barely does justice to the defining power of identity games – hide and seek and dressing-up – in Edgar's role. For even the apparently momentary and arbitrary ones (e.g. the Mummerset peasant in 4.6) can seem chosen to perform Edgar's most fiercely private, long-brewed necessities: Edgar's killing of Oswald seems all the more his own sweetly displaced revenge – and all the more brutal – for being couched in such pseudo-homely yokelisms ('Ch'ill pick your teeth, zir. Come, no matter vor your foins', 4.6.240).

Like many of Edgar's disguises, the details here cannot really be explained by the situation; as so often, the performance is in excess of the need. One consequence of this is that the disguises develop their own separate identity; another is that they work as allegories (here of a bluff provincial world, continuing his microcosmic panorama). But this excessiveness also suggests a tremendous neediness and loneliness: a sense of violent self-suppression, a life barely lived, producing these vast fictions that in protecting Edgar from discovery allow him his furtive agency. This explains the temptation to speculate about links between Edgar's visible role play and his hidden mind. How far we take such speculation probably depends upon how much we require a basically good, ethically transparent Edgar. To trace Edgar in his disguises – often a furious labyrinth of revenge and punishment, desire and recoil – is quickly to muddy such clarity; equally, it is to make him a far more interesting and indeed human character.

In a tragedy as raw as *Lear*, disguise necessarily resists attempts to explain it away, for instance as a generic trope, practical exigency, or social custom. The case of Edgar is quite different, say, from the masks worn at the ball in *Much Ado*: these allow for certain home truths to be spoken by Beatrice to Benedick, but as much as the disguise is a channel into candour, it also protects the situation from too much nakedness. In line with the comic genre, pretty much everyone can be excused their rudeness, folly, or even cruelty. In such a world, disguise works as a microcosm, almost a metaphor, of the comedy: a screen allowing for redeemable mistakes. The disguises of Edgar are no less conditioned by their context. But what this means is that there is precisely no escape hatch, no undressing from the possibilities therein embodied. Indeed, Edgar's trail of glimpsed lives might almost have emerged out of Lear's prayer in the storm for world destruction:

> Strike flat the thick rotundity o'the world,
> Crack nature's moulds, all germens spill at once
> That make ingrateful man!
>
> (3.2.7–9)

Lear wants it all to end, but instead the seeds ('germens') 'spill' out with newly chaotic fertility. Poor Tom is as though the first such seed, as the Edgar role cracks open one after another instance of surviving 'man'. Life goes on, in all sorts of tiny ways, even in the midst of catastrophe. Of course, this need not represent a particularly cheering message, any more than Edgar's larger survival at the end of the play represents a personal triumph. But what we need to see is that his disguises are no kind of improvised sideshow: they give to his role whatever substance it has.

If Edgar's disguises retain anything of social custom about them, then it is mainly to the extent that identity is radically uncertain, that it is only ever possessed precariously, and that too naked a 'presented' face (like Kent's or Cordelia's) is a profoundly dangerous and challenging thing. A screened face is not only politic, but also somehow necessary for sustainable community. The nakedness of Lear and Edgar, like the blind despair of Gloucester, has a terrifying sort of authenticity. But it is hardly a safe basis upon which to rebuild a society. Consequently, we might see his disguise's movement up the social scale as expressing just such prudence. It is as though nakedness is too frightening, too revealing. Edgar has to hide from what it shows himself as much as conceal what it shows others. Hence the way he gradually channels his primal wildness – as the betrayed brother and abandoned child – into disguises he can live with. At the same time as his disguises become more respectable – progressing as we have seen from birth, to beggary, to nobility – so too does their relationship to the concealed Edgar within them. Whereas the mania of Poor Tom suggests an inward labyrinth of sin, fury, and vengefulness (the 'foul fiend' merging into his father at 3.4.112–13), the later incarnations gradually normalise any hidden motives by dressing them up in much more generically appropriate ways: preacher to the despairing, true knight against false knight.

However, this doesn't mean that the play – as distinct from Edgar – trusts the later disguises more than the early ones. Edgar's hunger to escape compromising affiliations, his longing to cling on to some ethical clarity, is never quite shared by the play. Consider the way his attempts at philosophical rationalisation are repeatedly embarrassed by the sudden violence of experience (his father being led in blind, 4.1.1–13), or by their own deeply troubling complicities (identifying his father's blinding as the gods' justice and so Regan and Cornwall as divine agents, 5.3.168–71). Ultimately, Edgar as stoic philosopher or proto-Christian preacher is no less a disguise – improvising in the interests of sanity and survival – than any of his other mutations. Similarly, if his final survival embodies a tenuously restored order, then the possibilities this predicts have to be drawn from whatever Edgar's disguises have already traced.

Disguise here is always a whirligig of interpretive options. The disguise can be an indirect but basically sincere expression of (part of) the disguiser; the disguise itself can be the main thing at issue, peeling off into existential independence; or the significance of the disguise can be working in-between pretence and pretender: in the energies that generate the particular disguise, or in the energies produced by the connection. The example of Edgar reveals disguise to be no less a thing of process, and potentially no less internally variable and situationally dialectical, than any other of Shakespeare's dramatic languages.

## DOUBLES

Shakespeare loves antitheses and correspondences, identities that turn into oppositions or oppositions into identities: and nowhere more so than in his doubling or mirroring characterisations. There are basically two types of doubling. The first is when two or more actors play distinct parts which develop a mirroring relation with each other; the second is when the same actor plays more than one part. This second kind of doubling was a common recourse of any acting company, faced with enormous cast lists and necessary limitations upon budget and personnel. Particularly amongst lesser parts, doubling was routine. Doubled parts usually operated along the line of a particular 'type', and were almost always visible. It is difficult to hide the fact that the same man is playing here a young courtier and there a silly clown, or at one moment a vicious harridan and the next a bishop. A beard might be added or removed, a doublet altered, but the face and body and even the voice remain. The thing to recognise is that doubling becomes open to all kinds of archly posed speculations. Hence the ease with which doubles work as mirrors or shadows of one another, or provide a bridge between two strands of a double plot. Examples commonly exploited in productions include the Fool and Cordelia in *Lear*, and Oberon and Theseus in *Midsummer Night's Dream*.

At times this sort of doubling can work like an extension of disguise. (Indeed when an audience identifies a case of doubling they always have to make sure that it is not rather an instance of disguise.) Disguise and doubling can find common ground in being attributable to a single psyche: but a psyche that is under strain, or not fully visible to itself. Doubling becomes an economical technique for representing the layered or repressed self, or the subject with split levels of consciousness and unconsciousness.

Shakespeare builds a play around such a transparent doubling of parts by a single actor: the late romance, *Cymbeline*. The 'hero' Posthumus and 'villain' Cloten never appear in the same scene, but they are constantly going through identical motions. The founding similarity is in their competitive desire for the princess Imogen. Both idolise her; both want to marry her (Posthumus already has); both in due course become jealously and vengefully rapacious (2.3.156; 2.4.153–186; 3.5.131–47). We hear of duels between them when one body seems to invade or merge into the other (1.3); Posthumus's 'mean'st Garment' gets stolen by Cloten, and comes to symbolise the pair's transposable identity, as they likewise emerge as little more than mannequins of masculine obtuseness. Cloten assesses their 'single oppositions' in a mirror against the mental image of his rival (4.1), insults Posthumus as a 'squire's cloth' (2.3.123), obliviously punning upon his own name, and finally seeks to rape Imogen, dressed in his rival's suit, with his dead double serving as pillow. All of this is leading to the climactic moment (4.2.296–332) in which Imogen weeps over the wrong corpse: she thinks the decapitated trunk is her husband; we know it is Cloten, murdered on his path to raping her. So, Cloten acts out Posthumus's fantasy, and then suffers his punishment for him. The doubling helps clear the path (albeit savagely and ambivalently) for romance's programmed reconciliation: the same actor, different parts, but more profoundly facets of a single masculine consciousness. The technique of doubling is here bearing an awful strain.

Almost every play is structured around echoing circumstances, whereby two or more figures face similar provocations, trials, or temptations. For example, the killed fathers that link Hamlet, Fortinbras, and Laertes; the 'discovery' of the islander Caliban that unites as potential colonisers the drunken butler Stephano and the exiled duke Prospero (*The Tempest*); the perceptually blind Lear and the physically blind Gloucester in *Lear*; the rival lovers Proteus and Valentine in *Two Gentleman of Verona*; the Duke and his proxy Angelo in *Measure for Measure*; the rival 'sons' Hal and Hotspur in *1 Henry IV* (there are many more). Often each 'double' will both accumulate their own distinct identity while also working toward a virtual or corporate body that the relationship between them produces. So, the warring knights Hal and Hotspur, or the figures of justice Duke Vicentio and Angelo, provoke through their own individual inadequacies an idea of a desirable third figure. This figure will have something of the force or wistfulness of allegory, its function being critical, prophetic, or repairing.

Often it will be the case that a play's train of mirrors or substitutes emerge from and return to a central figure. This is particularly true of the big tragedies: *Hamlet, Othello, Lear,* and *Macbeth* all work partly through such patterns. In the comedies (or comi-histories like *1 & 2 Henry IV*) the patterns of correspondence are perhaps still more structurally governing, but not in a fashion that works toward filling out a single character's elevation. Instead, we get things like the doubled twins of *Comedy of Errors*, the worlds within worlds of *Midsummer Night's Dream*, the competing capitalists in *Merchant of Venice*, or the rival 'commonwealths' in *Henry IV*.

We might compare the similar techniques here of *Lear* and *Pericles*. Both plays present a number of different characters whose experiences resemble one another's. In *Lear* we get a roughly similar passage through loss, exile, suffering, and tenuous repossession endured by Cordelia, Kent, Edgar, Lear, Gloucester (and in some ways the Fool). The mirroring architecture both multiplies and magnifies the suffering. The mirrors are always a co-presence: in particular, we are never invited to lose sight of the king's suffering as we witness that of any of his subjects. The effect is at once socially panoramic and emotionally intensifying.

In *Pericles*, by way of contrast, the technique is one of substitution. In line with the comic-pastoral genre, we are released from any harrowing contemplation upon one figure's affliction by the repeated shift to a new object. One 'ruler' after another appears – Antiochus, Pericles, Creon, Cerimon, Simonides, the Bawd, Lysimachus – and repeats his predecessor's tropes or traumas. The same thing happens with the servants of this government – Helicanus, Leonine, Lychorida, Pandar, and Boult. A further line of recapitulation joins together the recipients of such government: Pericles (as suitor), Thaisa, and Marina. The mirroring is consecutive, like a stately dance in which temptation takes its turn with one then another courtier. *Pericles* is thus interestingly in-between the tragic and comic models – as befits the hybrid genre that the play is helping to develop. So, the doubling works in a broadly comic fashion. One scene subverts or shadows another, placing each local instance against its neighbour, lightening or darkening by turns, and building a cumulative civic portrait. But unlike the earlier comedies or histories, this method of scenic relief and cross-parody is also filling in for otherwise absent psychology. So, in bloc-by-bloc fashion it is building up, or rehearsing the possibilities for, the play's missing hero. In this way, romance allegory recovers something like the magnetic centrality of the tragic protagonist.

Accordingly, the whole play can be understood as the portrait of a single figure's fracturing. Pericles is never again as whole as in the first scene when, faced with the murderous riddle, he has to run away from full revelation. His eventual withdrawal into glum silence is already presaged in this early failure to be a conquering knight: as he says of his decision not to confront the incestuous Antiochus with the book of his crimes, 'He's more secure to keep it shut then shown' (1.1.96). But the play, as distinct from its hero, is not content with abdicating such things. So, Pericles' story is premised upon a style of self-departure or self-unravelling. In running away he becomes as though self-separated. This is the context for his various postures of withdrawal – his self-portrait to the fishers ('What I have been, I have forgot to know', 2.1.70); his scruffiness at Simonides' court (2.3); his divesting himself of one grown-up responsibility after another; his epically unkempt muteness. But it is equally the context for the way other characters bring to mind the absent protagonist. A typical example is Lysimachus' lecherous exclamation upon first seeing Pericles' daughter, Marina, in the brothel: 'Faith, she would serve after a long voyage at sea' (4.6.42–3). But it is Pericles who has been at sea, and Pericles who has been haunted throughout by fear of incest. We can push hard at these moments or not: we can see them as deep-hewn keys to the play's psychological structures, or as jokes about temptations *not* shared by the hero. But either way it is clear that the conflicts that move Pericles are as fully present in his absence and in his substitutes as in the things he actually says or does.

Accordingly, Pericles' misery is a civic, corporate thing as much as a personal feeling: and it demands representation. Hence his numerous surrogates. His silence requires the speech of others; his physical disappearance or inhospitality requires the physical presence of others. So, he spends years at sea in fear for his life, or in mourning for his wife, or plunges into incommunicado when he hears of his daughter's death. In each case we both allow him his grief *and* attend to the bodies that fill his lack. If Pericles has any kind of inwardness and self-responsibility, then it is provided by such techniques. The words and the bodies of his proxies supply his absences or ellipses. Others do his work for him (as father, ruler, lover, murderer, and so on). These diffused, fragmented functions patch together the diffuse and fragmented 'hero' into some kind of unified fabric. That is, he is a multiply augmented cipher, constructed not through 'vertically' revealing speech-acts but through horizontally accumulating scenes. It is only through his doubles that Pericles is any kind of 'character' in the modern sense of inwardness and dimensionality. Without them, he is a character only in the earlier sense of a single-branded type.

## SCENICALLY CONSTRUCTED DOUBLES AND TRAGIC EFFECT

Let's close this chapter by looking at a scene that shows how doubling can contribute to the fullest range of emotional and ethical affects. As we have seen, a doubling relationship can work to reconfigure the character on both sides of the mirror. It also produces a third thing in the mind of the reader or spectator, an idea of experience that owes debts to both sides but is fully possessed by neither. Doubling, that is, is always capable of pushing what we take as fact into new territory. It can make the boundaries between things uncertain; it can give to observable bodies a certain charge of transformation, of possibility, of exceeding apparent limits. In no sense need doubling leave behind basic emotional empathies, which continue to be overwhelmingly centred upon individual characters. But what it helps to do is exploit the potential of such empathy to be ethically or politically challenging: to surprise us in our pleasures; perhaps to implicate us in any hall of mirrors that we find. Doubling reinforces the fact that we cannot simply presuppose the freestanding existence of the figures on stage. They are not given, or static, or impenetrably separate from possession or invasion. To situate a character in a network of doubles or shadows is, in some very basic way, to render uncertain their grounds of being and identity. It is a powerful technique for representing the simple peril of existing. No character is a self-secure island. In a doubled world, our most grounded certainties – that I am who I am, that he is not me, that my life (or my death) is mine alone – become deeply vulnerable.

Let us therefore look at a disturbing scene from *Macbeth* in which the 'hero' Macduff is drawn disturbingly close to the 'anti-hero' Macbeth. This shadowing is brought to a head in one particularly chilling moment: Macduff's son has just been stabbed to death, his wife exits running for her life and screaming 'Murther!' Then Macduff himself, far away in England, unaware of his family's slaughter, enters with Malcolm to bemoan the misery in Scotland:

MALCOLM   Let us seek out some desolate shade, and there
    Weep our sad bosoms empty.
MACDUFF                  Let us rather
    Hold fast the mortal sword, and like good men
    Bestride our downfall birthdom. Each new morn,
    New widows howl, new orphans cry; new sorrows

> Strike heaven on the face, that it resounds
> As if it felt with Scotland, and yell'd out
> Like syllable of dolour.

(4.3.1–8)

Macduff offers here a striking image of universal suffering. The howl of orphans and widows echoes to heaven; heaven takes these cries as a blow to its own face, a sacrilege redoubling both the cause and the clamour of woe. Everything here is echoing and rebounding, an aural entrapment representing the claustrophobia of living beneath tyranny. But if the basic energy here is one of ricochet – of suffering and of voice – then Macduff himself is caught up in it. This is so in the obvious sense that his speech is itself offering 'syllable[s] of dolour'. But it is also so in a more insidious way. For Macduff here talks of how 'Scotland' is feeling, or of heaven feeling 'with Scotland'. But he is not in Scotland; he is hundreds of miles from home, explicitly not sharing in the devastating grief that we have just witnessed.

Shakespeare here sets up a savage irony. Macduff has abandoned his wife and children to their fate; Lady Macduff explicitly blames him for this ('to leave his wife, to leave his babes ... All is the fear, and nothing is the love', 4.2.6–12). In some sense they are exactly *now* being murdered, in that his frantic wife runs off stage to die just as her husband enters. How then should we take Macduff's words of brave patriotic compassion? At the very least, our response might be divided. He is ignorant of his family's destruction, and in this begs our pity; but this ignorance is his doing, the proof of his fault, and so less an invitation to sympathy than to sarcastic contempt. The scenic juxtaposition pre-emptively ironises Macduff's words. It opens his words up to radically discrepant perspectives. While he thinks he is talking about one thing – the general fate of his land – we apply it to another thing – the specific fate of his family. In other words, the whole speech is a kind of subdued pun, made so less by riddling language than by unequal measures of knowledge.

These very immediate framing ironies can draw us into searching out more explicitly punning language to feed off them. So, Macduff thinks he is talking about the death of men, of husbands and fathers murdered by tyranny; and of course he is. But in abandoning his family he has himself created a 'new' widow and 'new' orphans. This multiplies the speech's referents: the 'cry' is that of children both orphaned and murdered; the 'howl' that of wives both mourning and murdered. It becomes, thereby, less a report of grief than a cry of anticipatory guilt. Furthermore, although the 'downfall birthdom' is most obviously his suffering nation, it evokes various other things: spelt 'birth-*dome*' in the Folio, it suggests the darkening vault of the sky, and perhaps 'domesday' or doomsday. Here we might identify further connotations. Birth and doom are conflated; the beginning of time meets the end. His fantasy of repossession of his birthplace (Scotland) is also a fantasy about repossessing the terms of *his* birth. The 'downfall birthdom' therefore also describes the birth dome, or the rounded belly containing the growing child. Scotland merges imaginatively into Macduff's mother.

Accordingly, Macduff's picture of suffering Scotland can also evoke the simple facts of birth. The 'howl' may always attend childbirth, but it might more specifically evoke the final 'syllable of dolour' of the mother killed in the act: the 'cry' then becomes that of the newborn 'orphan'. Instead of childlike innocence, the baby invokes embeddedness in violence. Like Macbeth's earlier vision of 'Pity, like a naked new-born babe,/Striding the blast' and blowing the 'horrid deed in every eye' (1.7.21–2, 24), Macduff's 'orphan' owns a preternatural knowledge of atrocity. Later in the play we learn that Macduff's mother died in childbirth ('Macduff was from his mother's womb/Untimely ripp'd' (5.8.15–16). His life was only guaranteed by the 'mortal sword' of a doctor or midwife who cut open his mother and 'ripp'd' out the crying child.

If there were not this sense that Macduff's present avowals are shadowed by dark murmurings from the past, there would be no problem. He could be the simple saviour of all mothers and children. As it is, however, the half-buried allusions to his own birth make it possible to interpret Macduff's resolve in various ways. In wanting to 'Hold fast the mortal sword' and 'bestride our downfall birthdom', he might be assuming the place of the obstetrician. Macduff imagines delivering himself, or perhaps facilitating his own rebirth. Alternatively, it might be a form of vengeful infantilism, as though the only 'orphan' he is concerned with is himself: the grown man-child is now returning to the place that almost killed him. We may then hear in his martial rhetoric a 'phallocentric' male fantasy. Embodying mind and *virtu* in a single sword, honing the body into a weapon, his bravery is irredeemably phallic. There is a will here to be pure male. Macduff would dispel the androgyny of tears, shed any compromise with a body that encompasses or nurtures, and seize possession of the faculty of birth.

We might seem here to have shifted far away from any overt intent on the part of the speaker, down into the perilous territory of the unconscious; but we should also see that it is exactly such subterranean motive-forces that are the subject of the play. For if we seek to locate Macduff's 'character' in his speech-act, then it is clear that we simultaneously have to travel into acts and moments well beyond it. Shakespeare is absolutely orchestrating a scene in which echoes, murmurs, and under-voices, some of them slow and rumbling, some of whiplash violence, are at once the overriding context and the impelling energy. After all, if a particular speaker's conscious public knowledge were the principal measure of meaning, the scene would not be framed as cruelly and starkly as it is. And crucial here are the porous boundaries between one self and another. So: Macduff the man merges into Macduff the baby; Macduff the son becomes Macduff the mother; Macduff the deliverer evokes Macduff the life-denier; Macduff the innocent shadows Macbeth the guilty. The basic principle is one of connection and conflation across and between times, agents, and functions: it applies as much to the play's scenic, linguistic, and characterising techniques as it does to the play's men, ideas, and actions. All are connecting, all conflating. So, in returning with such fiercely welding imagination to a birthplace that has become a grave, Macduff both prepares for and shadows a similar speech moments later:

> Alas, poor country!
> Almost afraid to know itself. It cannot
> Be call'd our mother, but our grave; where nothing,

> But who knows nothing, is once seen to smile;
> Where sighs, and groans, and shrieks that rent the air
> Are made, not mark'd; where violent sorrow seems
> A modern ecstasy...

(4.3.164–70)

Rosse's speech recalls Macduff's similar picture of Scotland. But he takes things considerably further. Macduff's report of 'dolour' assumes an intact moral order, albeit under scandalous assault. In Macduff's account, the heavens are at one with the virtuous and the suffering; the present atrocities mainly accentuate the ethical division between good and evil. Rosse reports a much more troubling world. The shrieks and groans of suffering are so much the 'modern' soundtrack as to be a null backdrop to defeat. No one else's sorrow is 'mark'd', suggesting a world closed off to anyone's pain but one's own. But then the pain is also unanimous and de-individuating: 'violent sorrow seems/A modern ecstasy' evokes an El Greco-like tableau of fractured minds and morbid frenzy. The citizenry of Scotland, frozen in some crippling new dispensation, are astonished or catatonic sacrifices to violence. The hardy sense of order to which Macduff holds fast is simply gone. Instead, oppositions collapse into indistinction: order is inverted; a birthplace is a grave; language addresses no one; self-knowledge has become self-fear; identity is dissolution and alienation. Understood in these terms, we might see that Rosse describes the authentic world of *Macbeth*: this really is the dying days of a country gone to the dogs.

Equally, Rosse effectively describes the chief agent of such carnage: it is Macbeth who fiercely internalises all of this 'modern ecstasy'. But what about Macduff? Why does his report so differ from Rosse's? What *isn't* he seeing? What is he trying to hide, or to hide from? Why does he evoke a slaughtered mother and grave-like womb only through self-averting puns? Of course, we might answer some of this simply enough by appealing to gaps in time: Macduff has been away from Scotland, and reports what he saw when he was there; Rosse fills in the latest appalling news. But if indeed something has changed, or has triggered this absolute capitulation, then it is at the very least 'symbolised' by the slaughter of Macduff's family. Again, Macduff is somehow responsible for all that Rosse reports: he shadows Macbeth in culpability, and perhaps also in internalising a country 'almost afraid to know itself'.

Shakespeare is here setting up his two main characters as both mirror opposites and mirror images. For the suggestion carried by the language is that Macduff is some sort of double of or surrogate for Macbeth. They shadow one another, as act and idea. Each can be the other's cause or consequence; each can supply the other's past or future. Hence the fact that Macduff suffers precisely those losses that seem to so haunt Macbeth: most particularly the lost or absent children. This sharing of experience helps explain the ambiguity of Macduff's words after absorbing the news of his family's destruction: 'He has no children' (4.3.216). It is impossible to determine whether 'he' refers to Macbeth (or else how could he have done it?) or to Malcolm (or else how could he so blithely believe that 'great revenge' might ever 'cure this deadly grief'? 4.3.214–15), or even in stupefied fashion to Macduff himself (he frequently adopts the third person, as in 'Sinful Macduff!/They were all struck for thee', 'Macduff was from his mother's womb untimely ripped') 'He' is each and all, and the childlessness a shared inheritance of callow insufficiency.

Macduff is Macbeth's partner in more than vicarious or proxied slaughter. Like Macbeth, he traverses the boundaries of temptation and resolve. Both suffer doubt, nihilism, childlessness, self-alienation; each must prove and recover, or dare and lose, whatever 'man' he might be. To some extent the characters are each other's hinterland, filling in one another's context, consequence, or alternative lifelines. All of this draws Macduff – Macbeth's nemesis – uncannily close to Macbeth – as though the tyrant is *his* nemesis. We have seen how in abandoning his family Macduff in some awful sense becomes despotism's agent. For Macbeth too patriotic violence may be a screen for more primal fantasies of vengeance and repossession (in the report of the play's opening duel Macbeth's 'brandished steel' unseams Macdonwald 'from the nave to th'chops', an image often understood as one of bloody Caesarean section). The play is harping upon a particular type of sexual and familial lack, of which politics is more an effect than a cause. It is exploring the profoundest sources of masculine self-identity: the fears that underlie love, and the envy and violence, sublimated or not, that attends its expression. These great antagonists here play (or are played by) the same vibrating string.

Of course Macduff is not the only character to fulfil some such function in relation to Macbeth. So, he works similarly to Banquo, a character that is more notoriously a pale shadow of Macbeth. We might intermittently identify with Macduff or Banquo, and allow them to speak for our better natures. But the fit is never comfortable for long. Partly this is because Macbeth blasts them aside, or makes these characters so in debt to him that they are diminished. But it is also because they are not gifted with the candour of either humour or confession. Their speech is always in some way tucked away from easy access or sharing. We have seen how Macduff's speeches are full of secrets or evasions, and how both his wife and confederates struggle to penetrate his motives. Banquo is still more removed from clear knowledge. His only soliloquy meticulously balances suspicion of Macbeth's guilt and furtive hopes for his own consequent success. It then ends abruptly with 'But, hush; no more' (3.1.10) – an apt account of the silence into which he now descends.

In each case Shakespeare's characterisation is marked by taciturnity and diffidence, by a withholding of vigorous colour. This allows the characters' passivity to trace the more animated guilt of Macbeth. In the chronicle sources Banquo is straight-forwardly complicit with Macbeth in the regicide: Shakespeare's obscuring of this guilt is usually explained in terms of flattery to Banquo's ancestor, King James, patron of the King's Men. This may or may not have been a motive: more important here is the effect this has in terms of the distribution of ethical responsibility. In place of outright complicity, Banquo is represented as a shifty temporiser; his 'active inaction' is a perfect echo of Macbeth's wistful hope that 'chance' might see him crowned. Macduff meanwhile is at one with Macbeth in sublimating his guilt, or his failure as father and husband, into violence. Both 'goodies' thus do – or fail to do – just enough to leak out a sort of gas of guilt. They each belong surely enough in the play's 'filthy air'. It is a huge clue to the insidious, haunting reach of this play. No audience can avoid compromising affiliations. So, to find a mirror in Macbeth may be to see to the 'crack of doom'. But then to take refuge in another – Macduff, Banquo, indeed the shifty and oddly self-absent Malcolm – is to come upon someone who himself may merely be taking refuge. Ethical punch here lurks in the shadows.

These structures of correspondence and antithesis encapsulate the play's subject matter and methods: ethical equivocation; the unsettling of safe existential ground; the difficulty of interpretive closure. Such techniques of sharing, shadowing, or doubling serve the play's most basic tragic functions. For they do much of the work upon *our* emotional and ethical responses. In the simplest terms, it makes the anti-hero less anti and the saviours less safe. If we see on stage a surreptitious web of collusion and complicity, then we might see the same web of possibilities in our own responsive accounting. Shakespeare almost always works like this, surprising or seducing us out of easy detachments; this is particularly on show in *Macbeth*'s astonishing powers of ethical insinuation. The play makes us lean into, almost require, the most heinous acts and barefaced rationalisations. And what we should here recognise is the fundamental role of meticulously plotted technique in constructing character, and thereby harnessing our emotional and ethical responses: multiform figurative language, scenic juxtapositions, and characterological doubling. This sort of structuring machinery is always in motion: it is never a static infrastructure into which 'meaning' is poured. Exactly the same is true of character.

# 10

# IS DIRECT SELF-EXPRESSION POSSIBLE? THE SOLILOQUY

*This chapter explores the claims and possibilities of the soliloquy. Conventionally the soliloquy is seen as a device of truth-telling, when a character speaks directly to the audience about their thoughts or plans. In this way the soliloquy is identified with transparent self-expression. This chapter questions what kind of expression a soliloquy involves, and what kind of selves might thereby be represented. The first part of the chapter considers the different ways in which a soliloquy might address an audience, and therefore the different sorts of communication it might involve. How much is its form tied to rhetorical or other convention? How much is it a uniquely private confession? Is it an act of public address or private meditation? Are we being directly appealed to or are we overhearing a silent process of thinking? What difference do such things make to questions of the audience's engagement or complicity? And who exactly is the 'I' speaking in a soliloquy? Is it necessarily a self-consistent subject? The rest of the chapter explores these and other questions through the close analysis of certain parts of four famous soliloquies. Gloucester's opening speech in* Richard III – *concentrating upon the connection between rhetorical self-control and the speaker's state of mind; Hal's first soliloquy in* 1 Henry IV – *asking who exactly is addressed, and whether the speaker is identical to the self he talks about in the speech; Hamlet's 'to be or not to be' speech – exploring who we think the speaker thinks he is speaking to; and Brutus's meditation about whether to kill Caesar in* Julius Caesar – *analysing the movement between internal meditation and public speaking. Ultimately we see that soliloquy is as much a thing of drama and dialogue as any other speech-act. The task is to identify how it works as part of a moving dynamic.*

If so much that is vital about characters is mediated through more or less indirect techniques – absences, puns, doubles, metaphors – then what does this imply about supposedly more direct techniques? What about soliloquy, for instance, as a privileged medium of confidence and inward truth? For there is something uniquely self-confident – and self-confiding – about the basic premise of soliloquy: it purports to stop the clock on the play, stand outside of the action, and carve out a space and time all of its own. In this it presumes a kind of safety hatch, a location of truth and identity that subsists whatever the play elsewhere represents. This connects to its summative functions, drawing together bits and pieces, presenting a coherent account of motive and direction. It becomes almost a resting place, a brief respite from action that refreshes and clarifies. The overriding assumption is that there is an agreed place of shared understanding between audience and character. The candour of soliloquies is one that tacitly encourages us simply to relax and *believe*. This makes the soliloquist the closest thing the drama has to a narrator (especially if we include the rare 'prologues' and 'rumours' whose 'soliloquies' begin some plays). It also makes it – as conventionally understood – the most transparent location of self-present character.

The first recorded use of the term 'soliloquy' – from *solus* (alone) and *loqui* (to speak) – is by St Augustine in the fourth century. This is apt, in that Augustine is the author of the ancient world's most influential autobiography, his *Confessions*. Soliloquy is the act of conversing with oneself. Of course the word is not really coined to describe the mundane occurrence of talking aloud to oneself. A soliloquy's form is not at all random or accidental; it will rarely be rambling, circular, repetitive or banal. As its source in Augustine will suggest, soliloquy is something more measured and perhaps more mannered. For it is at its very roots a rhetorical activity. That is, rather than being a privately enclosed meditation, the soliloquy appeals to an audience.

The spoken or written form of a soliloquy will often conform to the standard formats of public discourse. We shouldn't expect it to be any kind of spontaneous outburst or naked record of emotions. It is likely to be organised by an armoury of rhetorical techniques designed to make a speech moving, exciting, or believable. Learnt thoroughly in Elizabethan schools, these techniques take effect at all levels of the speech: the individual image or clause, the sentence, the argumentative theses and antitheses, indeed its whole persuasive rhythm and momentum. These almost inevitable debts to rhetorical training may in turn be joined by other borrowings. A soliloquy might draw upon the conventions of lyric poetry, or upon the stock manners of plays, whether ancient, medieval, or contemporary. Alternatively, the soliloquy might borrow its forms from preaching, or from the rituals of the confession box. Or again, as we shall see, the single voice of the soliloquy might combine in self-arguing form two voices or attitudes that are traditionally identified with distinct characters: the good and bad angels of morality plays, for example. There are then lots of ways in which the particular form of the soliloquy might be sourced.

However, we might want here to question how far we can take this line of argument. After all, isn't it the case that, however much the bits and pieces inside a soliloquy might be influenced by prevailing cultural forms or rhetorical discourses, we still accept the soliloquy as a unique channel into something private and even secret? Indeed, isn't it the case that the basic convention of soliloquy is that there should be – again uniquely – no audience at all? Of course, we are listening in, and in some unavoidable sense there must always be an audience (or readership). But what we are listening in upon is not speech, but rather silence; it is not speaking out loud that we hear, but rather a character's thoughts. Hence the convention we often see in filmed Shakespeare, where the soliloquy is presented as a voice-over, the 'heard thoughts' of a non-speaking character.

Consequently, we need to consider the possibility of a soliloquy that does *not* solicit the audience. There will be gradations of this. Some will simply bear no direct appeal, but depend for their *raison d'etre* upon an assenting public ear. But what if the audience feels that they are not *supposed* to be listening? That the speaking is in some special way private? Macbeth, for instance, speaks in something akin to soliloquy when he is alone on stage: but equally he does so when he is accompanied by others, when it is unclear from the script whether he is alone or not, and indeed, when he is speaking directly to other characters but his speeches at the same time bear a relation to himself that only he can possibly recognise. We may be present only as a shadowy haunter of the speaker's self-meditation – as though tacitly embodying the concentrated self-attention of the speaker.

So, we always have to think carefully about what kind of appeal, if any, a soliloquy makes to an audience. This will often be measured by how overt or otherwise are the soliloquy's borrowings from public rhetoric. If the rhythms and methods of argument seem to be drawn very frankly from the handbook of persuasive oratory, then it will be clear that the audience is in some sense being asked to listen in, or to agree. This in turn can prompt the recognition in the same audience that the soliloquist is being 'political': that we are not listening in on somebody's innermost thoughts, but that we are instead being spoken to as part of a public act. Perhaps we are being spoken to simply as an audience at a play; perhaps we are being spoken to as a potential franchise, or potential supporters, or as a sounding board for possible options. A classic example of this is Hamlet's soliloquy, 'How all occasions do inform against me' (4.4.32–66): for instance the line 'Witness this army of such mass and charge' (47), which gives a clear direction to the audience, enacting an explicit sharing between soliloquist and addressed auditors. Either way, if the soliloquy directly appeals to the audience, then it is much more likely that we are thereby being framed as citizens with an implicitly political cachet, or as peers with a choice to approve or not. The speaker tells *us* something, and by including us our response becomes part of the soliloquy's meaning.

In such cases, the soliloquy will usually represent a moment of theatrical directness and emotional clarity. It will declare the speaker as either 'good' or 'bad', as more or less charismatic or sympathetic. It thereby organises the responses – fear, desire, sympathy, horror, complicity – that give a story its emotional magnetism. The simple audaciousness of a player stepping half-outside the fiction, half-undressing the naturalistic façade, is the most elegant means of drawing an audience closer. Such access is always a privilege: but its implications may be troubling. The whole transaction is insinuating: we can be drawn into complicity in crime (Iago in *Othello*, Cloten in *Cymbeline*), or collusion in voyeurism (Thersites in *Troilus*, Iachimo in *Cymbeline*), or seduced into ethical by-pass (Falstaff in *Henry IV*, Edmund in *Lear*). Alternatively, the intimacy might draw us into surprising resistance to established authority (Caliban in *The Tempest*). In this sense the soliloquy can suggest the affinity of popular theatre with types of sport, such as bear-baiting or gladiatorial combat, where part of the excitement is a very explicit self-identification with or against one party or another.

However, this sort of compact with the audience can also contribute to more subtle inward effects (in speaker and audience). If the basic tenor of the appeal is to seek approval for a certain course of action, then the alternatives to such a course of action will also be in play. They may or may not be spoken, but even if they are not the fact that the character is appealing for support is evidence that the alternatives remain possibilities. These alternatives will in such a case be in *our* possession. The audience may at once identify with the soliloquist and yet – of necessity – hold off from full agreement (Richard III, Macbeth). The audience can then embody something like the character's 'anti-self' or 'other-self' – perhaps pointing toward a lost, past, or future incarnation – which will be given shape and filled up according to our ethical predispositions. We may not conjure up such a figure in any methodical or even self-aware fashion, but we do it all the time. The apparent directness of soliloquy – inviting us in, asking us to contribute, without any other intermediaries – makes it a prime space for such constructions.

Ultimately, the same questions apply with soliloquy as with any speech-act. Who exactly is speaking? Who is being addressed? Who is listening (not always the same thing)? What is the purpose of the speech? But these simple questions may not produce simple answers. Here we can return to the origin of the term 'soliloquy' in Augustine's *Confessions*. So, Augustine writes his confessions for various reasons: to defend himself against his enemies, to provide support for allies, to tell his supporters how he got where he is; less tangibly, perhaps he writes to clear things in his own mind, to attest his faith to God, to declare continuing recognition of past and potential sinfulness; maybe to entertain himself, his friends, or future readers; who knows, perhaps as self-conceit, rhetorical exercise, a homage to his favourite Latin writers. In this case, where to locate any 'I'? Is it somehow 'in' every phrase? Does his presence differ according to the difference or similarity of his 'narrating self' (presumably virtuous, achieved, Christian, and so on) compared to his 'narrated self' (often flawed, sinful, dishonest, etc.)? In other words, his 'self' may be located at different stations in time. In some sense the autobiographer/soliloquist is always coming after everything they recount: they have survived it, and are now able to record it. In another sense they are in it, because expecting their readers/audience to inhabit imaginatively the moment of which they speak. But then if all they talk about derives its point from what they have become, it also looks ahead to something they are yet to become: in this sense there is also an 'I' that is 'not yet'. The consequence is clear enough: we need to be careful about assuming any self-identical, self-present 'I' in the first person voice. The first person of soliloquy, that is, always remains in history. At the very least this is the time-bend or time-arc represented by the plot of the play, and to which the soliloquy, as much as it often adopts a detached attitude, always contributes. Let's look at some examples.

## GLOUCESTER IN *RICHARD III*

The opening speech of *Richard III* is one of Shakespeare's most famous soliloquies: (or certainly its opening line is). It is a good example of Shakespeare's early soliloquies. It declares the speaker's 'character type', reveals his attitude and plans for action, and does so as a consummate exercise in *rhetoric*. This means that every turn of phrase and shift of rhythm is a gift to the eager audience. The speech is not a clear window onto Gloucester's thoughts. We are supposed to identify it as rhetoric. The manners of the speech itself, quite as much as its overt message, are the things that hold meaning – that is, humour, personality, dissidence, and menace. He knows that we know that he knows his address is deeply studied and artful: that it draws upon the stock tropes of oratory, and that it imitates the very popular recent plays of Marlowe, Kyd, and Shakespeare himself (in the *Henry VI* trilogy).

Accordingly, the soliloquy – occurring as the opening gambit of a big new play – therefore also assumes that this familiarity might well breed a kind of contempt:

> Now is the winter of our discontent
> Made glorious summer by this son of York;
> And all the clouds that lour'd upon our House
> In the deep bosom of the ocean buried.
> Now are our brows bound with victorious wreaths,
> Our bruised arms hung up for monuments,
> Our stern alarums chang'd to merry meetings,
> Our dreadful marches to delightful measures.
>
> (1.1.1–8)

It is impossible to quote these lines without remembering how simply famous the first line has become: *Now is the winter of our discontent*. Shakespeare cannot have known how iconic this drum roll of an opening was going to become. But would this fame have seemed to him an absurd betrayal of evident sense? For the fact is that this first line is only 'half' of the thought. The second line provides what, grammatically, is the thought's moving principle and shaping verb: '*Made* glorious summer *by* this son of York'. Gloucester's syntax is inverting and deferring. An easier and apparently more logical construction would be 'this son of York has now made a glorious summer out of our winter of discontent'. However, this translation is clearly unsatisfactory. This is not only because it sounds like dull reportage of an achieved fact (though that is part of it). The point is that the rhythm of Gloucester's syntax proposes a very particular relation of the speaker both to and *in* the events transcribed.

Taken at grammatical face value, the 'winter of our discontent' is in the past: and a shared past, represented by the communal 'our'. Taken as a self-describing single line, however, the 'winter of our discontent' is *now*, as Gloucester's urgent condition of mind. But if this is the reading, then 'our' has to denote Gloucester alone: he is simultaneously looking toward the future, when he can indeed possess the royal plural. The statement thus occupies present, past, and future. It offers potted history, immediate reportage, and implicit prediction as to what must be. This suggests why the line is so memorable. It is because it really does stand alone, a sort of pre-emptive anti-soliloquy at defiant odds with much of the rest that follows. So, Gloucester's time, his 'Now', is not anybody else's. He operates in his own space–time continuum, measuring his own history as the 'shadow' not so much of others' public movements as of his own lonely self-projections ('Have no delight to pass away the time,/Unless to spy my shadow in the sun', 1.1.25–6). The first line, intense with projective narcissism, is a predictive capsule of how Richard's egoism means the erasure of others.

The troubled density of this first line demands immediate compensatory release. This Gloucester finds through a parody of the force he 'should' be celebrating but would in truth have murdered. Hence the distinctively fake oratory that follows. So, we will see that the first line is terse and concentrated: 'the winter of our discontent'. The sense might be ironic but the phrasing has nothing mocking or borrowed about it. This is because it is Gloucester, deadly serious, who is hidden in its dual referents. Compare this to the succession of adjective–noun compounds that follow: 'glorious summer', 'deep bosom', 'victorious wreaths', 'bruised arms', 'stern alarums', 'merry meetings', 'dreadful marches', 'delightful measures'. It is not that any single such compound phrase is particularly silly. Taken together, however, one after another, the effect is one of gathering semantic indistinctiveness. Gloucester seems to quote from the obsequious eulogies and triumphant valedictions that belong to the happy victors. Each image is a stock one, and each organised around the unerring antitheses of knightly romance. Most of the lines have

two such symmetrical phrases, but even where they do not
Shakespeare uses some other effect of bathos: the fake reverential
pun upon sun/son; the rhymes of 'clouds that lour'd' or 'our
brows bound'; the alliteration of 'deep bosom' with 'ocean buried'.
The point is to deflate by inflation. To the extent that soliloquy is
here working toward self-revelation, it depends upon an audience's shared awareness, with the speaker, of generic cliché and
easy rhetorical appeal.

This does not mean that Gloucester despises rhetoric, or indeed
any arts: it is rather its gauche or plagiaristic use he despises. He
marks himself out from the start as a vicious aesthete, as proud of
taste and careful of decorum as Hamlet. Envy and emulation here
always go hand in hand. He dismisses what others do and he
cannot do as so much idle self-manicuring: he evokes their 'strut',
their 'capers nimbly', their 'sportive tricks' in the 'amorous
looking-glass' as though describing prize panting puppies. But
here there is a paradox. For what is this speech but an improvised
exercise in the same thing? The point therefore is to *outdo them*,
whether in their seductive narcissisms or – an instance of the same
– their rhetoric. So, Gloucester doesn't eschew rhetoric at all. He
just does it better than the style he first mocks:

> But I, that am not shap'd for sportive tricks,
> Nor made to court an amorous looking-glass;
> I, that am rudely stamp'd, and want love's majesty
> To strut before a wanton ambling nymph:
> I, that am curtail'd of this fair proportion,
> Cheated of feature by dissembling Nature,
> Deform'd, unfinish'd, sent before my time
> Into this breathing world scarce half made up –
> And that so lamely and unfashionable
> That dogs bark at me, as I halt by them –
> Why, I, in this weak piping time of peace,
> Have no delight to pass away the time,
> Unless to spy my shadow in the sun,
> And descant on mine own deformity.

> (1.1.14–27)

If this is exhilarating it is because of the way it combines a mastery
of rhetorical expectations – the way he uses familiar devices of

emphasis and delay – with a teasing ability to not quite deliver what is expected. There are here none of the bathetic repetitions of the first eight lines. Instead, this one long sentence is structured around the teasing return of its promised subject: 'I'. He begins here in diametric opposition to the way he begins the first line, declaring the subject – 'I' – immediately. He then sustains the single sentence for 12 lines, returning to the sentence's home ('I') a further four times before finally allowing himself a rest. Gloucester's basic technique is one of promise followed by withholding. The more the answer is delayed, the more eagerly we want to hear exactly what it is that so distinguishes him from the rest of the smugly self-congratulatory court.

However, there is something else in this speech that makes it more interesting than if it were merely a masterful winding up of the audience. It is to do with the way Gloucester's rhetorical prowess runs away from him, or is hijacked by the very thing he is intent upon communicating. So, this middle part of the soliloquy is built around a basic irony: Gloucester pretends to keep us waiting for something – the definition of his 'I' – that he is in fact the whole time, throughout his supposed digressions and teasing parentheses, supplying us with fourfold. There is no punch line here, nothing to cap or complete his delays, other than the thing that he is all the time delineating: his compulsion to 'descant' upon his 'deformity'. As rhetorically knowing as the speech is, it is also a confession of inescapable abjection: he is trapped in an echo chamber of self-loathing.

Consequently, as much as Gloucester can watch himself describe himself and find the solipsism grimly amusing, he is also powerless to prevent it. The only 'halt' he can here 'call' is his own comically lame walk: 'dogs bark at me, as I halt by them'. This is the secret to the way the soliloquy measures its psychology through rhetorical meta-reference. The first eight lines showed Gloucester firmly in control of his parody. These middle 12 lines show him try to seize the oratorical momentum for his own subversive purposes: as though to say that if he captures the rhythm-stick he captures the play's heartbeat. And in a basic way he succeeds. It is he who will put the play through its paces, and we are in some basic way 'with' him as the catalytic dramatic presence. But we must also remain partly outside him, as though watching a ghastly specimen in a bottle. Partly this is because the rhetorical flourishes and self-conscious comedy mean that he cannot truly hurt us. He cannot get into our bloodstreams (as Macbeth can). But it is also because even in the half-appalled stasis of our watching – we allow it all, we will not (emotionally, imaginatively, as we do with Iago) intervene – we remain led by Gloucester. For he looks at himself as just such a fly in a bottle: he is the captured insect *and* the jeering nose pressed against the glass. This suggests the crucial inside/outside nature of his rhetoric here. He plays with the opprobrium that he has long attracted, like a ball of endless string. But at the same time there is something that threatens to choke him, that he *cannot* let go, and that suggests how absolutely he has become the creature of the discourse that has for so long attended him. And the register of this is, once more, in the possession or loss of rhetorical decorum:

> But I, that am not shap'd for sportive tricks,
> Nor made to court an amorous looking-glass;
> I, that am rudely stamp'd, and want love's majesty
> To strut before a wanton ambling nymph:
> I, that am curtail'd of this fair proportion,
> Cheated of feature by dissembling Nature,
> Deform'd, unfinish'd, sent before my time
> Into this breathing world scarce half made up –
> And that so lamely and unfashionable
> That dogs bark at me, as I halt by them –
> Why, I...

What we need to notice is how the speech by turns satisfies or upsets expectations as to its timing, or to the symmetry of its periods. So, this sentence is timed by the repeated 'I', returning as it does to the beginning and centre of the thought. The first two times have the same rhythm: 'I' followed by two lines of parenthetical self-observation (ridicule, disgust, excoriation). The third 'I' is different, however. Instead of two lines, we get six lines of such observation. The rhythm chops and alters, stutters and splurges rather than flows ('by dissembling Nature, Deform'd, unfinish'd, sent before my time into this breathing world scarce half made up – And that so lamely...'), as though mimicking the hurried, harrying limp of his gait. He cannot close the thought; there is always another humiliation that he endures, that he clocks up, as he stands by watching.

This is marked above all by an arrest of oratorical panache, best seen in the line, 'That dogs bark at me, as I halt by them'. The first half of this line is in fact a satisfying close to the theme: 'And that so lamely and unfashionable/That dogs bark at me'. It scans neatly, and closes with an image of dogs just generalised enough to remain comic. But the second half of the line quite upsets this poise. It is rhythmically unnecessary: it is one more masochistic breath; one more unkind cut. It is as though Gloucester *needs* to add the situational specificity that transforms self-deprecating comedy into self-mortifying historical document. Why does he 'halt' by the dogs? Is he in such desperate need of companions? Of course he knows that even the dogs won't have him – hence the pun on 'halt', meaning both to 'cease' and to 'limp'. But why does he need to tell us? There is an awful helplessness and abjection in the forethought of 'halt': it carries the sense of him watching himself limp by, and of how he has decided to do just that, has made joining the dogs his particular aim, but which he already knows will fail because of his unfitness.

This effect is clinched by the closing and rather diminishing repetition of 'I': diminishing because at the *end* rather than the beginning of the line; it is therefore out of time, deflating of rhetorical punch and prowess. This explains the further pun in 'halt', which in rhetorical terms means to be defective in rhyme or rhythm (as Hamlet has it, 'the lady shall say her mind freely – or the blank verse shall halt for't', 2.2.326–7). Again, Gloucester's self-possession is absolutely tied up with rhetorical self-possession. This control is advertised most obviously in the ostentatious self-confidence of 'But I'. He declares complete faith that this 'I' can control the sense, sustain audience attention, disappear and return at its own whim; that it will always assume the dominant position at the start of the line and as the subject of the clause.

Here, however, the 'I' comes belatedly and almost apologetically. It is a crucial sign of the helplessness and indeed mortification inhering in his motivation. The prosodic line is both a working metaphor and creator of the plot-line; the oratory is at once masterfully detached and auto-compelled.

The effect of all of this is paradoxical. On the one hand, it reinforces Gloucester's demonic control. He can string anything out, and yet still everything is at the tips of his fingers. On the other hand, it suggests some pathological kind of self-loathing. For the thing he keeps on stringing out, refusing to allow limits to as either physical phenomena, psychic provocation, or cognitive subject, is his defining state of prematurity and deformity. The endlessly shifting rhythms show him recall one insult, hurry into another, relapse into yet another, each insult like a creating slap to his clay. There is nothing tired or humdrum about this obsession. Indeed his recollections embody a sort of shock of recognition and surprise: the news they bear remains so arresting, so recoilingly self-defining. But then memory shades into, or is indistinguishable from, repeated anecdote. And it is these anecdotes that to all intents take over the soliloquy: anecdotes of himself or others of him, of the kind that he is again caught here rehearsing, of being born too early, or being barked at by dogs, or being scorned by love or mocked by mirrors. Hence the itching, chafing recognition that for all of his knowledge that he is what he is it still retains the power to hurt.

Any such inferences about Gloucester's inwardness depend, as so often, upon rhetorical organisation. Of course in many ways it is not an 'inward' speech at all. For one thing it is obsessed by outward appearances, and for another its basic ambition is mass arousal (simultaneously horror and seduction, as he repeats soon with Queen Anne). But these things are Gloucester. His 'character', as literally as such a thing can be, is 'rudely stamp'd'. This physical branding, as though from a pre-cut stencil signifying foulness, determines his everything, and not least his identification of how to channel his revenge and consolation: *publicly*, by necessity. With this persona at least, public rhetoric is revelation.

## POLITICAL SOLILOQUY: HAL

Because the soliloquy is the context-shaping speech of a single individual before an audience, it always implies a political relation or energy. Much will depend upon the sort of audience, or subset within it, being played to. The soliloquist might lead the crowd into new and dangerous dispensations, like Edmund in *Lear* (1.2.1–22). S/he might base the appeal upon an already defined contract, so that the figure on stage seems to emerge out of an existing social group: the disenfranchised aspirant (the Bastard in *King John*, 2.1.561–98) or courtier wishing for a less foolish or whimsical government (Enobarbus in *Antony and Cleopatra*, 3.13.29–47). S/he might be a more inclusively microcosmic figure, embodying the nation as a prince (Henry V in *Henry V*, 4.1.226–80), or pastoral heroine (Imogen in *Cymbeline*, 3.6.1–27), or nostalgic warrior (Hotspur in *1 Henry IV*, 2.3.1–34). S/he might be more frankly carnivalesque, drawing upon the audience's holidaying irreverence and a festive teasing with subversion (Falstaff in *1 Henry IV*, 4.2.11–47, 5.4.110–27; *2 Henry IV*, 3.2.297–327, 4.3.85–124; Autolycus in *The Winter's Tale*, 4.3.1–31, 4.4.597–620, 672–85, 834–45). It is important that we don't presuppose any glib association of the soliloquy's form – *solus* to an audience – with any predefined and necessary politics or ideology. Soliloquy can take the place of a retarded or discredited political system, one for instance dazzled by spurious ceremony or obedience to ritual (*Hamlet, Julius Caesar*). Alternatively, it may be the sabotaging thing itself, blocking an alternative source of due process or social organisation (*Macbeth, Richard III, Othello*). The mere framework of the speech – stopping the action, stepping outside of it, offering monologue *as* the dialogue – can suggest a radical challenge to generic forms and coercive momentums. Equally, it can embody a conservative refuge in monological authority and declamatory principle.

Context is all – and perhaps three things above all. First, the relation of the speaker to the soliloquy's 'I'; second, the identification of the addressee; third, the relation of the speaker to this addressee.

In the speech of Gloucester's discussed above there is no real ambiguity of address. It is clear to whom he is speaking. This is not always the case – or even if it is Shakespeare can play subtle tricks that complicate the assumption that soliloquies speak directly and fundamentally respectfully toward an audience. The audience need not be on an equal footing with an 'opened' character and an unfolded situation. A good example of this is Hal's first soliloquy in *1 Henry IV*.

The situation is this. We have heard the King talk of his own weariness, of rebellious murmurs and the gallantry of young Hotspur. This motivates King Henry's shame that his son Harry (Hal) should be so comparatively wasteful and dissolute. We see Hal in boisterous spirits with his low-life companions, trading wits and planning a robbery. These companions leave the stage to execute Hal's wishes. The Prince, alone on stage, then says this:

> I know you all, and will awhile uphold
> The unyok'd humour of your idleness.
> Yet herein will I imitate the sun,
> Who doth permit the base contagious clouds
> To smother up his beauty from the world,
> That, when he please again to be himself,
> Being wanted he may be more wonder'd at
> By breaking through the foul and ugly mists
> Of vapours that did seem to strangle him.
>
> (1.2.190–98)

This soliloquy is notoriously troubling, and like the whole of Hal's role evokes very disparate responses. The questions have long been fought over. Are these sentiments necessary and kingly? Or is the speech childish and callous? Is it politic or vain, smug or transcendent? Is it the ethical key to the play's vision or a crass subverting of its appeal? These questions cannot be explored here. But we should see how it is the *address* of this soliloquy that so deftly allows them.

The whole speech is premised upon a shifting, and indeed shifty, possession of the apportioned roles of speaker–auditor. This is best seen in the soliloquy's opening gambit: 'I know you all'. Exactly who is the *you* that he *knows*? The obvious answer would seem to be his companions. They have left the stage, but their talk and atmosphere remain, and Hal is now quick to denounce it. But there are problems with this solution: partly that there were at most only two of them, Falstaff and Poins – a small 'all' – and indeed for the last few minutes only himself and Poins; partly that they have indeed left the stage and so can only be an inferred absent addressee.

This points to the more insidious effect of Hal's address. Remember, he is alone on stage: alone, that is, in front of thousands of people. He is the heir to the throne; the king is ghostly and declining; the rebels have a mortgage upon virility: Hal has to be the hero in waiting, the chevalier about to reveal his glittering armour. And this is exactly what the speech is performing: 'like bright metal on a sullen ground,/My reformation, glitt'ring o'er my fault,/Shall show more goodly' (207–9). But if this is the intention, why not begin the speech like this:

> I know *them* all, and will awhile uphold
> The unyok'd humour of *their* idleness.

If he spoke in this way, we might still feel he is a little bit cunning or manipulative. But it feels different. Why? Because everything at issue is suddenly clearly in place: Poins and Falstaff are the idle ones, and we join the prince in detached anticipatory rejection. If he says 'I know them all', we watch *with* him. The soliloquy becomes an invitation. It draws in the audience, who then stand for the populace that will in time endorse his sovereignty. He can be 'our' hero. If he has to do dirty work he is doing it so that we don't have to; his cruel kindness is then a model of virtue that we are asked to follow and assumed to be worthy of.

What difference does it make if he says 'I know *you* all'? It means that *our* position is no longer clearly defined. 'You all' might include us all. The prince goes to the edge of the stage, casts his eyes over his auditors, and speaks his words of disdain. We are then 'with' the reprobates. Our 'idleness' is the fact that here we are, in the middle of the day, at the theatre. Our 'unyok'd humour' is that we have just heard ourselves laughing – the prince has just witnessed us laughing – at these no less 'idle' good-for-nothings on stage. The prince recognises our affinity with the comedians, and says it will do for a while but not for very much longer. The claims of good sober rule become an anti-theatrical tract.

It is in this fashion that the soliloquy makes problematic its own grounds of appeal. It is positioned at the perfect moment to do what soliloquies are supposed to do. We have had lots of action and variety of voices but alarmingly little in the way of a moral compass. We can take a breather and be assured of where the play finds its 'home'. Part of this means telling us what sort of a play it will be. But one effect of Hal's ambiguously dismissive, ambiguously taunting address is to disdain the enjoyments that we have so far embraced. We can see how difficult this might be for our own sense of orientation if we think of other such malcontents resentful toward festive play: Malvolio in *Twelfth Night*, Don John in *Much Ado About Nothing*, Egeus in *A Midsummer Night's Dream*. Hal is very different from all of these. He cannot remotely be dismissed from account; he doesn't frame the comic action, or counter it, or catalyse it. Instead, he forces 'humour' exactly to come to account. This of course means that he is in a history play as much as in a comedy. He is thereby (both historically and generically) exemplary in insisting that there are indeed consequences of irresponsibility, fecklessness, and so on. But he does so by projecting forward to a play's end that we can hardly not resent or resist, even if as obedient subjects we immediately swallow such resentments (or as lovers of the powerful we embrace our implicit abasement).

This uneasiness is achieved through effects that we are more likely to intuit than identify. But the basic technique is one of invoking expectations – basically that as the prince he will be *satisfying* – that are more imitated than achieved, and that in the imitation can seem flagrantly and even sneeringly violated:

> Yet herein will I imitate the sun,
> Who doth permit the base contagious clouds
> To smother up his beauty from the world,
> That, when he please again to be himself,
> Being wanted he may be more wonder'd at
> By breaking through the foul and ugly mists
> Of vapours that did seem to strangle him.

Hal does not attempt transparent self-presentation; nor does he permit blithe or confident access. Instead, he flatly acknowledges the regal symbol and energy as a thing he will 'imitate', whilst offering himself only through the further detachment of a nameless third person: 'when he please again to be himself,/ Being wanted he may be more wonder'd at'. The calculating self-detachment is chilling enough in its narcissism. But equally to the point is the way the audience too is rendered detached from the moment. The ones to whom he appeals are not here and now but in the future; it is not 'you' that I address (that I *know* and scorn) but something other whose 'wonder' 'he' shall one day allow. He does not embrace any listeners as his real confidants: rather, we are either part of his present denunciation (as idle and unyoked) or overhearing him as he imagines a future and better audience.

It is a remarkable speech in being so hostile to its supposed franchise – the hero supposedly needing and serving the audience as much as vice versa – and subverting of its customary function. Shakespeare delivers Hal the consummate occasion for soliloquy, but then has him refuse all of its easy channels and comforts. Of course, indirectly, the speech is immensely revealing about Hal's character and about his function in the play. But the revelations emerge precisely counter to the supposed candour of soliloquy. Again, this basically means that Shakespeare is playing with the possibilities of rhetoric, and again in quite an audacious way. Rhetoric is supposed to be for the crowd, to cajole and persuade. This might include as part of its method a rebuke of the crowd. Hal may well do this, but he does absolutely nothing to invite them back in or to give them a lead. They remain resolutely outside his projections: 'I'll so offend, to make offence a skill,/Redeeming time when men least think I will' (211–12). Hal's methods here are then these: first, making obtuse rather than direct his immediate angle of address; second, making himself either as 'he' or 'I' *not* identical with himself as the speaker in the moment; and third, making the 'men' to whose opinion he ultimately appeals not the same as the people to whom he now speaks. Together they signify a striking example of a soliloquy that subverts conventional soliloquy: the speaker is split and made hypothetical; and the audience *too* is split and made hypothetical.

This evokes a fundamental refusal of self-presence. Hal is not yet here; nor is the audience he would reveal himself to. In this sense the speech withholds the usual inferential trust of soliloquy, whereby we fill up the gap between words and the mind behind them. These gaps – between speaker and audience, one audience and another audience, and above all between the speaker as present first person, addressed second person, and dramatised or metaphorised third person – open up all sorts of possibilities for Shakespeare's future deployment of soliloquy.

## HAMLET

Hal's speech is a good example of a soliloquy that exploits the inherent tension in a soliloquy as to who exactly is being addressed. Is it a speech to oneself, or to an audience, or to both? This is a particularly fertile tension in a political play, where the audience can so easily shade into 'the people' or a subset within the people. But what about soliloquies that do not double as political oratory? Who then is being addressed?

The most famous soliloquy of all – Hamlet's 'To be or not to be' – is a fascinating example of just how far Shakespeare enjoyed toying with the grounds of any trust in soliloquy. Probably the best-known crux in the speech is the doubt as to its object: is he talking about killing himself, or killing Claudius, or the movement between being and non-being in general – or a bit of all of these? Perhaps less well recognised is how any answers to this depend upon our understanding as to whom exactly Hamlet addresses. For Shakespeare so sets up the speech that it is impossible quite to know.

The scene begins with the King questioning Rosencrantz and Guildenstern about Hamlet's 'true state': is it 'confusion', 'dangerous lunacy', 'crafty madness' (3.1.4–10)? It is a question we also ask, and seek to answer. We then learn that Claudius and Polonius have arranged for Ophelia to meet Hamlet 'as 'twere by accident'. The king and his counsellor will then 'bestow' themselves in some secret place where, 'seeing unseen', they can try to gather what afflicts Hamlet. Polonius instructs Ophelia to pretend to be reading a book; the King has his own brief soliloquy confessing his heavy conscience and reminding us of his crime; Polonius hears Hamlet coming, and he and the king then hide. It is after this that Hamlet begins his soliloquy.

However, what is not at all clear is when exactly Hamlet enters, or what if anything of all these preparations he hears. All of the three different versions of *Hamlet* provide different entrance points. In the First Quarto (probably based upon at least one performed version of the play) he enters after the king says 'see where he comes poring upon a book'. He is then on stage as Corambis (Polonius) arranges for the Queen to leave them, for Ophelia to read a book and 'walk aloof', and for he and the king to hide 'unseen'. In the Second Quarto, Hamlet is marked to enter at some point during or immediately after the King's long penitent 'aside', and before Polonius says 'I heare him coming, withdraw my Lord'. In the Folio, Hamlet is not marked to enter until after the king and Polonius have hidden themselves. Consequently, there is no sure evidence as to how the scene might have been played. Indeed the script seems designed to remain ambiguous whatever the instructions for entrance. Whether he enters early or late, Hamlet doesn't overtly mention that he has seen or heard anything. He may have seen and/or heard everything. He may be prepared for Ophelia's falsely reading appearance ('Are you honest?' as he asks in a moment) but unaware of the king: or the other way around. Of course it is open to any performance of the scene to make a decision for us here. However, the only certainty that the scripts as given seem to offer is that Hamlet *may* know that something is afoot. It is not really an option to ignore the possibility: but no reading of the scene can decide either way.

But the uncertainty doesn't end here. For we need to decide what we take a soliloquy to represent. Is it a silent meditation that the audience is allowed to 'hear'? Or is it a character talking to himself? If the king and company are listening in, when do they start hearing? Do they hear all of Hamlet's speech from 'To be or nor to be' on? Do they tap into the exchange as soon as he addresses Ophelia (after 30-odd lines of 'silent' dialogue)? Might Hamlet, in the way of so many people when they think that they are alone, move back and forth between silent and enunciated thoughts?

First, Hamlet might be speaking aloud, oblivious to the fact that he is being spied on. In this case, there is a further layer of doubt in that we, the audience, have to negotiate the consequent irony: who do *we* look at? How does it alter the dramatic meaning of what he says if we are anticipating how these overhearers will interpret it almost before we interpret it for ourselves, or as it were 'for' Hamlet? Second, he might be speaking aloud, fully aware that they are listening, and directing his 'meditation' accordingly. Third, he might be silently 'thinking', beyond anyone's access but our own. Or fourth, he might, as always, shift and wax from one mode to another, taunting his overhearers ('by opposing end them'), appealing to the crowd ('who would bear the whips and scorns of time'), acting as the citizenry's common agent ('the law's delay,/The insolence of office'), before losing interest in such play and ending as he started, neck up in his own enveloping desolation ('their currents turn awry and lose the name of action').

If soliloquy is the representation of inwardness, then nowhere, we might suggest, can there be a more faithful sense of just how besieged, how doubtful, and indeed how intersubjective such a thing might be: drawn from the voices of others, or unable to avoid the ears and eyes of others. Traditional notions of soliloquy assume a mind that always knows itself, that communicates itself, that is happily separate from its addressee whilst being transparent to this addressee. But examples such as Hamlet's suggest that this understanding is little better than an idealist and mystifying fiction. A more interesting conclusion suggests itself: Shakespeare teases with different options of rhetorical address so as to get closer to the way the mind might be even when it is most alone.

## BRUTUS

The very existence of a soliloquy often presupposes some kind of struggle. This may be an external struggle, where the soliloquy shows the character declaring his hand against this or that opposition. Often, though, it is some sort of internal struggle, where the soliloquy represents a self-divided, self-deluded, or self-quarrelling mind. In these cases, where exactly do we locate the primal, directing 'I'? Is there such a thing? Might the fact that the speaker needs to externalise their thoughts in such a form suggest that the soliloquy in itself is a way of *detaching* the form from the mind? The soliloquy becomes a mask, or a presentation, or an aesthetic experiment. Again, Hamlet is exemplary: his 'O what a rogue and peasant slave am I' soliloquy (2.2.550–607) shows him try on a whole sequence of parts that both stand for and fail to measure up to his 'true' self (see Chapter 12). Indeed, we might question whether the soliloquist necessarily possesses any more privileged control over intention than any other speaker. Part of a soliloquy might represent the intensive unfolding of self-consciousness, whilst other parts embody the refusal, evasion, or interpretation of such unfolding.

How can we tell the extent to which a soliloquy is appealing to an audience, and how much it is an internal meditation? There is no hard and fast rule here, but the basic thing we have to look out for is the adherence paid to the conventions of oratory. These conventions are designed to *lead* the attending ear: the rhythms are measured, made regular or ascending as the sense requires; each line, accordingly, tends to contain a single thought, a block of sense to be heard and processed. So, if one line is enjambed with another it is to engineer acceleration and climax; if figures such as extended similes are used, then they will point a clear moral. The larger unit of the speech block will be similarly measured, dividing into subunits of question, proof, and assertion, gathering momentum and definition as persuasiveness moves toward decisiveness.

But let's compare such general guidelines to a famous soliloquy of Brutus in *Julius Caesar*, as he rehearses the arguments for assassinating Caesar:

> It must be by his death: and for my part
> I know no personal cause to spurn at him
> But for the general. He would be crowned:
> How that might change his nature, there's the question.

It is the bright day that brings forth the adder,
And that craves wary walking. Crown him that,
And then I grant we put a sting in him
That at his will he may do danger with.

(Julius Caesar, 2.1.10–17)

We will notice that many of the thoughts stop halfway through the line, and that when the line does end the thought it really *ends* it: there is little here in the way of a lulling or galvanising rhythm. The fifth and sixth lines offer a brief metaphor of the adder, but its conclusion is ambiguous: 'that craves wary walking' is hardly an emboldening to tyrannicide, and is more than anything a sort of holding gesture. The metaphor concludes nothing, instead beckoning further and, one hopes, more decisive reasons. The rhythms of the speech as a block are similarly stop–start. He twice avers to the idea that Caesar would or may be crowned: this of course is supposedly the 'big' idea, the clinching argument that Caesar wants to ride roughshod over the republican constitution. But both times that Brutus invokes this ambition he does so as the cold re-ignition of a line after he has stopped it halfway through. Rather than a climactic assertion it becomes a hesitant hypothesis: a would-be 'predicate' caught between hopeful and fearful.

Similarly, on both occasions that he raises the 'crown' idea he immediately veers into arguing from analogy. But these attempts to argue from analogy are interrupted by repeating – with still greater indirection – Caesar's links to a 'crown'. So, 'Crown him that' is Brutus's very weak attempt to join assertion with analogical reasoning. It fails through the imprecision of 'that': what does 'that' refer to exactly? Probably nothing (or at least nothing exactly): 'that' seems to be the general idea, vaguely sketched in the parable of the bright day, the snake, and wary walking, that Caesar needs to be – what? It makes no sense: this second invoking of 'crown' is therefore strung out between evasion and some sort of half-dreamy, half-somnambulistic reiteration. It is as though he has to repeat the killing word, rehearse the transgression it signifies over and over, and eventually the word will mutate into a terrifying enough 'fact' to demand action.

This all suggests something almost occult about this speech. The words of supposed 'reason' are in fact closer to incantation, as the soliloquy begins to resemble a drifting echo, as though the aural leftover of a night-long commune with the nearly dead. The speech begins with 'It must be by his death' and ends 24 lines later with 'kill him in the shell'. We might see from this circularity that the speech, for all of its imitation of rhetorical persuasion, is more to do with pleasing the speaker through an observed ritual of pseudo-argumentation. Hence, again, the laxative rather than tightening sequence of Brutus's 'doing' words: 'at his *will* he *may* do danger with'. Again the effect is thoroughly subverting of rhetorical momentum. He wants to assert that Caesar's 'will' – his arbitrary prerogative – is dangerously absolute. But because 'will' is so quickly succeeded by 'may', he turns this political application of 'will' into its promissory sense – what shall or must happen – which is then contradicted and undermined by the doubtful contingency of 'may'. Even if 'will' is still taken to refer to Caesar's untrammelled power, it is 'may' that takes the burden of predicting his exercise of that power. It becomes a prerogative that 'may' be defined exactly by *not* being exercised. Instead of invoking inevitable autocracy, Brutus outlines what might just as easily be taken as a 'princely' sort of discretion.

As the speech unwinds these rhetorical sleights of hand grow in flagrancy. So, after another lengthy and indecisive metaphor, this time of a climber scorning his ladder upon reaching the top, he continues:

> So Caesar *may.*
> Then, *lest he may*, prevent. And since the quarrel
> Will bear no colour for the thing he is,
> *Fashion it thus*: that what he is, *augmented*,
> Would run to *these and these* extremities.
>
> (2.1.27–31; my italics)

Brutus here reaches climax by almost overtly giving up on the tools he uses to get there. The repetition of 'may' is the turning point. We have seen how this weak auxiliary word disables his previous attempt at self-persuasion. Here he says it twice more. At best the word indicates a possibility: but by the time we hear 'lest he may', the 'may' has vanished into a hinterland of wistful scaremongering. This is oratory at the pitch of exhaustion, or at a point of self-annulment. So, the terse finality of *'prevent'* – full stop – signifies both a decision for action and an end to the pretence, wanly imitated throughout this speech, that private thought need have any greater claim to ethical scrupulousness or semantic transparency than public rhetoric. The point here for Brutus, as for an orator before a crowd, is simply to satisfy due process (the imitation of honesty) and to clear the decks for action.

In other words, soliloquy here is not about the direct expression of inward thoughts. It is much more of a *dramatised* phenomenon. Brutus is playing a part to himself, finding a voice and gesture that will pass for real even though he, like any audience, knows throughout that it is all a game: more or less fanciful, more or less obedient to generic boundaries. This is the import of his final teeing up, 'Fashion it thus'. He is sorting out what he is going to say to other people to justify the decision he has just now hedged around. Hence the careful inexactness, the deferring to another time for articulation, of 'what he is, augmented' ('augmented' by exactly what he hasn't quite worked out yet) and 'these and these extremities (which can similarly be clarified later). Understood in this way, the soliloquy becomes a kind of rehearsal for the act of public rhetoric that it all along appears to imitate. It gestures toward a future moment – one when he might have sorted out exactly what tales he will tell.

However, we can also read 'Fashion it thus' as the act of this very moment. He is doing the fashioning *right now*. So, 'these and these extremities' is its expression – self-politic, perhaps, but adequate in the circumstances – and works as a mediating bridge between Brutus as performer and Brutus as audience. Accordingly, 'these and these' works to evaporate precise reference, or gestures toward an impenetrable inward silence. This inner space might be quite empty of content; alternatively, it might be full of motivating 'extremities' that we infer but which he does not or cannot here enunciate. Either way, the power of public rhetoric to organise and express inward truth is so deferred as to evaporate.

At the same time, we should notice that the supposed subject of the soliloquy – Caesar – has all but disappeared. Indeed by the end of the speech Caesar has not even been born ('And therefore *think him* as a serpent's egg/Which *hatched*, would *as his kind grow* mischievous,/And kill him in the shell', 2.1.32–4: the italics showing how the same tricks of false reasoning, spurious proof, and facts subverted by contingency recur). In a basic sense Caesar has indeed gone by the end of this speech; there is from here no turning back from the decision to assassinate. The soliloquy thereby also poses in miniature what the play dramatises: after Caesar, then what? The answers are all here. The thing that remains is this sort of speaking, and this sort of 'Roman' as its embodiment. The real subject of the soliloquy, that is, is not Caesar at all. It is Brutus, and the way Brutus here speaks. The thing at issue becomes the failure of rhetoric, and in this failure it becomes Brutus, as a sort of shadow man, haunting his own words, a 'little kingdom' (2.1.68) both symbolising and facilitating the breakdown of the bigger one.

Ironically, therefore, the very failure of this rhetoric to speak inward truth is what allows Brutus's private mind to be so revealed. There could hardly be a weaker example of the great republican virtue of persuasive speech. But this failure of rhetoric does nothing to reduce its centrality. That Brutus *cannot* fit his thoughts into due rhetorical form is the proof of a mental turmoil that is pre-eminently defined by the chaos it presages for the body politic. For part of the theme of Brutus's speech is that virtue has to remain a 'general' thing. There is barely any identity here, or none that Brutus wishes to let in, that is not civic in origin and orientation: man is here a little Rome. If Brutus suffers cognitive shutdown and the release it affords, then so too will Rome; one chaos mirrors and produces the other. The soliloquy shows very explicitly the sort of wilfully jaundiced and manipulative rhetoric that will now run the civil wars ('what he is, augmented'). Just as the soliloquy foretells the rest of the play, Brutus's private breakdown here works as public predicate and prophecy.

The soliloquy raises the same questions about its authority as any other speech-act. Just as no history can be written after history, so too can no soliloquy be spoken above and beyond the play. The soliloquist is shot through with connections and allegiances, acknowledged or not. The soliloquist remains in character: the monologue always remains a mode of dialogue. As the examples in this chapter suggest, the soliloquy may indeed not be a place of safety (for character and audience), of consensus amid strife and clarity amid contention. A soliloquy's peculiar mode of address – direct to the audience, unable to be interrupted – pretends to break free from the circumstances and consequences seen everywhere else in the play. But as the example of Brutus suggests, even this pretence at separation begs difficult questions. How to achieve such transcendence without one or another kind of violence, forgetfulness or deluding mystification? It might be an interruption – or indeed an irruption – as much as resting place; it might signal a banishing of oneself or others; it might be a refuge *from* one's emerging self as much as for it. The challenge is always to retrieve the place of soliloquy within a moving dynamic.

# 11

# DID THEY DO IT?
# SEX AND HEROINES

*This chapter considers the role of supposedly naive questions or illicit curiosity in constructing and placing characters. It is a common experience to want to know things about characters that the play simply doesn't tell us. But it is hardly likely that Shakespeare was unaware that such questions will be asked – not least because these unanswerable curiosities often lead us to the nerve centre of a play's ethical or emotional tensions. This chapter looks at how he plots these questions, often by not presenting important scenes, or by not clarifying important facts about a character's life 'before' the play. Often these curiosities are to do with sex – particularly the sexual experience or temper of the young heroines. We want to know more than we are given; our hunger to know more can become prurient or voyeuristic. In this way, our experience of the character frequently involves uneasy complicities, particularly with the (usually) male characters that are seeking, possessing, or endangering these young women. The simplistic or illegitimate question (did she do it? does she want it?) becomes a channel to a play's most pressing ethical challenges. So, the bulk of the chapter looks at three examples of such compromising curiosities, the detail of the analysis increasing with each one: Ophelia, Desdemona, and Cressida. We see how such prying curiosity always contributes to making the heroines whatever it is that they are. We see how it can limit them as characters in deference to the primary male character (Ophelia); or conversely, how our curiosity can be turned against us, in a way that makes the heroine fuller than voyeuristic possession might seem to allow (Cressida). We also see how our speculative filling out of the heroines is fundamental to how the plays represent the big questions of identity and politics. Above all, the sexual prurience felt by reader or spectator typifies the seductive but often dangerously insinuating powers of empathy.*

Every play of Shakespeare gives us questions that cry out to be asked, that are invariably asked by readers or viewers when they first meet the plays, but that resist any direct appeal to the evidence of the script. The unanswered curiosity is of course a staple of popular narrative, whether suspense, mystery, or romance. It is the most basic hook there is: leave something dangling and we will seek to pluck it, leave it in darkness and we will hope to illuminate it. The aim is to get the reader or viewer leaning forward, desperate to peep into undisclosed spaces.

These questions are almost always about character: the reasons why someone acts as they do, or (still more basic) the facts of what they have done or might do. In *Measure for Measure*, for example, why does Isabella enter the nunnery? What does Barnardine's silence to the Duke's pardon mean? What does Isabella's silence to the Duke's proposal mean? In *Othello*, what did or did not Othello and Desdemona get up to on their wedding night? In *Romeo and Juliet*, did Romeo really love Rosaline? In *The Tempest*, what happens to Caliban when all the rest leave the island? In *The Merchant of Venice*, where does Shylock go after the trial? In *The Winter's Tale*, what happens to Hermione? Most infamous of all, perhaps: did the Macbeths have any children, or what has happened to the child to whom Lady Macbeth claims to have 'given suck'?

We could conclude that the reason these things are not clear is that we are not supposed to know. If we needed to know, Shakespeare would have told us – or will tell us in the end. But an alternative explanation seems more appropriate to the way drama works. The coincidence of not being told, and wanting very much to know, means that we dwell upon these things with whatever ethical or imaginative sympathy we can. It can take on the contours of our desires – but often our disguised or furtive ones, hidden from view just as these scenes are. It can force us into speculation, all the more urgent and tantalising for lacking evidence. Or it can seem to take us uncannily close to a work's latent heartbeat. Take the question of missing children in *Macbeth*: in one form or another all sorts of absent, murdered, unborn, or undead infants ghost through the play, connecting intimately to the play's haunting preoccupations. Repeatedly the missing scene or unshared secret beckons as a promise-crammed nestling place: a place where bonds and debts breed, or anxiety and appetite beat.

Unsurprisingly, questions about sex are among the most common of all. Occasionally the prurience is homoerotic, as at times in *Twelfth Night* and *Merchant of Venice* (aren't *both* Antonios gay?). More usually, the gaze is searching out the woman's secret spaces. Often such sexuality is frank and admirable, and no kind of puzzle for the audience: this is so in most of the comedies. But from around *Hamlet* on sexual questions increasingly take over as the dark secret into which our 'extra-textual' speculations are provoked to roam. The disturbing bed-tricks of *All's Well* and *Measure for Measure* – models of the unseen scene – can stand as metaphors for the way oblique, occluded, vicarious or deflected female sexuality increasingly becomes the off-stage pivot of motive or theme. It can feel like presumptuous speculation or illicit curiosity. But Shakespeare plots such questions as surely as he seeds many other kinds of suspense or desire. The fact is that (Cordelia possibly excepted) there is barely a single Shakespeare female whose function or inwardness is not bound up in the question of her sexual predilections, whether past, present, or possible. This is true even of the definitively chaste (consider the provoking body denial of Isabella in *Measure* or Marina in *Pericles*) or the mature (consider the exultantly perverse mothering of Volumnia in *Coriolanus* – or indeed Lady Macbeth). But as much as the questions often begin with sex, they rarely end with it. More often than not they return us to something like the generating premises of the play.

## OPHELIA

*Hamlet* is a play that breeds puzzled questions, but perhaps the most irresistible of all involves curiosity about the true status of

Hamlet's relationship with Ophelia. Does he really love her? Did they have sex? (The best answer to this latter question is perhaps the one attributed to Laurence Olivier: 'in my productions, *always*, darling'.) Olivier's answer is witty, but also appropriate: it recognises both the question's magnetism and its basic absurdity. If you are going to answer the question, you are not going to find your rationale for doing so in the text. It has to be answered at some extra-textual level, in the space where a play gathers a life of its own, for instance in the private mind of a reader or the practice of a company. But if the question is literally absurd, it is also clear that Shakespeare expects us to ask the question. The first scene with Ophelia (1.3) shows her father and brother obsessed about Hamlet's intentions and Ophelia's chastity. She in turn responds enigmatically, with ironic hints of knowledge in reserve. When Hamlet and Ophelia meet he circles aggressively around her questionable 'honesty' (truth/chastity); he says in quick succession how he loved her and how he loved her not, suggesting how the word 'love' can equally house adoration and lust; her presence provokes him into general abuse of painted 'wantonness' and sinful breeding; he demands that she get to a 'nunnery', suggesting less a religious community than a brothel, or a place of confinement for unmarried mothers (3.1.103–50). Most famously, when Ophelia goes mad (4.5) her songs are full of bawdy (*Young men will do't, if they come to't/By Cock they are to blame./Quoth she, 'Before you tumbled me,/You promis'd me to wed.'/ 'So would I a done, by yonder sun,/And thou hadst not come to my bed'*, and so on). But the more we are showered with aspersions, the more it is clear that Ophelia will not quite be caught by any of them. Identifying any kind of specific personal history is flatly impossible. Ophelia remains tantalisingly unknowable.

It is therefore not surprising that it is Ophelia that provokes the best explanation of how Shakespeare's mixture of hints and withholding works upon an audience:

> Her speech is nothing,
> Yet the unshaped use of it doth move
> The hearers to collection. They aim at it,
> And botch the words up fit to their own thoughts,

> Which, as her winks and nods and gestures yield them,
> Indeed would make one think there might be thought,
> Though nothing sure, yet much unhappily.
>
> (4.5.7–13)

The gentleman here offers a sort of charter for romantic inference, for deeply interested appropriations of characters for our own purposes. And Ophelia has indeed become a prime object of such passionate dwelling. Particularly in her 'mermaid-like' absorption into the 'weeping brook' (4.7.175–6), she is an enigmatic and even mesmerising figure. Indeed she can seem to have been composed with an eye to future form-bestowing idolaters (like the nineteenth-century pre-Raphaelite painters). But the fact that she almost has more life beyond the play than in it can suggest just where the questions about her sexuality are leading. For in some almost callous sense Shakespeare lets her go 'for' Hamlet. Throughout the play her grief has to give way to his, and so it is in her songs, her secrets, and her dying. Shakespeare seems content to leave her vaporous or 'weedy' (4.7.174), with altogether 'too much of water' about her (4.7.185). And the effect of this (if not the reason) is that her mystery becomes a channel into Hamlet's. As the grave scene shows, the significance of her death passes away from her possession and into whatever he cares to do with it. This is always the way with speculation about Ophelia's secrets: first and foremost, they are Hamlet's.

Accordingly, all of the questions about her sexual knowledge send us back to 'before' the play. This is the place where, if only we could get access, secrets would be revealed. And the real secret is not whether Hamlet and Ophelia had sex or not, or whether he loved her or not, or whether his courting of her was intended to end in marriage, as his mother hoped, or in her bed, as her father feared. All of these unanswerable questions are collateral narratives, just outside the frame of the play itself, which contribute via their absence to the play's primary narrative: the question as to what makes Hamlet, what has unmade him, and whether he can be put back together again. Above all, they point to the basic premise of his characterisation: the 'real' Hamlet only ever existed just before we get to meet him. In other words, the supposedly naive and illicit question so often asked of *Hamlet* – did they do it or not? – is in some ways a screen for that still more vexed question: who exactly is Hamlet, and how can we possibly know?

## DESDEMONA

The tragedy of *Othello* pivots around speculation concerning Desdemona's sexuality. The question that obsesses Othello is whether she has slept with Cassio. We might think we know the answer to that one. But there are other questions, hovering at the edges of our vision, that are less easily answered – and indeed less easily asked. For instance, has she slept with Othello? If she has, *why*? Such questions might seem crude and ugly. But they are as hard to resist as they are to acknowledge. This will seem a paradox, but it is one that gets at the most elemental qualities of this peculiarly disquieting play. Again, then, the point is to see how supposedly inadmissible curiosity about character's 'secret truths' can be a pathway to ethical or thematic purpose.

The clue to this paradox is Iago, in many ways the play's directing spirit. So, he has his own distinctive way of telling stories. This involves a mixture of declaration and deferral. He is at once in our face and oblique, turned away as though half in shadow. The effect of this is quite devastating. We see horrors, and then find ourselves straining to see still more. It is a narrative style established in the play's opening words. 'Tush, never tell me', says Roderigo to Iago: and Iago will not. Repeatedly, Iago's apparent candour in fact masks false promise and indirection. He is a master of evasion and frustration. So, not only does Iago 'never tell' Roderigo: but he never tells us. For instance, we never definitively learn what the subject matter of the play's first exchange is: 'I take it much unkindly/That thou ... shouldst know of *this*', 'If ever I did dream of *such a matter*,/Abhor me' (1.1.1–5). The audience is left chasing after clarity. But what do we get instead? We get Iago, in his next two, very long speeches, not supplying such clarity. We hear successively of 'him', 'his', 'him', 'he', 'he', 'his', before the closing coup de grace, 'his Moorship'. The speech conveys some information. Iago has been passed over, someone else has got his place, and an unnamed man has made the decision. But above all it establishes *Iago*, his wit, aptitudes, prejudices. Whatever else we are in the dark about, Iago is crystal clear.

So, he displays from the start a hypersensitivity toward styles of speech. He mocks the way others talk, what they read, setting himself up as a kind of policeman of both linguistic and ideological manners. Nothing, we are somehow certain, can escape him. Almost uniquely in Shakespeare, Iago seems to be in assured possession of all of the meanings given him. His own swift speech, so unlike his report of the bombastic Moor and the prattling Michael Cassio, ensures that it is Iago who will seem the one with knowledge in reserve. He is impatient, but this is a good thing: here is a man of no-nonsense experience. It works similarly with his misogyny and racism. Even if we aren't seduced into collusion with his prejudices, they might work almost as recommendations: after all, what can there be left to hide? With this mix of authority, familiarity, and scorn, he is irresistibly trustworthy: we *know* him already.

The play here begins as it goes on. That is, constructed around ironic discrepancies of knowledge. His 'Moorship' is always such irony's dupe. But what is less often recognised is that Shakespeare sets it up so that we, the audience, are similarly marooned. We are unable quite to get our bearings even as it seems that we are entirely secure. Telling us whatever he wants, all the while refusing to 'answer' to anyone's expectation, Iago establishes that there will be only one source of audience satisfaction: him, in good time, as he chooses. He has us in his pocket, telling us whatever and whenever he wishes. We are locked from the start in an unholy bargain. The play's very foundations are in his gift.

Accordingly, it is also Iago who first gives us the play's heroine. He does so by offering rich and repeated images of a sexual act happening *now*. We hear of an unnamed daughter who has escaped to the 'gross clasps of a lascivious Moor' (1.1.124). What is stressed is her revolt from parental authority and, even more, her enjoyment, 'now, now, very now', in frankly animalistic sex (1.1.87). Iago stokes the father's horror with pornographic vignettes: 'an old black ram/Is tupping your white ewe' (87–8), 'your daughter covered with a Barbary horse' (110), 'daughter and the Moor are now making the beast with two backs' (114–15). To her father, she has become a monstrous example of feminine duplicity and filial ingratitude: 'O, she deceives me/Past thought' (163–4), 'Fathers, from hence trust not your daughters' minds/By what you see them act' (168–9). Desdemona is the unknown soul, unknown even to her own father, silent of motive and treacherous of act. We have to see just how rebellious she is painted. Revolting from her childhood dwelling ('O heaven, how got she out?', 167), she discovers a horribly natural home in the primitivism and urgency of sex. The effect of the repeated animal imagery is partly to make us see what is normally hidden. Sheep and horses fornicate in public; anyone might witness its stupendous, absurd intensity. But a young Venetian noblewoman! Through exhilarating, returning shafts of lightning, Iago has these domestic beasts reveal what must not be seen. The daughter is becoming an animal; it is the most awful return to basics.

The thought of Desdemona might evoke the 'joy' of paradise (70): but here she embodies a carnal version of the same thing. She suggests the secret haunts of the imagination, the secret throb of desire, the secret place of satisfaction, and the secret urge for an abandoning of 'duty, beauty, wit, and fortunes' (133). And such secrets remain the hidden centre of the play. Figuratively, imaginatively, and indeed theatrically, they are the place where curiosity peers. They are what we seek to penetrate and, lacking the means, which we make up, steal, or otherwise steal into. They are Desdemona's body, handkerchief, and, finally, bedroom.

For there is a further narrative trick here at work. Iago's action in describing their lovemaking ensures that the wedding night gets interrupted. The same thing happens the next night the lovers are together (2.3), when Iago's ruse again draws Othello away from his pleasures. The question 'have they or haven't they?' hangs in the air, at the same time as we have been invited to imagine rampant sex. Just as Iago's narration uses interruption and deferral, their sexual satisfaction is interrupted and deferred. The analogy recurs again and again: between Iago's way of dictating what we hear, and other characters' 'actual' experiences. It isn't that Iago always writes the script (although he does so often enough). It is more like Shakespeare is making the action resemble Iago's motives. We only know what the play gives us: but the play will not give us more than Iago fundamentally allows.

The effect is that speculative voyeurism takes the place of evidence. The play constantly tests the ability of the senses – the faculties of hearing, seeing, touch, taste – to provide knowledge. But the knowledge at stake simply will not remain in any way mathematical, judicious, or bloodless. It is sexual, and compulsively so. Iago makes it this way. We might say that this is because he needs it to be this way. After all, his cynicism gathers almost the force of a desperate and even needy ideology: 'She must change for youth; when she is sated with his body . . . she must have change, she must' (1.3.351–3). But if Iago seeds our prurience, so too does Shakespeare. Hence the string of tiny hints (often intuited by readers and exploited in productions) that Desdemona might just share in furtive or even self-unravelling desires. To run away with Othello is evidence enough; an astonishing thing to do. She herself 'trumpet[s]' the 'downright violence' of her action, and her will to be sacrificed to the 'utmost pleasure' of her man (1.3.250–4). It is suggestive that Desdemona's defence here of her actions differs in the two versions (First Quarto and Folio) of the play. In the Folio she speaks of deferring to Othello's 'very quality' rather than his 'utmost pleasure'. We cannot know which is a revision of which, or which (if either) is closest to Shakespeare's first or later intentions regarding Desdemona's erotic abandon: but these small tunings surely enough attest to the tenderness of the question. This tang of sexual appetite persists in her active role in the courtship, as she feeds Othello his lines; or in her request for 'praise' from Iago when he is acting as her bawdy clown (2.1); or in the odd moment when, getting undressed, her thoughts dwell upon the very 'proper' Lodovico. In this case Emilia takes her mistress's cue: Desdemona can both enjoy and abjure the erotic speculation that follows (4.3.33–8). Desdemona's part is both perfect innocence and impenetrable complicity. In this, Shakespeare acts like Iago does. He dares us to draw out the string as far as we will have it: perhaps it becomes her necklace; perhaps her rope.

Shakespeare and Iago are in this point one. Each reveals his plot completely, showing us all the machinery of 'tragedy'. At the same time, they bed within us a barely acknowledged striving for more, for a closer examination of hidden chambers. To the extent that we are one with Iago, we are so in this fact above all: he turns us into stalkers, voyeurs, priers. But equally, of course, we are one with the hero Othello: and here what is specifically shared is the simple groundlessness of knowing. There is absolutely no sure foothold for our certainties. It is part of the audacity of *Othello* that both of these identities (with Iago and with Othello) are in this sense not only unwelcome, but invariably unacknowledged. We don't want either. We don't want to be sadistic voyeurs; we don't want to be certain of nothing. But in order not to fall into one of these unwelcome empathies, we have to take refuge in the other. There is nowhere else to go.

The example of Desdemona therefore shows how Iago establishes the terms by which we attend. Of course it is possible to resist a lot of what Iago says. As the Vice figure he works in a familiar tradition. However amusing and intimate he is, an audience is well aware they must keep the best part of themselves aloof from his seductions. Indeed Iago himself commands it, insisting at every turn upon his malice and dishonesty. But it is not quite so easy. Iago's candour in such matters also releases us in a way to trust him. There isn't much we can throw at him that he hasn't already thrown at himself. Iago's narration keeps on pre-empting possible responses, neutering the potency of any rejection of him. Exactly because he is so self-confessedly not honest, we go along with him.

Here then is where supposedly prurient or illicit speculations enable the play's ethical punch. We become complicit in the violations we abhor, yet we remain determined to protect the innocent from them. We long to interrupt the action and tell Othello to stop believing him; it can be still more horrifying to see Desdemona insulted as a whore and killed because of her trust. It is terrible for her to suffer, and unfair to feel in any way implicated. There is indeed much to lament. Nonetheless, it is hard in this play to do so with clarity, or to receive any kind of reward for our mourning. A balanced moral ledger, healthy self-forgetfulness, a breaking through to some ethical clearing? Not here; not once we have really experienced *Othello*. For the difficult point remains: this kind of tragedy depends upon this kind of horror. We expect it, wait for it, watch it, require it. It may almost always be thus in tragedy, but in *Othello* we are made to feel it – even if we don't quite acknowledge it. Iago does, absolutely. He unblushingly sees through to the consequences (if not the sources) of his desires. If we cannot, if we do not see how thoroughly all of these figures are our agents, then perhaps we are here even less 'honest' than Iago is.

## CRESSIDA

In *Troilus and Cressida*, Shakespeare seems to supply the answers for which in other plays we secretively hunger: yes, the heroine is indeed promiscuous. But it is somehow no answer at all. Cressida is twice publicly witnessed as lewd or promiscuous, and yet her mind remains tantalisingly elusive. The example of Cressida can suggest that, far from being the endlessly sublimated primal hunger, sex might itself be a translation of a still more insatiable desire: to really know another. All 'character reading' perhaps teases with voyeurism, a longing to see more than is quite shown. If so, perhaps the quixotic aim is to overcome any tawdry satisfactions and locate the something else that inheres in fascination.

The politician Ulysses would scoff at any thought of Cressida's depths. For him, nothing she is or owns can be hidden:

> There's a language in her eye, her cheek, her lip,
> Nay, her foot speaks; her wanton spirits look out
> At every joint and motive of her body.
> O, these encounterers, so glib of tongue,
> That give accosting [F: a coasting] welcome ere it comes;
> And wide unclasp the tables of their thoughts
> To every tickling reader! Set them down
> For sluttish spoils of opportunity
> And daughters of the game.

(4.5.56–64)

Cressida is a flirt and a tart. Every limb has a tongue, every movement is a motive. She moves for men like a cat before cream. Ulysses' judgement is often taken as gospel (as his earlier 'degree' speech is often taken as speaking for Shakespeare's politics), being expressed with his habitually persuasive confidence. However, his whole speech is undercut by dramatic ironies: not least, he has just been publicly embarrassed, bested in wit by this girl and left groping for a kiss like some superannuated lecher. Furthermore, the whole summary is brazenly self-forgetful: if she is a 'spoil', then it is he and his confederates who make her one; if she is a daughter of the 'game', then he is among her adoptive parents, and the 'game' she serves nothing less than his war.

We then come upon a typical Shakespeare irony. Ulysses purports to summarise the [anti-]heroine. If our reading is directed by a concern for conventional moral order, and we want to dismiss her for ethical turpitude or sexual looseness, then here we have a neat package of reasons. And there can be little doubt that Cressida, measured against the standards of a policing patriarchy, is contemptible. She may or may not be thought a victim, but either way she is worth no more serious consideration than any other counter in trade. However, there can be equally no doubt that Cressida is *not* defined by this moral framework – any more than the play is. Indeed summary judgements like Ulysses' – because so situationally ironic, so responsive only to surfaces, so absorbed by the very clichés that the play is deconstructing – seem almost designed to protect whatever 'lies within' from invasive knowledge.

We might here return to Ulysses' 'tickling reader'. So, his meaning is crudely sexual: a mere tickle and she's open. But Ulysses' metaphor rather subverts his disdain. He evokes Cressida as a book, but would limit its application to the physical correspondence ('wide unclasp') between opened book and spread legs. To complete his metaphor he invokes the 'thoughts' appropriate to a book. But as the whole speech amply declares, Ulysses cares nothing for Cressida's mind, indeed argues that she has none that is not thoroughly embodied in her 'wanton' pliancy ('her eye, her cheek, her lip,/Nay, her foot speaks'). But we of course do care for her thoughts. If anyone is a 'tickling reader', we are. Yet throughout the play the book of her mind has been anything but 'unclasped'.

Similarly, the basic social status of Shakespeare's Cressida is unclear. In the sources (principally Chaucer) she is a widow. In Shakespeare's play, however, she seems far more defined by her absent father – but a father whom she claims to 'have forgot', knowing 'no touch of consanguinity;/No kin, no love, no blood' (4.2.97–9). She hovers in-between various forms of definition and possession. Cressida is neither daughter nor orphan, wife nor widow, virgin nor courtesan. She floats provokingly free from patriarchy's usual categories for womankind. Still more ambiguously, Shakespeare does not push through her story to any of its customary exemplary conclusions. So, her fabled unfaithfulness attracted various narrative additions, ranging from torturous punishment (leprosy, incarceration, beggary) to some reclaiming of spiritual dignity (for example in repentant death). She became a ballad-maker's by-word for wantonness and inconstancy. Shakespeare's Cressida is unfaithful to Troilus. But he simply leaves her 'in' this unfaithfulness. There is no shortage of judgements offered about her: but none of them get the confirming endorsement of generic closure. Her function and character are therefore at some defining level elusive, or inconclusive.

From her first scene Cressida withholds things, making a fool of ardent eulogies and the rhetoric of absolutes. She lies outside anybody's confident possession. The ignorance shared by Troilus and Pandarus is less to do with whether or not Troilus will ever bed her, or the perils ahead, than it is about the very substance of the thing they both seek. 'Tell me, Apollo, for thy Daphne's love,/ What Cressid is, what Pandar, and what we?' (1.1.97–8). Everything is in doubt here: knowledge of another, knowledge of self, knowledge of path, agents, and possibilities. Shakespeare is writing here around the same time as he wrote *Hamlet*, and the questions are familiar ones. 'Let her be as she is', 'she has the mends in her own hands' (1.1.65–7). From the perspective of her witnesses, on-stage or off-stage, the challenge is one of mental access: how can we know her? But Cressida herself shares in this puzzle. If Troilus and the audience struggle to locate her, then so too does Cressida herself. She takes on as her own dilemma this quest for possession and fear of absence.

This is not immediately apparent. In Cressida's first scene she exudes self-possession. As she and Pandarus watch the passing soldiers, Cressida adopts the role of a 'fencing' jester. She returns all Pandarus's attempts at flattery, insinuation, or intimacy with the dead bat of flat literalisms or vaporising quibbles: 'Is he so young a man, and so old a lifter?', 'If you love an addle egg as well as you love an idle head, you would eat chickens i'th' shell', 'Alas poor chin! Many a wart is richer', 'Without the rack' (1.2.115, 130–1, 135). The sense is of an open-eyed woman, assessing the games that men and women play, the measures that mark failure or success, and keeping herself carefully beyond the fray. Above all, she refuses access. Her manners would not be remarkable in some other type: a widow, a shrew, the witty companion of the romantic heroine. But if she is anything, she is this romantic principal. It is her mind that we need to enter. But instead of candour we get the willed opacity of literalising puns.

Pandarus's exasperation might almost be our own: 'You are such another woman! One knows not at what ward you lie' (1.2.251–2). But at this point, as though the switch of object from the soldiers to Cressida suddenly cues her into commission, she 'herself' enters the picture:

> Upon my back to defend my belly, upon my wit to defend my wiles, upon my secrecy to defend mine honesty, my mask to defend my beauty, and you to defend all these; and at all these wards I lie at, at a thousand watches.

> (1.2.253–7)

This is her first self-analysis, and it summarises the part perfectly. She seems to be saying something fairly consistent: that she is wary of approach and wary of giving; that she knows the world to be full of dangers, and that a single loss might end all she has of value. Basically, it is the wisdom of the virgin abroad (or at court). In line with this prudence, each part of the speech proposes a certain self-splitting. She invokes a forward self-agent (back, wit, secrecy, mask) whose role is to deflect challenge and protect more indigenous self-possession. In other words, she proclaims a certain latent inwardness, one that, like Hamlet's, is defined by its refusal to show. But in fact the speech is still trickier. For a start, any 'I' here being proposed is multiple: 'at all these wards I lie, at a thousand watches'. She is eternally sleepless, but the price of her vigilance is that she can never rest in any achieved self-truth. Her eyes dart out at angles, spy into every corner, but there is no single 'I' either directing or gathering in the glances. Instead, these 'watches' are she: Cressida is made, remade – and potentially unmade – by the things she sees or fears. Consequently, we might identify an almost haunted account of a subject taken hostage by the objects it perceives, and by the fact that it might know *itself* only as the object of these others.

But if there are any such intimations of self-erasure, then they co-exist with an assured display of self-possession. Her tone alone demands faith in a presiding consciousness fully able to both set up and elude the dizzying puns of her riposte. Hence the defining pun upon 'lie': it continues Pandarus' fencing metaphor, and therein the awareness of sex as combat; it invokes lying down, for sex or sleep, and more broadly as a posture of concealment; and it reminds any who doubted it that her every act, including this one, might be a 'lie', a knowing deception. For indeed the whole self-description has a strangely oxymoronic quality. She describes supposedly substantive essences (belly, wiles, honesty, beauty) as the things protected by her siege mentality and stratagems of deflection. However, on closer inspection these turn out to be repetitions of the deflections. So, 'upon my back, to defend my belly' might mean that she is always facing forward and able to rebuff any 'hits'; equally, it can mean that she is lying recumbent, inviting an assault upon her belly. '[U]pon my wit, to defend my wiles' implies that beneath the 'wit' is not so much unvarnished truth as further trickery. Similarly, 'upon my secrecy, to defend mine honesty' invokes something like 'I keep my own counsel', but it more penetratingly offers the key to her performance throughout: if honesty is secret then it is logically never spoken; if 'honesty' also means chastity, then 'secrecy' can be the dark place where sinful deeds find furtive commission. Finally, 'my mask, to defend my beauty' again acknowledges that what she shows is a false face. Cressida surely enough invokes the convention of ladies wearing masks to protect against the elements, but the more pregnant point is that her 'beauty' remains unseen. Like her 'honesty', it is a thing only of inference and reputation. If no one sees it, what can be evidence of it except the mask?

The cumulative effect of the explanations is one of compounding rather than clarifying suspicion. Insofar as her quibbling indirections are not hopelessly vaporising, they hint at a back-stairs life of secret assignations and smoke-and-mirrors illusion. However, at the same time as she drip-feeds some such narrative, the import of the speech as a whole remains aversion to sexual advances and to any kind of invasive presumption of knowledge. Through 'self-watchings' like Cressida's here, Shakespeare explores just how changeable a 'self' might be *to* oneself, and how unknowable it might be to those who would love it.

The playful, almost experimental temper is as crucial to Cressida's part as the power of secretion and hoarding it attends. She knows herself to be a piece of property, but of a kind that eludes hackneyed notions of the woman as commodity. So, she can 'let' part of herself out, sublet another part, she can without notice break the lease and, insofar as she is judge, get away with it: and she can do so because if she is her own tenant she is also, ipso facto, her own landlady. This can be easily taken for simple craft, for instance in the seduction scene with Troilus (3.2). So, she offers something, withdraws it, confesses her wrong, regrets the confession, mocks the regret as still further shifting, and so on: all to the end, it is often assumed, of bringing on the man. But we might equally suggest that Cressida invites just such a dismissive reading – ''Twas not my purpose thus to beg a kiss' (3.2.134), 'Perchance, my lord, I show more craft than love' (149) – precisely so as to forge for herself a place of inscrutability and survival. This is much to do with the sleepless policing she does of her own discourse:

TROILUS   Why was my Cressid then so hard to win?
CRESSIDA   Hard to seem won; but I was won, my lord,
   With the first glance that ever – *pardon me*;
   *If I confess much, you will play the tyrant.*

I love you now, but till now not so much
But I might master it. *In faith, I lie;*
*My thoughts were like unbridled children, grown*
*Too headstrong for their mother. See, we fools,*
*Why have I blabbed? Who shall be true to us*
*When we are so unsecret to ourselves?*
But though I loved you well, I wooed you not;
*And yet, good faith, I wished myself a man,*
*Or that we women had men's privilege*
*Of speaking first.* Sweet, bid me hold my tongue,
*For in this rapture I shall surely speak*
*The thing I shall repent.* See, see, your silence,
Cunning [F: coming] in dumbness, in [F: from] my weakness draws
My soul of counsel from me! Stop my mouth.

(3.2.113–30; my italics)

Everything here in italics is at least potentially an aside to the audience. Equally, everything might be said baldly to and for Troilus. The speech asks us to make a choice. We can think that Cressida is 'playing' Troilus, hinting at retraction or regret so as to elicit praise or stoke ardour. Or we can accept that her stops and starts are a genuine record of hesitancy. The two interpretations are difficult to square with each other, although not quite impossible: Cressida shows herself entirely aware of the effect of rhetorical craft, and even if her parentheses are sincere markers of turmoil she might recognise how they can be seen (and indeed used) as artful 'angling'. She both loves and angles, she is earnest and crafty, just as later on she is faithful to Troilus within her need for another.

The speech therefore asserts two of the qualities that the play's first scene prepares us to expect: an 'off-stage' Cressida, alone with her secrets; and, precisely in this aloneness, a subversive Cressida, totting up possibilities, rehearsing options, assessing the lay of the land, and in all of this presenting an implicit challenge to ruling masteries. That is, each parenthesis is a turning back towards, or a quick cross-reference to, constructions or conclusions pondered elsewhere. As with Hamlet, we are cajoled into imagining a more fully fleshed off-stage Cressida.

The clue to this is how her words communicate at once publicly and privately – shelves of meaning that correspond respectively to a proverbial and a literalising use of metaphor. Consider 'who shall be true to us/When we are so unsecret to ourselves?' By 'unsecret to ourselves' she refers to her vow not to tell anyone of her private feelings. But a further implication is that she should be 'secret' not only with herself, but also to herself. Cressida might be bemoaning self-knowledge. She wishes she might not see into herself quite as clearly as she does, knowing that to see one's motives is to live knowingly in error and inauthenticity (a theme that returns in her departing analysis, 'Ah, poor our sex! The fault in us I find:/The error of our eye directs our mind', 5.2.115–16). Or consider, 'my thoughts were like unbridled children grown/Too headstrong for their mother'. Again, the meaning is both immediately lucid and complicatedly self-generating. She means that her love for Troilus grew too big to be contained. But again Cressida is populating her inner self with multiple and perhaps incompatible agents. She is the 'mother' of the 'thought', but then the thought gathers an independent life of its own; in turn, it becomes not one child but plural 'children'. This image of filial disobedience fissions into a whole sequence of Cressidas quarrelling over the beloved – or perhaps more than one beloved. Furthermore, her self-image as a 'mother' is no less potentially unsettling than her self-image as her own 'children'. She is once more evoked either as the parentless self-creator or as the 'unbridled' child. See, she now says, 'we fools,/Why have I blabbed?': 'fools' is overtly a reference to womankind, and her sex's inveterate failure to keep good counsel. But it also means simply her, Cressida. She is a 'house of fools' that (returning to her self-image as her own baby) has 'blabbed'.

The kind of rhetorical organisation suggests a self in process: one that is consciously self-constituting, and because of this fearful of some material vacancy at its heart:

TROILUS                    What offends you, lady?
CRESSIDA   Sir, mine own company.
TROILUS   You cannot shun yourself.
CRESSIDA   Let me go and try:
    I have a kind of self resides with you,
    But an unkind self that itself will leave

To be another's fool. Where is my wit?
I would be gone. I speak I know not what.
TROILUS   Well know they what they speak that speak so wisely.

(3.2.140–8)

This is perhaps Cressida's most plaintive moment in the play. The pathos comes from knowing herself so pre-scripted, and so much her own unwilling prophet. She inhabits different moments, now and in the future. So, her commitment to this moment with Troilus is as absolute as can be. However, it is also mortgaged to rival truths and desires that when the time comes will not be denied. This is her tragedy: that to achieve desire can be so allied to renunciation and diminishment. She identifies a self that – just like her rhetoric – is coherent only insofar as it is multiple. Accordingly, she is the 'fool' of 'another' – a sexual pawn, puppet, or plaything – but also her own fool, self-subverting in her self-service. She is a 'kind of self', implying an approximation or shadowing of any essence; or she is an 'unkind' self, implying cruelty to her 'self' or her suitors; or, if 'unkind' means unlike, then she is simply different from her 'self'. Her self-consciousness here comes upon a sort of auto-peril. Hence her attempt at departure: 'Where is my wit?/I would be gone. I speak I know not what'. Of course she is here retracting or regretting her confession (or pretending to do so), and so displaying her familiar discursive and political self-consciousness. But if we allow her words the full metaphysical weight that the context invokes, then Cressida is also cataloguing a sequence of comprehensive self-disappearance: her 'wit' (mind), her speech, and indeed her 'I' are all on a path toward erasure.

Ultimately, the point of such moments is less to do with metaphysics than more mundane difficulties of knowledge, power, and sex. Throughout the play such difficulties are experienced equally by Cressida, her lovers, and her audiences. Must we hide from self-understanding to survive? Can we know what we love? Can we love what we know? Is promiscuity openness or mystery? Does it demand disgust or awe? Can anyone's behaviour be consistent? Can anyone's being ever really achieve coherence?

Cressida is not finally to be pinned by any of these questions. Throughout the play she is thoroughly 'clapper-clawed', and yet still she slips through sundry grasping fingers. The voyeurs' scene (5.2) epitomises this, when Cressida's teasing and lovemaking with Diomedes is spied upon by a number of very different eyes. The voyeurs are Troilus, Thersites, and Ulysses – and perhaps Diomedes too, strung as he is between witness and player. However, even as a sum of distinct perspectives they cannot capture Cressida. For she too is present, by her words and actions proving, confusing, or eluding their judgements. (Thersites' masturbatory eagerness to see *more* – 'Now the pledge; now, now, now!' (5.2.67) – blurts out a common longing that she be more decisively betraying, and therefore more easily dismissed.) For there is always an inductive space where evidence simply lacks. Cressida says things we cannot hear ('Hark, a word with you', 'one word in your ear', 5.2.8, 36), writes things we cannot read, and all the time directs her discourse along multiple lines, some to Diomedes, some to herself, some to an undefined absent party who might yet understand her better than she can. All of these disparate positions of investment or detachment can then approximate to an audience's similar variety of response.

Cressida's part finally tempts us toward a rather postmodern conclusion: the thing at issue becomes the instability or unknowability of any object. The interpreters on- or off-stage can do little but discover as 'Cressida' some refraction of their own prejudices or desires. We might choose to conclude that it is these framing facts – the fact of discrepant perspectives, the fact of objectifying violence – that here becomes the effective thing at issue. But it is doubtful whether such a conclusion can quite account for the dramatic experience or audience hunger here in motion. For the questions really remain all about her. How many 'eyes' has she? Does her mind go with her body? Why does she still say 'come' when she knows she shall be 'plagued' (5.2.111)? This last may be a reference to the leprosy that tortures her in some of the sources: if so, it is typical that Shakespeare's 'plagued' seems to refer most pointedly to Cressida's private expectation of anguish, remorse, or pining. Shakespeare's manipulation of perspective is seen throughout the play, and brought to bear upon all sorts of things as well as Cressida (particularly the war). But it is the voyeurs' scene that most emphatically stages this irresolvably ironic approach to the facts. One consequence is the thorough deconstruction of essentially knowable character. Nonetheless – and ironically – Shakespeare's irony here renews the need for and hedges the privacy of just such inwardness.

For perhaps the clinching point about Cressida is, very simply, that she survives her supposed crime, and in this survival in some sense exceeds it. Her failure to die, whether by her own contrite hand or her lover's enraged one, is the great scandal of Shakespeare's version (repaired for example in Dryden's version 70 years later). But it is also an illustration of her recurring condition: never finally to be defined by her body, her actions, or her witnesses. Instead, her speech repeatedly invokes thoughts of a world elsewhere, hovering moments above her even as she acts contrarywise, just as she speaks jokes that at once know her entrapment, cast beyond it, and compound it. There is then 'somewhere' for her to disappear into as she survives the opprobrium of men: we don't really know what or where this is, but we do intuit that it exists. If this is bourgeois neediness, then it is equally the pleasure of play. Her character is a surprising vessel of such possessive desire.

# 12

# IN SEARCH OF
# SHAKESPEARE'S
# CHARACTERS:
# IAGO AND HAMLET

*This chapter concludes the book by offering set-piece explorations of two of Shakespeare's most enigmatic characters: Iago and Hamlet. These analyses are not intended to be in any way final. They are meant to illustrate the potential interplay between two different ways of approaching character. The first way is to approach the character as a textual or dramatic construct. The character is in no sense real. It is a network of signs, dictated by the limitations and conventions of Shakespeare's medium. So, both Iago and Hamlet are collections of dialogue, bearing relationships to various types and genres, animated by their place in particular plots (etc.). But not only does Shakespeare (inevitably) construct them out of the materials of drama: these characters construct themselves out of such materials. Specific dramatic machinery takes the place of psychology, motivation, and self-image. Inwardness gets built up from an often accidental collection of such techniques. Any individuality is not simply given and present in any single speech or act. It is inferred from this patchwork of effects; it is found in what is not present as much as in what is present. This leads us to the second way of approaching character: as a distinctive coherent individuality. Both Iago and Hamlet suggest that any such coherence must be built up precisely out of the signs and absences that mark the character's inessentiality and fictiveness. The recognition that they are pre-scripted or bounded by dramatic materials leads to a search for that which lies within or beyond such materials; similarly, the absence of explanation or evidence makes us supply both. The characters we locate are our constructions, without substance outside our experience of them (which of course may in various ways be a shared experience). But in that they are hardly less real than any other thing we call our own.*

## IAGO

We have seen how Iago directs our sense of other characters. We have also seen how Iago presents himself as at once bluffly reliable and impregnably dishonest. But can we locate Iago 'himself' in this? If his functions and rhetoric are defined by such a paradox – he is our only guide to the facts, but he is a sworn liar – then does the essence of his character fall similarly into an unknowable abyss? Is his 'character' perhaps no more than this rhetorical shiftiness?

Iago can be a test case for some basic questions about Shakespearean character. How much is any coherent persona our construction, pieced together from textual hints? How much do we have to fill in absences that Shakespeare simply leaves unexplained? Is there any speech-act that is free from the basic dramatic transaction: that is, a piece of dialogue, inherently ironical, and open to be taken by different audiences, on-stage and off-stage, in different ways? If a character is always created out of the materials of theatre (dialogue, scenes, stage, audience, etc.) then how can any coherent persona be identified that is independent of such materials? Is there any distinction between the methods of characterisation and the substance of character?

Here let's make some first steps in a search for Iago, concentrating only upon what might be gathered from his opening conversation and two early soliloquies. First, we'll consider Iago's identity in terms of its textual placement; second, as a personality with (inferable) psychological depths and human reality.

The conventional place to look for authentic self-presence is (as we have seen) the soliloquy. Unsurprisingly, however, Iago's are less than transparent. In his first soliloquy he says that it is 'thought abroad' that Othello has slept with Emilia: 'I know not if't be true', says Iago, 'But I for mere suspicion' will act as though it is (1.3.385–8). The role of revenger pleases him, just as does the pretence of groundless jealousy: what for others is a tragic compulsion is for Iago a rhetorical choice, as he casually dresses up his plot in appropriate trappings of cause. But as much as his motive seems whimsical, it is also somehow all he has got. In a terrible way there is no substance to Iago except such theatrical stuffing. Hence the way his next soliloquy seems to take as a self-determining insult what moments earlier was merely exploitable gossip: 'I do suspect the lusty Moor/Hath leaped into my seat; the thought whereof/Doth like a poisonous mineral gnaw my inwards' (2.1.292–4). How can we explain the inconsistency, whereby he seems casual and ironic one moment, tortured and possessed the next? One explanation is simply to reply with the terms of the question: so, Iago simply is capricious and unstable; thoughts he barely credits turn in a blink of an eye to horrifying truths.

But this kind of mental movement is more than one of Iago's distinguishing characteristics. It is a (literally) self-constituting narrative technique. So, Iago has a rare capability of imagination and projection. He needs merely to envisage a hypothesis to proclaim a fact. He gets presented with seeds of possibility – a coincidence, a conceit, another's weakness – which instantaneously flower into seemingly pre-scripted stories. Most often the seed is simply something that someone else says. This becomes a kind of super-narrative convenience, giving form, gravity, and momentum to his plot. As though with the full force of history and psychology behind it, the accident of opportunity takes the place of motive. In other words, Iago's motive, and therefore his inwardness, is nothing less than his own moment-by-moment improvising.

Consider Iago's very first words: 'But you'll not hear me. If ever I did dream/Of such a matter, abhor me' (1.1.4–5). Iago's deceptive self-description suggests the central deception to come. So, he anticipates what will happen to Othello, who fatally finds proof in absence and magnifies nothingness into crime; he jokes about being abused falsely as a 'whore' ('abhor me'), preparing for the true scapegoat to come. But equally tellingly, Iago is positing himself by withdrawing himself. He claims that he has done nothing, been nowhere, thought or dreamt nothing, and in such absence he asserts his unblemished interior. It is a knowingly self-vaporising method of asserting veracity. The tragic plot surely enough here spins out of Iago's self-spinning. But if Iago gives the plot its substance, the plot gives him his.

So it is that when Iago appeals to an authentic inward truth, the terms of his appeal still evoke something manufactured by theatrical arts:

> For when my outward action doth demonstrate
> The *native act and figure* of my heart
> In complement extern, 'tis not long after
> But I will wear my heart upon my sleeve
> For daws to peck at: I am not what I am.
>
> (1.1.60–4; my italics)

The thing that is 'native' here – meaning original, natural, unadorned – is not so much the heart as its 'act' and 'figure'. Its substance is definitively theatrical. In place of a secret chamber of truth, we get the plastic arts. Iago is explicitly claiming that his 'outward action' is not his inward heart. But his inward heart remains constructed out of 'extern' acts and figures. If we are wondering whether Iago has any interiority at all, then here perhaps is our answer. Look closely, and see what you have already been seeing. His inwardness *is* his actions. If he is not transparent, or simply opaque, then he is a mere actor. And perhaps this is what is so fearful about his role, its efficiency, its intimacy, its seductiveness: that 'at heart' it is no more than a chain of more or less taken cues.

Iago, that is, discovers his own substance via serendipitous cue-taking. It is his basic animating trait. We witness it in the self-dialogue of soliloquy: we see it still more in his dialogue with others. He catches whatever is floating upon the air, and this somehow becomes him. The play's very first speech establishes the terms: 'I take it much unkindly/That thou, Iago, who hast had my purse/As if the strings were thine, shouldst know of this'. Iago has taken Roderigo's money, but his 'purse' is more than that. It is also Roderigo's brains and balls: the 'strings' Iago pulls are those of his marionette, Roderigo. Iago is the puppeteer behind the curtain, stealing the mind and animating the body. The relationship recurs again and again. Iago moves in and out of those he encounters, drawing from them, combining with them, taking them hostage. Within moments he is insinuated into another, who again becomes his agent. It is in this sense that Iago can be talked of as devilish. A power of invisible habitation makes him a kind of male succubus, feeding on his own sex.

However, if Iago possesses others, then logically they also become part of whatever he is. He absorbs them, is nourished and shaped by their diminishing. We see the same thing when he starts to talk about Othello. 'I would not follow him then', says Roderigo. Iago once more accepts the image given him and transforms it into his own self-constituting action:

> O, sir, content you!
> I follow him to serve my turn upon him.
> We cannot all be masters, nor all masters
> Cannot be truly followed … For, sir,
> It is as sure as you are Roderigo,
> Were I the Moor, I would not be Iago.
> In following him, I follow but myself…
> (1.1.40–57)

The impetus for the self-description comes from Roderigo's cue-phrase. Iago repeats Roderigo's keyword ('follow'), but utterly distinctively. He intensifies it, making it equivocal and menacing. He does so by framing the word 'follow' with 'serve my turn'. This phrase similarly picks up on Roderigo's dim assumptions: here, that to 'follow' is to 'serve'. I 'serve', says Iago, but not as you suggest. Iago has served his turn, and now he will turn his service to advancement. So, from behind Othello's back he will plot his revenge, perform unseen deeds, haul his master in. It suggests rotating a lever, like that of a pre-scripted plot; or the nautical 'turn' of a rope, twisting around the great masthead, his master; or a figure from hunting or coursing, with Iago the dog, Othello the game, and the plot he is laying Iago's cruel sport. He takes the merely descriptive word and invests it with all the energies of self-making narration. Accordingly, he momentarily becomes a dog, a rope, a lever, a plot-maker. This is the other recurring manifestation of Iago's power of habitation: just as he possesses his adversaries, he finds endlessly provisional form in his intensely dwelt-upon language. This language has a quality almost of metastasis: full of rhetorical transitions which mark his own restless mutations from one pose or possibility to another; but also truly pathological, spreading disease from one body to another, as his words divide and conquer like cancerous cells. These characters become to him no more than laboratory rats, in which he can inject his malignancy; in turn, he derives substance precisely from the uncontrollable divisions he causes in his specimens (in their selves, their reputations, their relationships).

So, Iago's identity uncoils out of a combination of his improvised conceits and the objects whom he 'follows': 'In following him, I follow but myself', 'Were I the Moor, I would not be Iago'. Of course words such as these convey a cold threat. But they also perfectly describe Iago's take on individuality. Consider 'Were I the Moor, I would not be Iago'. It breeds with self-obliterating, self-swapping menace. In due course we see Othello becoming possessed precisely by his ensign's language, sexual horror, and paranoia. Iago here sets this morphing in motion. So, he projects himself into the Moor, mentally steals him from himself; if he knew what was best for him, Iago hints, Othello would do the same to his ensign. The battle for power is a battle for basic self-identity; it is a fight to the death, made all the more perilous because the self-substance at issue is always a blink away from nothingness.

For Iago to speak in this way points to how willing he is *not* to believe in 'essential' characteristics; how much his plot will exploit both the elasticity and fragility of the self. Individual characteristics – trustingness, honesty, valour, vanity – are in Iago's vision little but endearing follies, temporary ornaments of occasion. Iago's own radical emptiness gets projected onto others, who consequently have no substance worth respecting or protecting. Individuality recedes, replaced by a nest of borrowed terms, imitative concepts, plagiarised discourses. A pithy example of this is the way Iago distinguishes himself from Othello:

> I know my price, I am worth no worse a place.
> But he, as loving his own pride and purposes,
> Evades them with a bombast circumstance,
> Horribly stuffed with epithets of war...
>
> (1.1.10–13)

Iago is a semantic and political ironist. 'I know my price' captures his attitude perfectly. It recalls a certain humanist faith in his abilities, but at the same time is a cynical deconstructing of any such intrinsic worth. He speaks of himself as a commodity, able to be bought, sold, measured. But at the same time it is impossible to quite place any private self-estimation. The words might as easily be derogatory as assertive. The brisk homophony of 'worth no worse' tends to collapse the words into one (worth is worse, worse is worth). Furthermore, in the mouth of the misanthrope 'man' can represent a crumbling foundation for 'faith'.

Indeed, what exactly is there to have faith in? Iago's keyword here is 'bombast'. Iago is ridiculing his general's habit of pompous bragging, seeing it as the hot air of bloated gravity and borrowed authority. For Iago, Othello's 'bombast' both prefigures and deflates his tragedy: the false sublime. But he is also playing upon the word's more primary referent, which is cotton-wool. This is the connecting thread between 'bombast' and 'stuff'd'. Most particularly, this wool was used to fill out doublets, making the wearer seem more imposing; they might also be used as a form of armour, cushioning the harmless arrows. Iago is effectively unpacking the very 'stuff' out of which Othello's character – any character – is constituted. The great general is both a puffed-up piece of air (bombast as language) and a grotesque doll (bombast as stuffing). His whole being is 'horribly stuff'd' with nothingness. In Iago's construction, self-creation is simultaneously self-evacuation. Word and body conflate and collapse in each other. Words are air, bodies are vessels, and any inhering self is as empty as rhetoric, or a mannequin, or a joke.

We might conclude, therefore, that Iago embodies and exploits the idea that a self is nothing but an arbitrary and accidental collection of signs. But is this satisfying? Is it true to the experience of the part or the play? Almost certainly not: for a start, to accept such a view is to endorse Iago's vision of humankind, fatally lacking as it is in affect and love, and in recognition of the claims of others upon us. Furthermore, if we retain a faith in the connections that Iago would so destroy, then we are likely to apply such humanism in our attempt to come to terms with his actions. So, if he is cruel, what hurt has made him so? If he seems impossibly shallow, what depths lurk below? And after all, doesn't Iago invite just such speculation? He advertises his negative identity – 'I am not what I am' – in a manner that can equally be taken to mean his identity is hidden (and therefore must be searched for) as to mean literally that his identity is 'not'. Similarly, he might describe his 'heart' as an enacted thing ('act and figure'): but still he twice insists upon his 'heart' as the hidden truth that he must protect. We have seen how Iago turns us all to some degree into voyeurs. But one of the places we are led to pry into is Iago himself. Of course he resists any such prying as insolent intrusion. But still he receives it. Perhaps in one thing Iago's mastery is indeed compromised: in his power entirely to hide (if not hide from) himself.

We might therefore propose a different response to Iago's boast that his 'outward action' will never express the 'native act and figure' of his 'heart'. The 'act and figure' return us precisely to his actions: if we want to see what lies within, we have to study what lies without. Rather than affirming the textual and theatrical substance of the self, we might infer that such symptoms are a sign of something elusive, repressed, and defining.

The notorious elusiveness of Iago is most often talked about in terms of his obscure motives (Coleridge's 'motiveless malignity'). Why does he do what he does? Because he has been passed over for promotion, he suspects Othello with his wife, he hates blacks, he's jealous, envious, contemptuous, bored? We quickly leave evidence behind and enter the realms of psychological speculation. Productions of the play invariably revel in such speculation. So, Iago is played as a repressed homosexual or reactive puritan, whose recoil from sex gets sublimated into military efficiency and plotting; or he is a smooth charmer wrapped (rather like Richard III) in an unlovely body. These versions of Iago make attractive stage sense, but they are hardly the only ones possible. Two things are sure if we want to locate a coherent Iago: there will be more than one of them, and we have to build it up out of absences. Let us here experiment with an alternative speculation.

As we have already seen, Iago's words often give an impression of tremendous mental forethought, or a tightly bound nervous energy. We might consider the 'heart' statement more closely, noting here a striking difference between the Quarto and Folio readings: 'For when my outward action doth demonstrate/The native act and figure of my heart/In complement extern, 'tis not long after/But I will wear my heart upon my sleeve/For daws [Folio]/doves [Quarto] to peck at'. Iago envisages a heart, worn raw on his coat, and being eaten by birds. The different readings suggest that here again is a point of particular tension. In popular lore the two birds are polar opposites: the daw being thievish, dark like a crow, dim-witted or sluttish; the dove invoking whiteness, peace, the Holy Spirit, and a gentlewoman. In one version, therefore, Iago imagines his inwardness being eaten by cravenness and stupidity; in the other, his heart is being eaten by love. One version (daws) suggests a fierce and contemptuous privacy – the sort of attitude Iago enjoys declaring – in which the whole of the public world is disgustingly beneath him; the other (doves) suggests a much more specific aversion to one particular thing. This thing is white, beautiful, and noble; it is also a sadist. It is a surprising image, but one that exemplifies Iago's world of ethical inversion. Here the guise of innocence is a screen for the most inveterate depravity. This dove preys upon the masochistic drive of love, cruelly wounding any too open heart. But the context – Iago's scornful refusal of openness, his mixture of ferocity and concealment – seems to scream some kind of impelling hurt. A specific experience beats in this 'heart', compelling both his privacy and his plots. And if we are seeking a particular 'dove', then who can it be but Desdemona?

There may be some memory here of Shakespeare's primary source for *Othello*, the story by Cinthio called *Hecatommithi*. In Cinthio, the Iago figure is hopelessly in love with Desdemona. Correspondingly, in Iago's image Desdemona is the dove, consuming his heart, punishing him for daring to love above his station. To wear one's heart upon one's sleeve is an invitation to be sacrificed. So, confession is impossible. Secrecy and conceal-ment are imperative. In response, Iago discovers his own vengeful calling. With this bitter knowledge in safekeeping, Iago will take *his* tragic story – the move toward sacrifice for love – and in revenge turn it back upon its cause (the 'dove' Desdemona). He is thus getting his revenge in early: his plot is a super-rational, overcompensating escape from the rage of love ('If the balance of our lives had not one scale of reason to poise another of sensuality, the blood and baseness of our natures would conduct us to most preposterous conclusions. But we have reason to cool our raging motions, our carnal stings, our unbitted lusts; whereof I take this, that you call love, to be a sect or scion', 1.3.328–34). Iago's socially 'preposterous' love is buried in the fierce germ warfare of his language. This language, in turn, will attack the still more preposterous love which has replaced his own. For the love between Othello and Desdemona is multiply insulting, to be revenged correspondingly. It defeats, mocks, and repeats his own. Iago's loathing for others is motivated by shame and disgust with himself (or with the sensual self that feels). His concentrated language is therefore jam-packed with this urge to purge and to destroy:

> And, though he in a fertile climate dwell,
> Plague him with flies! Though that his joy be joy
> Yet throw such changes of vexation on't
> As it may lose some colour.
>
> (1.1.69–72)

The pivotal repetition is the apparent tautology: 'joy be joy'. Once again, by repeating the word he divides it, here by expecting us to dwell in the space between 'joy' and 'joy'. As Othello's 'joy', Desdemona is his darling, his 'sweet'; as 'joy' per se, she is also a symbol of ultimate bliss, beatitude, indeed paradise. Character-istically, however, here the word starts to turn. For such innocent connotations can barely survive the context of voyeuristic relish. The 'fertile climate' evokes Europe, as distinct from the rocks and deserts of Africa; and Iago is as gaudily fixated here as anywhere upon Othello as the foreigner ('it may lose some *colour*'). However, the primary meaning is gynaecological: the fertile space is Desdemona's vagina, as 'joy' becomes flatly carnal. Certainly there is something lip-smacking about Iago's imagination here. But there is also disgust. This is seen in his wish to 'Plague him with flies', meaning the censure that will ruin Othello. For it is clear that Iago's language has an abundance that goes far beyond the efficiencies of plot. So, the 'flies' spread germs, just like Iago; they feed upon the flesh, like Iago's nudge-and-wink conversations; they are attracted by things putrid and decaying; they feed upon, indeed spawn upon, rotting flesh and discarded rubbish. Iago's image moves from one consummation (sex) to another (death). The bride and groom are imagined as the carcasses they shall soon become. The 'flies', that is, are Iago's active agents.

The particular sort of 'flies' he imagines is the 'flesh-fly': one that feeds, breeds, and hatches in the skin of its hostage. Iago wants no one to escape the almost cellular vandalism for which he prays. Desdemona, Othello, and himself must all share in the sweltering meltdown of this 'joy'. Appropriately, the flesh-fly is also the penis (it is a common enough pun during the period). Othello's sex organ is 'now, very now', a 'joy' for the loving couple: for Iago, it is a 'plague'. Imminently, however, the roles should be reversed; hence the simple transfer of referent in 'joy be joy'. For in an awful sense, Iago speaks the most basic truth. Othello's present bliss *is* also Iago's, because it will be the cause of all that Iago longs for. It is the most insidious, grimly comic transforming of the idea that 'joy' is paradise, that it is ripe with promise. This 'joy' might not promise everything in the world to Iago: but it will do as compensation.

Of course a different Iago, one who barely gives a thought to Desdemona, can be perfectly coherent: but only by piecing together some other more or less plausible story from the web of hints and absences that the play gives us. There is a very simple paradox here, basic to Shakespeare's characterisations. That is, we create fullness from absence; we conjure reality from textual traces and palpable pretence. The hunger to know more about things that do not strictly exist – a character's unspoken motives, their past, their secrets – is a product of dramatic ellipses and textual withholding. It is also why the substance of many of Shakespeare's most interesting characters so often resembles the theatrical arts that make them. It is done this way so that we pour into the gaps – so that we pore over the art – hoping to find or form what we're after. Such theatrical immediacy – for nothing is more immediate than this more or less instinctive reaching after reasons – is a prime channel into his work's ethical difficulty. It is also a basic pleasure of any story. The conviction that a character has depth, has some kind of coherent moving soul, is invariably created precisely by the play-form's deferring and deconstruction of any such thing.

## HAMLET

Let's close with Shakespeare's most famous character, Hamlet, again searching out the connections between the textual and theatrical techniques that make him and the recognisable persona that we identify. For Hamlet is the dramatic character that, perhaps more than any other, has attracted possessive empathies and passionate appropriations. He has become a key model of the three-dimensional character: someone whose troubles appear both to live in the moment and to have a past; who is unique in isolation and existentially self-accounting. However, Hamlet's role is also profoundly indebted to the stock stage figure of the revenger. The part draws much of its shape and impetus from its relation to theatrical precedent. And if this is true of the Hamlet part, it is equally true of any Hamlet-inwardness that we like to identify with this part.

Neurotically aware of literary, mythic, and theatrical cliché, Hamlet spends much of the play bemoaning the fact that he is being asked to play roles that he can never quite believe in. He tries on all kinds of parts, usually consciously but sometimes not, in the effort to reconstruct some kind of appropriate role. Hamlet can be understood as an actor never at one with his part. He knowingly puts on roles that allow him an ironic gap wherein he can hide or brood: the 'antic disposition' being the most famous but hardly the only one. More profoundly, the play presents him as always non-identical to any part supposed to define him. Consider the roles that he is 'born' into: he is the [non]-revenger in a revenge play, the [non]-heir to the throne, the [non]-lover of the heroine, the [non]-son to the [non]-father. But the same basic non-identity applies equally to the parts that Hamlet *chooses* to play. In various ways he goes through the motions of being a fool, a comedian, an actor/director/playwright, a preacher, an assassin, a philosopher, a clown, a fencing knight, and, in his own estimation, a 'drab' (whore). He is and is not each such type; he is the aggregate of them all and none of them at all.

Consequently, we might see a peculiar appropriateness in Hamlet's response to the players' arrival (perhaps his only cheerful and – seemingly – self-forgetful moment in the play):

> He that plays the king shall be welcome – his Majesty shall have tribute on me, the adventurous knight shall use his foil and target, the lover shall not sigh gratis, the humorous man shall end his part in peace, the clown shall make those laugh whose lungs are tickled a'th' sear, and the lady shall say her mind freely – or the blank verse shall halt for't. What players are they?

> (2.2.321–8)

Hamlet here rushes through various clichés of the popular stage, each type he invokes being a staple of every company and all genres. His delight in so doing can be played as more or less mocking and ironic: but either way, he hardly here forgets himself. For we might notice that the types he summarises uncannily correspond to the types that he at one time or another plays: 'king ... knight ... lover ... humorous man ... clown ... and the lady [who] shall say her mind freely – or the blank verse shall halt for't'. Hamlet's own field of possibilities resembles those of an actors' troupe. The playing company becomes the macro-version of the individual; the individual the micro-version of the company. Hamlet is teasing popular stage stereotypes: but he is also predicting himself. So, he says that the 'blank verse' will limp, stutter or cease ('halt') if the players are put out of their parts. Hamlet is joking: but he is also anticipating exactly what he performs in his very next soliloquy. In this soliloquy Hamlet rages through a sequence of inappropriate parts – rogue, peasant, rascal, John-a-dreams, coward, villain, ass – that he has found himself playing only because he keeps missing 'the motive and the cue' that he has been given (2.2.561: as with Iago, Hamlet's hendiadys here suggests how 'cue' can stand for, produce, or derail one's 'motive'). He ends up expiring in disgust at the contrast between his scripted role – 'the son of a dear father murder'd' – and the role he finds himself helplessly improvising – an indulgent, loquacious 'whore': 'I . . . Must like a whore unpack my heart with words/And fall a-cursing like a very drab,/A scullion! Fie upon't! Foh!' (2.2.587–9). It is no accident that Hamlet moves from this furious curse to thoughts of playgoing: 'Fie upon't! Foh!/About, my brains. Hum – I have heard/That guilty creatures sitting at a play. . .' (2.2.589–91). If he cannot adequately compound himself of the appropriate parts, then it is *he* who will indeed 'halt for't'. For the verb 'halt' concentrates the dangers facing Hamlet: his verse will lose measure and time (as in the imploding rhythms of 'Fie . . . Foh . . . Hum'); his very being will be fatally crippled, devolving into his notorious condition of pause, suspension, or paralysis. It is much more than defeat in a plot that he intimates; much more in an odd way even than death. It is his own dissolution, as though he literally is nothing, an undressed mannequin in an empty tiring house ('to be or not to be, that is the question. . .').

Hamlet's very existence is at stake at such moments, but he has nothing but the repertoires of theatre to draw upon. The point to notice is how captive Hamlet is to the very things he despises. He curses himself for mincing words like a whore; for seeming so false, second-hand, and self-prostituting in his discourse. But his only medium for restoring integrity is a play. This is why Hamlet's mocking rejection of theatrical cliché works alongside his need (by turns affectionate and contemptuous) for just such borrowed garments.

Hamlet is condemned to rehearse and repeat something akin to what early modern actors were paid to rehearse and repeat: 'This day one playes a Monarch, the next a private person. Heere one Acts a Tyrant, on the morrow an Exile: A Parasite this man too night, to morrow a Prescisian'. Hamlet dips into the stock of both minor and major part-players. His particular mix might be unique, but his passage through the play compresses something close to a season in an actor's life. Shakespeare's task is then Hamlet's, which in turn is that of the players (at least as Hamlet would direct them): to construct a new part from old parts; a sustainable compound from typecast materials. Any whole and coherent Hamlet is made from such parts.

It might seem that to identify Hamlet so directly with theatrical materials is to resist any approach that feels for the character as though 'he' were real. But the opposite is more the case. Hamlet can seem so real precisely because the suffering revenger was already a cliché by the time the play was first performed. So, Hamlet understands this coercive and stereotyping tradition as yet another kind of false parent. He comments upon this role that he is born into, criticising its clichés, questioning its precepts, parodying other's expectations. In turn, this awareness of precedent both separates Hamlet from what he is 'supposed' to be, and asserts a rival – and prior – authenticity. He and we treasure a more intimate, less pre-empted self, one that is both framed and validated by Hamlet's instinct to reject a merely fictional and borrowed role.

But if we do treasure some such individuality, it is far from glibly given to us, and far from simply present. Hamlet is the most talkative of all Shakespeare's characters, and dominates his play like no one else. No character seems more present in or defined by soliloquy. Nevertheless, our relationship with him (like his with Ophelia) is marked by recurring uncertainty, ignorance, and disappointment. As much as we are given various qualities upon which to hang our faith (his wit, honesty, distrust of tyranny, etc.), it may be that the things that are most distinctive about Hamlet are less to do with what we get than with what we don't. If Hamlet has an essence, perhaps it is defined by separateness and exclusion: from the audience, and from himself.

This need not imply profound metaphysical puzzles. It can be an effect once more of one of Shakespeare's most basic theatrical techniques: not presenting a reported action or character on stage, and thereby creating hunger, curiosity, and need. For example, the play's first scene is a long one, but Hamlet is not in it. Indeed he is not mentioned until the very last speech of substance (Horatio's 'Let us impart what we have seen tonight/Unto young Hamlet; for upon my life/This spirit, dumb to us, will speak to him', 1.1.174–6). This opening scene is all frustration and groping. The opening parley, 'Who's there?', is answered by the equally suggestive deferral, 'Nay, answer me: Stand and unfold yourself'. It sets the tone for a scene of question and counter-question, demand and refusal, in which attempts at understanding are little but barks in the dark. The entrance of the Ghost clinches this feeling of ignorance, alienation, and mystery. So, we get Marcellus' torrent of questions ('tell me, he that knows,/Why . . . why . . . Why . . . What might be toward . . . Who is't that can inform me?', 1.1.73–82), 'answered' by Horatio's circumspect offering ('At least the whisper goes so', 83). Nine times Horatio charges the Ghost to 'speak' (52–4, 132–42), the imperative command echoing like the world's first and only desire. But the Ghost will say nothing.

This is the context for the force of expectation that lands in the lap of young Hamlet: 'for upon my life,/This spirit dumb to us, will speak to him' (175–6). He will be the romantic hero, blessed with the charisma of decisiveness, destined to fill our lack and satisfy our hopes. Hamlet has not yet entered; we know nothing about him; but we need and trust him absolutely.

The second scene continues the effect. The whole court is on stage. We should picture a majestic display of colour and finery. But amidst these signs of splendour is Hamlet, dressed in the 'inky cloak' of mourning. There could barely be a more ostentatious show of dissidence. And again he is present in silence. He does not speak until the new regime has asserted, at great length, its oratorical mastery, and all the other business is completed. An audience will surely know that the man in black is young Hamlet. They will not quite be sure who to look at, the king or this silent malcontent. We listen as the business proceeds – but at the same time we are waiting, ready to magnify his smallest fidget. The effect is one of bated breath, of ratcheting up the expectation.

When Hamlet finally does speak, these are his words: 'A little more than kin, and less than kind (1.2.65). Expectant as we are, we will hear plenty in his terse rebuke. So, he is dissenting from the king's normalising rhetoric, and recoiling from the hints of scandal and incest in Claudius's yoking of 'cousin' to 'son'. He is scrupulous, perhaps pedantic, about the use and the misuse of words. We hear a refusal to be bullied or fooled; we smell knowledge of transgression, as yet dangerous to speak of too openly. We hear too a certain fierceness of compression, as though within the intense and lonely privacy that we have already come to expect of him, his mind turns in cramped, self-meeting circles. And the wordplay itself suggests a ruling culture disturbingly out of focus. Kin should be kin, kind should be kind, each should be the other: but here there is a bit missing, there a bit added on, and either way there is a violence done to decorum and order. Hamlet's pedantry refuses to let the words merge into or rhyme with one another. 'Kin' can be divided or added to; so too 'kind'. Everything is both more and less than it should be.

The basic impression of a world out of joint seems clear enough. But the more we ponder these first words, the more they start to beg questions. So, of whom exactly does Hamlet speak? To whom exactly does he speak? Editors usually gloss Hamlet's words as an aside. But what does this mean? Is he acknowledging our presence or not? Perhaps he appeals to us as supporters in the revenge tragedy tradition. Or perhaps we are overhearing something unshared with anyone. Indeed it needn't be an aside at all. Hamlet's next three comments are all sarcastic or dissenting, so it is hardly out of character for him to be directly rebuking the king's attempts to pacify him. Alternatively, he may speak in the ear of one or more people on the stage: the king, his mother, Ophelia, Polonius, Laertes, some other courtier. Clearly any such choice would alter the meaning of the words: to Ophelia it might appear intimate or conspiratorial; to Polonius mischievous; to his mother an ethical rebuke; to the king a flat threat. Similarly, the words apply equally well to himself ('I am not as you think'), or to Claudius ('you are not as you pretend'), or to their shared circumstance (oblique incest). He is saying that one of them is dangerous to the other ('less than kind'), but which one is ambiguous. Or perhaps it is a riddle with an answer. More than 'kin', less than 'kind': what else but *king*? But who is this unkin, unkind king? Is he satirising the present impostor (King Claudius) or predicting the true inheritor (King Hamlet)?

Clearly a production is faced with interesting decisions; and these are not casual matters. The remarkable thing is just how little we are gifted. These are our hero's first words: we have waited for them, we depend on them, but we don't quite know to whom or of what he is talking.

For all of our trust in Hamlet, it is never quite returned. We are not confided in. We are not privy to all and any ironies. We are left at least partly on the outside, speculating, inferring, filling in the gaps with our best or most attractive guesses. It is the basic principle of Hamlet's characterisation. We know there is a fullness 'in' him; he appeals to exactly such a thing when he declares 'I have that within which passes show' (1.2.85). We know that he has been much admired, that he is much loved, and so on. Other characters attest to his qualities all the time. But it is a Hamlet that we never witness. In some crucial sense, this Hamlet has gone before the play starts. We piece bits of him together from the report of others, but these reports are, increasingly, of what has been lost. He might be in mourning for his father: but the play is in this sense an act of mourning for him.

The consequences are huge. For it is this absence that is the cause and the corollary of Hamlet's methods – peculiar to himself – of self-representation. Most particularly, this means his intense scepticism about the pretensions of any kind of language. Hence Hamlet's basic disposition: the compulsion to be precise and scrupulous; the linked awareness of the uselessness of words; the need to resort to obscure conceits or extravagant onomatopoeia, and then their evasiveness and illusoriness; the seductiveness of 'show' and 'play' that, as fictions, are the only kind of language worth bothering with; the pathos, therefore, of masks, and yet their bogusness; the vanishing line between the 'dejected havior' and buffoonery. He has tried them all – 'all forms, moods, shapes of grief' – but nothing can 'denote' anything truly (1.2.76–86).

Essentially refusing recognition in the here and now, Hamlet seduces us into reaching for an inwardness that must be taken merely on trust.

Nonetheless, much of the allure and magic of the play comes from the fact that we do not in fact renounce belief in the 'real' Hamlet. After all, revenge might precisely be an act of rebirth. Achieve that, cleanse the slate, and this perfect soul might return. This is why Hamlet is so powerful a mirror or vessel of those who engage with him. The more impassioned this engagement, the more subtle and magnetic the connections. For we fill the gaps with our own best intentions, with all of the excuses and explanations that *our* experience can muster. Hamlet becomes a character recreated out of the most basic instincts of self-permission and survival: that rationalisation and furtiveness are sometimes just and necessary; that there are always reasons that cannot be told; that no action can ever satisfy or truly express the teem of stuff within us; that cruelty comes from weakness rather than malice, that the weakness is not our fault, and that we make victims because we were made one; that there are more thoughts in the world than moments to act them; that we are born to a mother and she leaves us; that we are born to a life and it leaves us: and so on. It makes Hamlet, because he is the most simply disappointing of all characters – because he will not and *cannot* satisfy our hopes – also, very often, the most urgently familiar.

Hence the way Hamlet is here born to us, and the particular address of his first speech-acts. The manners of 'a little more than kin, and less than kind' are twice immediately reproduced ('I am too much in the sun', 'Ay, madam, it is common', 1.2.67, 74). It is enough to establish not only a manner of speaking, but also a way of making. His opening statements are rude, belligerent, riddling, obscure, sarcastic, insolent, mean-minded, and evasive; they are perhaps cowardly, certainly boasting, coiled up with malice and secretiveness and brooding bad health. There is no way, we might conclude, that this can 'be' the 'young Hamlet'. However, the multiplicity of his barbs, the way his meanings breed and divide, is at the same time the trumpet of absolute secrecy. Because he is so flagrantly refusing confession, he points us toward it.

His deadpan obtuseness is also the diffidence of pained sensitivity. The stylised folds of his words speak the care of a pedant, in some crucial sense silent because no words can do the job. In being so absent, Hamlet bleeds – or perhaps rather haemorrhages – something like the authenticity of presence.

The technique is in evidence to the very end. So, if Shakespeare famously builds *Hamlet* around not-doing, he closes it in a maze of not-saying. The justice of any revenge is never spoken. Claudius is never accused, or shamed, or revealed in his guilt. Instead, there is an avalanche of accident and mischance, and a series of statements which first promise and immediately withdraw the promise of revelation: 'You that look pale and tremble at this chance,/That are but mutes or audience to this act,/Had I but time – as this fell sergeant, Death,/Is strict in his arrest – O, I could tell you –/But let it be' (5.2.341–5). The urgency of Hamlet's dying commands to Horatio suggest that he is well aware of this failure of accounting: 'Report me and my cause aright/To the unsatisfied', 'what a wounded name,/Things standing thus unknown, shall I leave behind me', 'in this harsh world draw thy breath in pain/To tell my story', 'tell my story', 'tell him' (5.2.346–63).

This is the context for Hamlet's final statement: 'The rest is silence'. It is a context that makes it certain that the character's basic trope of being – presence through absence – will survive even his death. So, these famous words are an almost paralysed joke (a bon mort) about ineffectuality and unspeakability. As such they provide the perfect mock-epitaph to his role. So, the 'rest' is everything to come; it is the sleep he is about to embark upon; and it is what he was about to say – what Hamlet is *always* about to say. In other words, it evokes the impossibility of saying what 'is': whether this 'is' invokes the meaning of this play, this life, or the next. The joke is partly that the punch line will never be heard. Or – hence the dark comedy – that *this is it*. The 'rest' is either nothing or repetition. The best Hamlet can do is pass the narrative baton to Horatio, who has no more access to any secrets than the rest of us. The best we can do, therefore, is to watch the play all over again. Hamlet thereby returns us to the play's beginning. Only this time it is 'young Hamlet' who will be the ghost, finally and ironically inheriting his father's mantle. He is now the one who will be borne 'like a soldier' upon the 'stage' (5.2.403), hinting at untellable but portentous truths.

There is consequently no closure, and even silence is racked with doubtful content. But so, interestingly, is the nature of Hamlet's last utterance. For 'The rest is silence' is Hamlet's last statement in only one of the play's three early versions. The 'good' quarto (Q2) is the one with this seemingly appropriate finality, as Hamlet's sonorous enigma reaches out to one or another kind of symmetry. The Folio text, however, gives us four great wails to shatter any glassy silence: 'The rest is silence. O, o, o, o'. These wails are usually (quietly) left out by editors. But as sure as day they record at least one early incarnation of the play in performance. Indeed there could hardly be a more immediate type of communication, or one that will more inevitably be taken in by an audience as the hero's parting deliverance. But what might such wails mean?

Of course, the repeated moans, or growls, might merely be some secretary's fastidious report of performance: Burbage as Hamlet, simulating the agony of dying. But even to think of Hamlet after his last words is to think about the substance in his moans, and to feel with the mind inside them. The awe and horror is that Hamlet cannot reach to words. 'O, o, o, o' is Hamlet's movement into death: and therefore, with due astonishment, momentarily back through life. The speech-act, like so many, invites empathising inference. So perhaps it all starts rushing in, like a world-ending wave, the mourning for what has been and now so suddenly is going: the whole mess of never to be reconciled parties, split purposes, corrupted authenticity, unfulfilled desire, lost hope. At the same time he looks ahead, to whatever lies beyond. And (as for Joseph Conrad's Kurtz) the horror is unspeakable.

In this sense, the repeated 'O' brings to a climax those things that supply Hamlet's inwardness: varieties of absence; the failure of words; and the linked insistence upon absolute scrupulousness of vocabulary. Of course in a sense the 'Os' represent the despairing renunciation of any such pedantic pride. But in another way they are Hamlet's perfectly self-correspondent syllables. Consider the sheer punch of the communication here, and the way it leaves behind all dilemmas as to how to express one's self or situation. No audience can fail to know what is happening. Yet, as immediate a dramatic moment as it is, it is also the most emphatic instance in the play of the audience or reader needing to supply the gaps themselves. The 'Os' can be cumulative, identical, divisible, dilated, sudden, isolated, self-collapsing; they can be piteous, enraged, violent, wistful, weeping, booming, tiny. They can form one speech-act, a corporate wail or moan or sigh; or they can be each of them distinct, as demarcated as a moment in time: a capsule of memory, a pocket of experience, as the hero moves into death and recalls it all. Each 'O' can be a cause for grief and a test-tube of mourning. They might pile up one on top of another, a monument to the ruin of life and language. Or the four 'Os' might be the single moment that is every moment, in which the impotence of speech and the fact of death force the mind into simple, empty, cul-de-sacs like this.

And yet at the same time the 'O, o, o, o' is a typical Shakespeare joke. You thought I'd finished? – think again. The rest is silence? In Shakespeare's world of echoes, it never quite is. The barest, most voided space – like the 'O' of Hamlet's pain, or the 'rounded O' of the stage itself – is always full with possibilities.

# SUGGESTIONS FOR FURTHER READING

There are thousands of books and articles on Shakespeare, and all of the passages, plays, and characters discussed in this book have been analysed in endless ways elsewhere. There are simply too many to list usefully, so nothing is listed below specifically for its close readings of the plays (although many contain excellent such readings). What follows is instead limited mainly to a selection of works that might help fill out those contexts only briefly alluded to in *Doing Shakespeare*. There are also a few suggestions for further reading on particular dramatic techniques. Most of the listed books are recent publications that will supply excellent histories of their various subjects. All will have their own bibliographies that can be consulted for more specialised reading. There are also comprehensive bibliographies in most scholarly collected editions of the plays.

No journal articles are listed below, although journals are an excellent place to start looking for interesting material. See in particular the yearly *Shakespeare Survey* and *Shakespeare Studies*, and the *Shakespeare Quarterly*. The *Shakespeare Quarterly* has a yearly Bibliography which is immensely useful for tracing what has been written recently about any of the plays, genres, or characters, and about recent stage productions, films, adaptations, and so on.

The canonical neo-classical and romantic critics, editors, and adaptors of Shakespeare are always worth reading, starting with Ben Jonson, and including John Dryden, Alexander Pope, Samuel Johnson, Samuel Taylor Coleridge, William Hazlitt, and Goethe.

See under individual authors; for selections see Brian Vickers (ed.) *Shakespeare: The Critical Heritage*, 6 vols (Routledge, 1976–96); Jonathan Bate, *The Romantics of Shakespeare* (Penguin, 1992).

Useful starting-points for criticism of particular plays, genres, or performances are: the Oxford Shakespeare Topics series, edited by Peter Holland and Stanley Wells; the Cambridge Companions to Shakespeare, which include volumes on Shakespearean tragedy (ed. Claire McEachern, 2003), the history plays (ed. Michael Hattaway, 2002), Shakespeare on stage (eds Stanley Wells and Sarah Stanton, 2002), comedy (ed. Alexander Leggatt, 2001), and Shakespeare on film (ed. Russell Jackson, 2000); and Blackwell's four-volume *Companion to Shakespeare's Works* (eds Richard Dutton and Jean E. Howard, 2003).

There is an ever-expanding amount of textual and critical material online. A convenient gateway to this abundance is the reference site Mr. William Shakespeare and the Internet. This and many other sites are conveniently listed at http://www.shakespeare. bham.ac.uk/resources. For the RSC's archive catalogue and database see www.shakespeare.org.uk/main/3/313. For Shakespeare productions 1960–2000 see http://ahds.ac.uk/performingarts/designing-shakespeare.

On the First Folio, see W.W. Greg, *The Shakespeare First Folio* (Oxford University Press, 1955). On the actors, see Andrew Gurr, *The Shakespeare Company, 1594–1642* (Cambridge University Press, 2004); Tiffany Stern, *Rehearsal from Shakespeare to Sheridan* (Oxford University Press, 2000).

On the production of texts, see W.W. Greg, *The Editorial Problem in Shakespeare* (Oxford University Press, 1955); Margreta De Grazia, *Shakespeare Verbatim* (Oxford University Press, 1991); David Scott Kastan, *Shakespeare and the Book* (Cambridge University Press, 2001); Laurie Maguire, *Shakespearean Suspect Texts* (Cambridge University Press, 1996); Gary Taylor and John Jowett, *Shakespeare Reshaped 1606–1623* (Oxford University Press, 1993).

For arguments that Shakespeare wrote for page as much as stage, see Lukas Erne, *Shakespeare as Literary Dramatist* (Cambridge University Press, 2002).

On Shakespeare's audiences, see Andrew Gurr, *Playgoing in*

*Shakespeare's London*, 3rd edn. (Cambridge University Press, 2004); Ann Jennalie Cook, *The Privileged Playgoers of Shakespeare's London 1576–1642* (Princeton, 1981); Martin Butler, *Theatre and Crisis 1632–42* (Cambridge University Press, 1984).

On Shakespeare's theatrical contexts, see E.K. Chambers, *William Shakespeare*, 2 vols (Oxford University Press, 1930); Andrew Gurr, *The Shakespearean Stage, 1574–1642* (Cambridge University Press, 1992); Peter Thomson, *Shakespeare's Theatre* (London, 1992); Robert Weimann, *Author's Pen and Actor's Voice* (Cambridge University Press, 2000).

On rhetorical training, see Brian Vickers, *In Defence of Rhetoric* (Oxford University Press, 1988); Peter Mack (ed.) *Renaissance Rhetoric* (St Martin's Press, 1994).

On aesthetic form and history, see Theodor Adorno, *Aesthetic Theory*, trans. Robert Hullot-Kentor (1970; repr. Continuum, London, 2002); Stephen Greenblatt, *Shakespearean Negotiations* (California University Press, 1988); Stephen Orgel, *Imagining Shakespeare* (Palgrave, 2003) and *The Authentic Shakespeare* (Routledge, 2002).

For a glossary of Shakespeare's word use, see David Crystal and Ben Crystal, *Shakespeare's Words* (Penguin, 2003).

On language in general, see Russ McDonald, *Shakespeare and the Arts of Language* (Oxford University Press, 2001); Sylvia Adamson, Lynette Hunter, Lynne Magnusson, Ann Thompson and Katie Wales (eds) *Reading Shakespeare's Dramatic Language: A Guide* (Arden, 2000).

On metaphor, see I.A. Richards, *The Philosophy of Rhetoric* (1936); William Empson, *Seven Types of Ambiguity* (Chatto & Windus, 1930) and *The Structure of Complex Words* (Chatto & Windus, 1951); Terence Hawkes, *Metaphor* (Methuen, 1972); Christopher Ricks, *Allusion to the Poets* (Oxford University Press, 2002); George Lakoff and Mark Johnson, *Metaphors We Live By*, 2nd edn. (Chicago, 2003).

On grammar, see N.F. Blake, *Shakespeare's Language: An Introduction;* Jonathan Hope, *Shakespeare's Grammar* (Arden, 2003).

On prose, prosody, and rhyme, see George T. Wright, *Shakespeare's Metrical Art* (California University Press, 1991); John

Hollander, *Vision and Resonance* (Oxford University Press, 1975); Brian Vickers, *The Artistry of Shakespeare's Prose* (Methuen, 1968).

On puns, see William Empson, *Seven Types of Ambiguity* (Chatto & Windus, 1930); M.M. Mahood, *Shakespeare's Wordplay* (Methuen, 1957); Patricia Parker, *Literary Fat Ladies* (Methuen, 1987) and *Shakespeare from the Margins* (Chicago University Press, 1996); Jonathan Culler (ed.) *On Puns* (Blackwell, 1988).

On defining character, see Catherine Belsey, *The Subject of Tragedy* (Methuen, 1985); Jonathan Goldberg, *Shakespeare's Hand* (Minnesota University Press, 2003); Edward Burns, *Character: Acting and Being on the Pre-modern Stage* (Macmillan, 1989); Katherine Eisman Maus, *Inwardness and Theater in the English Renaissance* (Chicago, 1995).

On actor's parts, see Simon Palfrey and Tiffany Stern, *Shakespeare in Parts* (Oxford University Press, 2005).

On text and performance, see Peter Brook, *The Shifting Point* (Methuen, 1995); Jean E. Howard, *Shakespeare's Art of Orchestration* (Illinois University Press, 1984); Alan C. Dessen, *Recovering Shakespeare's Theatrical Vocabulary* (Cambridge University Press, 1995); W.B. Worthen, *Shakespeare and the Authority of Performance* (Cambridge University Press, 1997); Barbara Hodgdon and W.B. Worthen (eds) *A Companion to Shakespeare and Performance* (Blackwell, 2004).

On characters and empathy, see A.C. Bradley, *Shakespearean Tragedy* (1904; Penguin, 1991); John Bayley, *Shakespeare and Tragedy* (Routledge, 1981); Harold Bloom, *Shakespeare and the Invention of the Human*; Harry Berger Jr, *Making Trifles of Terrors* (Stanford University Press, 1977).

On female characters, see Dympna Callaghan (ed.) *A Feminist Companion to Shakespeare* (Blackwell, 2000).

# INDEX OF CHARACTERS

# INDEX OF PLAYS

# GENERAL INDEX